Laboratory Approaches to Spanish Phonology

Phonology and Phonetics
7

Editor

Aditi Lahiri

Mouton de Gruyter
Berlin · New York

Laboratory Approaches to Spanish Phonology

edited by

Timothy L. Face

Mouton de Gruyter
Berlin · New York

Mouton de Gruyter (formerly Mouton, The Hague)
is a Division of Walter de Gruyter GmbH & Co. KG, Berlin.

♾ Printed on acid-free paper which falls within the guidelines
of the ANSI to ensure permanence and durability.

Library of Congress Cataloging-in-Publication Data

Laboratory approaches to Spanish phonology / edited by Timothy
L. Face.
    p.   cm. − (Phonology and phonetics ; 7)
  Includes bibliographical references and index.
  ISBN 3-11-018176-2 (cloth : alk. paper)
1. Spanish language − Phonology.   I. Face, Timothy Lee, 1974−
II. Series.
PC4131.L33 2004
461'.5−dc22   2004008876

ISBN 3-11-018176-2

Bibliographic information published by Die Deutsche Bibliothek

Die Deutsche Bibliothek lists this publication in the Deutsche Nationalbibliografie;
detailed bibliographic data is available in the Internet at <http://dnb.ddb.de>.

Acknowledgments

This volume would not have been possible without the assistance of a number of people. First and foremost, I would like to thank Scott Alvord for his many hours of collaboration and hard work on the formatting of the volume. In addition to the formatting, Scott was my right-hand man throughout this endeavor, collaborating on many aspects of the editorial process, and for his energy, enthusiasm and friendship I am extremely grateful.

Secondly, I would like to acknowledge series editor Aditi Lahiri and Mouton de Gruyter editor Ursula Kleinhenz. Both Aditi and Ursula were essential to this publication. I am grateful for their support of the initial idea for the volume, their evaluation of the papers under consideration for inclusion in the volume, and for their willingness to provide endless guidance and consultation whenever required. They have certainly made it easier for me to navigate through the editorial process.

Finally, I am indebted to those individuals who served as reviewers of the papers considered for inclusion in this volume. Without the voluntary aid of these individuals, the quality of the final product would not be what it now is. For their assistance in the review process, I am grateful to Travis Bradley, Laura Colantoni, Manuel Díaz-Campos, David Eddington, Robert Hammond, José Ignacio Hualde, Carol Klee, Anthony Lewis, Pilar Prieto, and Erik Willis.

Table of Contents

Introduction

Timothy L. Face

Laboratory phonology is the study of the sound systems of languages using experiments to collect concrete data that motivate the phonological analysis. The types of experiments, however, are numerous, and each offers insight into different phonological issues. Quoting from the call for papers for the Laboratory Approaches to Spanish Phonology conference that I organized at the University of Minnesota in September 2002 (and which motivated the publication of this volume), "The phrase 'laboratory approaches' is intended in its broadest possible sense and includes any experimental work that offers insight into the sound structure of Spanish. This may include, but is not limited to, data from phonetic, perception, language acquisition, psycholinguistic, and speech disorder studies." Because of the breadth of experiment types employed, studies in laboratory phonology address a wide array of phonological issues – a glance at the table of contents of this volume offers just a glimpse at the variety of issues being addressed by scholars employing a laboratory phonology approach.

The notion of laboratory phonology developed about two decades ago with a community of scholars dedicated to investigating phonology using experimental methods. While experimental studies have always been the basis for phonetic studies, applying both traditional phonetic methods and new innovative methods to the study of phonology allowed for new perspectives on existing issues, access to previously untapped data sources, and new insights into the phonological systems of human languages. Laboratory phonology, over the past two decades, has developed from a new approach to phonological issues into a full-fledged, and increasingly popular, field of linguistic inquiry. In 1987 the first Lab Phon conference was held at The Ohio State University to provide a forum for scholars using experimental approaches to phonology. This became the first of a now prestigious conference series that has been hosted by institutions both in the United States and in Europe. Following each Lab Phon conference a volume of selected papers has been published, and these publications have led the field of laboratory phonology forward. But laboratory phonology is by no means limited to one conference series or set of publications. In fact, laboratory phonology is now as mainstream as any other approach to linguistic investigation, and is represented in many conferences of more general themes and in the most prestigious journals and publications dedicated to linguistics, psychology, cognition, and other areas.

Despite the fact that work within the field of laboratory phonology has been growing in popularity within the Hispanic Linguistics community for several years, until the Laboratory Approaches to Spanish Phonology conference in September 2002, there had been no common forum for the presentation of this work. While experimental studies of Spanish phonology had appeared in Hispanic, Romance and general linguistics conferences, they were, and continue to be, only a handful of the papers presented and did not bring together the community of Spanish laboratory phonologists. And until now, neither has any publication been dedicated to presenting the wide array of experimental work being carried out on Spanish phonology. As was the intention of the conference, it is also the intention of this volume to provide a forum for scholars employing experimental approaches to the phonological investigation of Spanish. It is a forum to share individual research with a community of scholars interested in similar issues and approaches, to present a representative sample of the various laboratory approaches that are being employed and the issues they can address, to bring for the first time recognition to the body of experimental work on Spanish phonology, and to generate ideas in the reader that may eventually lead to further growth of the community of scholars of laboratory phonology in general, and of Spanish laboratory phonology in particular.

As is clear by now, the Laboratory Approaches to Spanish Phonology conference that I organized at the University of Minnesota in September 2002 has close ties to this volume. In addition to the nearly identical intentions of the conference and the volume, as discussed above, there is an even more direct tie between the papers in this volume and the conference. Of the ten papers included in this volume, eight of them were originally presented at the conference. Furthermore, many of the participants in the conference graciously offered their time to review the papers that were considered for inclusion in this volume. While the papers in the volume represent the work of only a portion of the community of scholars employing laboratory approaches in their work on Spanish phonology, the volume would not have been possible without the larger community, and especially without the members of that community that participated in the Laboratory Approaches to Spanish Phonology conference.

The papers included in this volume are organized into three parts, dealing with intonation, syllables and stress, and segmental constraints. Within each of these parts, each paper approaches a different issue and/or takes a different approach to an issue than do the other papers. Part 1, "Intonation", contains three papers. Conxita Lleó, Martin Krakow, and Margaret Kehoe, in their paper "Acquisition of language-specific pitch accent by Spanish and German monolingual and bilingual children", find that monolingual speakers of Spanish and German acquire language-specific pitch accents before the age of three. Bilingual children acquire both the Spanish and German pitch accents by the same age, though the ability to use them appropriately varies between the children. In her paper "The search for phonological targets in the tonal space: H1 scaling and alignment in five sentence-types in Peninsular Spanish", Pilar Prieto examines the scaling and alignment of the first F0 peak in declaratives, absolute interrogatives, pronominal interrogatives, and exclamatives. Her results lend support to the target-based hypothesis of intonational production and indicate the speakers most likely use cues as early as the first pitch accent gesture to identify phrasal type. In the final paper of Part 1, "Dominican Spanish absolute interrogatives in broad focus", Erik W. Willis investigates each tonal movement in the intonational contours of Dominican Spanish absolute interrogatives. The results reveal four differences between the intonation of Dominican Spanish interrogatives and previous accounts of Caribbean Spanish interrogative intonation, and the identification of this new contour raises questions for the phonological analysis of Spanish interrogatives.

Part 2, "Syllables and stress", contains four papers. In the first paper, "A computational approach to resolving certain issues in Spanish stress placement", David Eddington runs computer simulations of an analogical model in order to determine what factors most influence stress placement in Spanish. He finds that the best success rates are obtained when at least some phonemic information is included, the more abstract information such as the CV tier and syllable weight may also be involved. These results indicate that speakers may make use of phonemic representation in determining stress placement. My own contribution, "Perceiving what isn't there: Non-acoustic cues for perceiving Spanish stress", examines four factors other than acoustic cues that may influence stress perception. The results show that of the four factors examined, the stress pattern of segmentally similar words, lexical subregularities, and morphological category influence stress perception. The fourth factor, syllable weight, was found not to affect stress perception, though segmental factors tend to mimic syllable weight effects in certain contexts. Sharon Gerlach's paper, "Another look at effects of environment on L2 epenthesis: Evidence for transfer of ranked constraints", investigates the role of preceding context on word-initial epenthesis in English by native speakers of Spanish. A more detailed analysis of preceding environment is undertaken than in previous studies, leading to a more well-refined understanding of its effects. In addition, it is shown that stage of acquisition is an important factor and earlier stages result in epenthesis patterns unattested in previous studies. Stages of acquisition are analyzed as different constraint rankings within Optimality Theory. The final paper of Part 2 is Mark Waltermire's contribution, "The effect of syllable weight on the determination of spoken stress in Spanish". A questionnaire was employed to collect data on where subjects would stress words with different syllable weight combinations. The results indicate that syllable weight is a factor in Spanish stress placement, but more importantly that there is a complex interaction of the weights of different syllables in determining stress placement. This goes against claims that only the final syllable is a factor in determining stress placement, though its weight is consistently the most powerful factor in this study.

Part 3, "Segmental constraints", contains three papers. Travis G. Bradley's contribution, "Gestural timing and rhotic variation in Spanish codas", considers the role of gestural alignment in the realization of heterosyllabic consonant clusters beginning with a rhotic. A spectrographic analysis demonstrates assibilation of coda rhotics in the Spanish of highland Ecuador, which differentiates this dialect from others studied experimentally. Cross-dialectal differences are analyzed within Optimality Theory as the different ranking of competing constraints. In "Acquisition of sociolinguistic variables in Spanish: Do children acquire individual lexical forms or variable rules?", Manuel Díaz-Campos investigates whether children acquire sociolinguistically variable phonology as a rule or as a case-by-case copying of adults' surface forms. In studying the variable pronunciation of intervocalic /d/ in Venezuelan children's speech, it is found that variability exists in all age groups, and for each age group in the most frequent words more than in the less frequent words. Dictionary frequency and corpus frequency are found to be the most important predictors of the pronunciation of /d/, and this lends support to the case-by-case hypothesis. The final paper in Part 3 is Marta Ortega-Llebaria's contribution, "Interplay between phonetic and inventory constraints in the degree of spirantization of voiced stops: Comparing intervocalic /b/ and intervocalic /g/ in Spanish and English". The findings show that stress and vowel context had similar effects on both /b/ and /g/. In both Spanish and English, the two consonants were most lenited in trochees than in iambs. However, inventory constraints limited the effect of phonetic factors accounting for cross-linguistic and speaker variation. This leads to the conclusion that lenition of intervocalic consonants is a gradient phenomenon whose variability is best described by the interaction of phonetic factors and inventory constraints.

It is my sincere desire that the currently growing interest in Spanish laboratory phonology will continue for years to come, and that this will be the first of many volumes dedicated to the empirical investigation and analysis of the Spanish sound system. I draw hope from the success of the Laboratory Approaches to Spanish Phonology conference held in 2002, from Mouton's desire to publish this volume, and perhaps most of all from the knowledge that a second conference dedicated to this topic will be hosted by Indiana University in Fall 2004, with another volume to follow. May this start be a building block for more laboratory approaches to Spanish phonology in the years to come.

List of contributors

Travis G. Bradley	University of California at Davis, Davis, California, USA
Manuel Díaz-Campos	Indiana University, Bloomington, Indiana, USA
David Eddington	Brigham Young University, Provo, Utah, USA
Timothy L. Face	University of Minnesota, Minneapolis, Minnesota, USA
Sharon Gerlach	University of Minnesota, Minneapolis, Minnesota, USA
Margaret Kehoe	Universität Hamburg, Hamburg, Germany
Martin Krakow	Universität Hamburg, Hamburg, Germany
Conxita Lleó	Universität Hamburg, Hamburg, Germany
Marta Ortega-Llebaria	University of Northern Colorado, Greeley, Colorado, USA
Pilar Prieto	Universitat Autònoma de Barcelona, Barcelona, Spain
Mark Waltermire	University of New Mexico, Albuquerque, New Mexico, USA
Erik W. Willis	New Mexico State University, Las Cruces, New Mexico, USA

Part I

Intonation

Acquisition of language-specific pitch accent by Spanish and German monolingual and bilingual children

Conxita Lleó
Martin Rakow
Margaret Kehoe

1. Introduction

Although in recent years the study of intonation has seen a flourishing development in relation to innumerable languages, it has not undergone a parallel development as far as first language acquisition is concerned. It is not to be denied that prosody in general has attracted much attention from first language acquisition researchers, especially in the realm of perception, although many results are not yet clear. Such lack of clarity is especially true as far as production is concerned. On the one hand, it is often claimed that suprasegmentals are learned very early in first language acquisition. Children seem to be able to tune in to the prosody of their target language earlier than to segments. In the realm of perception, Mehler and Christophe (1994) have presented evidence that new-borns can distinguish their language as belonging to a certain rhythm group, as stress-timed or syllable-timed, and Bosch and Sebastián-Gallés (2001) have shown that at the age of 4 months children can distinguish their own native language on the basis of prosody, distinguishing it even from another language belonging to the same rhythmic group. As soon as at the babbling stage, children have certain rhythmic preferences in their productions depending on their target language: Children acquiring English have a preference for trochees, whereas children acquiring French have a preference for iambs (Whalen, Levitt, and Wang 1991; Vihman, De Paolis, and Davis 1998). On the other hand, it has also been claimed that other prosodic aspects like vowel length and lexical tone are acquired relatively late by children growing up in a language that distinguishes vowels by length or has contrastive tones (Fikkert 1994; Clumeck 1980). These latter opinions have been questioned, though, by Kehoe and colleagues (Kehoe, and Stoel-Gammon 2001; Kehoe 2002; Kehoe, and Lleó 2003) as regards vowel length. Other researchers have argued that pitch contours may be learned before certain segmental oppositions are acquired (Snow and Stoel-Gammon 1993; Vihman 1996).

With respect to intonation, research has barely begun. In order to find out whether children acquire the intonation units of their target language from the earliest stage on, the child must produce relatively long utterances, with a fair number of syllables. This implies that research on the acquisition of intonation in production must wait until children are about 2;6 and, thus, cannot observe the earliest stages. Research on the earlier stages would be limited to a few syllables, and therefore would not allow us to observe full intonational patterns; we would only be able to observe some partial aspects, as in Snow and Stoel-Gammon (1993), who analyzed productions of English learning children at 18 and at 24 months, limiting their study to final phrases. Such studies nevertheless, enable us to find out whether from the production of the first sentences on, intonation is target-like or whether certain substitutions take place, as in the segmental realm.

Until recently, cross-linguistic investigation of intonation was hampered by the lack of common representational tools for intonation. Comparisons between languages were done, but they were based on phonetic properties, not on systematic or phonemic ones, and this made comparative results difficult. Since the advent of the Autosegmental-Metrical Model of representation, based on Pierrehumbert (1980), we have a tool for cross-linguistic comparison of intonational systems. Although this representational system may, in some instances, be ambiguous or unclear (Hualde 2003), it leads to the search of the basic patterns of pitch accents in languages, i.e. the phonological units of intonation, and thus provides a good basis for comparison.

Many questions have not even begun to be asked as regards intonation. For instance, are there universals in intonational phonology? What should they be? Are there certain pitch accents which are more marked than others? If there are, which are the (un)marked patterns? Candidates for universals seem to be e.g. the lowering tone at the end of declarative sentences. There is also a tendency in many languages to produce rising tones in interrogative sentences, but this depends on the type of interrogative (yes/no vs. wh-questions) and on the language. Downtrend might also be a general tendency, but only in declaratives. According to Snow and Stoel-Gammon (1993: 82), who attribute their claim to Cruttenden (1986), "final lengthening and one of the major intonation patterns (falling contour) are among the few universals or near universals of speech prosody in the world's languages". At this stage of our limited knowledge on intonation, we have to constrain our questions to very concrete issues, to punctual comparisons between specific aspects that are distinct in different languages. In this context, the comparison between different pitch accents in two languages, like German and Spanish, can help us to know whether both patterns are learned equally well and at the same time point in both languages. In that case, the comparison of the acquisition of those same patterns in the bilingual child will shed light on the possible markedness of one of the patterns over the other.

German and Spanish share a falling tone pattern at the end of declarative sentences and a rising tone pattern towards the end of yes/no questions, although there are also important differences in the phonetic realization of such falling and rising tones, which will not be dealt with in this paper. For the purpose of this study, we have isolated a non-final or prenuclear tone pattern, which can be characterized as falling for German (H*L) and as rising for Spanish (L*H), and we intend to find out whether they are produced target-like by monolingual German and monolingual Spanish children, and by German-Spanish bilinguals. Both tones occur in equivalent prosodic contexts, namely in prenuclear position within declarative broad-focus utterances. The study of the development of these two distinct tone patterns in the bilinguals will not only show whether there is interaction between the two languages of the bilinguals (as influence has been proven in many realms of the simultaneous acquisition of the two languages, German and Spanish). It will also show whether markedness might play a role in the direction of the influence.

The paper is organized as follows. After presenting the two prenuclear pitch accents in German and Spanish declarative broad-focus phrases, the acquisition of the two patterns by monolinguals as well as bilinguals is analyzed. Monolinguals produce each pattern in a quasi-target-like fashion in both languages, but bilinguals do not necessarily do so: whereas one of the bilinguals develops in a way parallel to the monolinguals, the other bilingual child analyzed here shows a tendency to mutually substitute the falling pattern of German and the rising pattern of Spanish, manifesting a stronger tendency to substitute the Spanish pattern with the German one. These results are discussed by considering issues of markedness and frequency of occurrence, and conclusions are drawn.

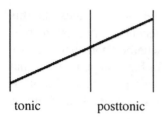

tonic   posttonic

Figure 1. Spanish: L*H

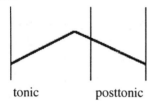

tonic   posttonic

Figure 2. German: H*L (H* or LH*)

2. Two different language-specific pitch accents

A comparison of prenuclear accents comprised within declarative broad-focus utterances shows that the normal tonal pattern in German is a falling one, whereas in Spanish it is a rising one. These two patterns (exemplified in Fig. 1 for German and Fig. 2 for Spanish) have been represented by means of two different pitch accents: H*L in German, i.e. High pitch on the stressed syllable and Low pitch on the following unstressed one (Féry 1993), and L*H in Spanish, that is, the Low pitch is aligned with the stressed syllable, whereas the High pitch is postponed to the following posttonic syllable (Sosa 1999; Face 2002). Since Navarro Tomás' (1944) pioneering work on Spanish Intonation it has been noticed that the latter rising pattern is very common in Spanish; when no contrastive focus is involved, it reaches a frequency of about 70%, according to Garrido et al. (1993) and Sosa (1999), whereby they did not exclude nuclear accents from their counts.

Although there has been some debate about the adequacy of representing the rising pattern of Spanish by means of L*H, and especially about the phonological status of this pitch accent (e.g. Hualde 2002; Prieto 1998; and Prieto, van Santen and Hirschberg 1995 interpreted it as a mere phonetic variant), nowadays a certain consensus has been reached about the correctness of the L*H representation in Spanish (Hualde 2003). In German, the pitch accent characteristic of declarative utterances is considered to be H*L in nuclear as well as in prenuclear position (see Féry 1993; Grabe 1998). The characterization of the German pattern by means of H*L is debatable, though, as shown in Hualde (2003). If we look at Fig. 2, we can see that the H tone is in fact rising, in the same sense that the Spanish pattern in Fig. 1 is rising, too. We could thus represent the German pattern as LH* or just as H*, not including the L tone of the posttonic syllable as part of the pitch accent. The crucial difference between these two representations concerns the posttonic syllable. Whereas the posttonic syllable in Spanish continues the rising trend initiated in the tonic syllable, in German the rising trend ends towards the point at which the tonic syllable ends, and the posttonic is low, i.e., from the tonic to the posttonic there is a falling movement. The difference between the two pitch accents can thus be best characterized by a difference in alignment of tones to text: In the German pattern H is aligned with the stressed syllable, whereas in the Spanish pattern H is aligned with the posttonic. This means that the tone peak occurs within the stressed syllable in German, and within the posttonic syllable in Spanish. If we consider the end of the stressed syllable as the reference null-point for measuring the occurrence of H, the values in ms (corresponding to the distances between the occurrence of the peak and the reference null-point) will tend to be negative in German and positive in Spanish. This contrast in alignment has been used to compare different pitch accents within a single language. For instance, Face (2001, 2002) has shown that in Spanish L*H is the normal prenuclear pitch accent in broad focus declaratives, whereas an early peak alignment, which we label here as H*L, appears in final position and in contrastive focus. In this paper we will apply the measurement of peak alignment cross-linguistically.[1] Nevertheless, we will keep the relatively standard representation H*L for the German pattern.

The cross-linguistic difference shown schematically in Figs. 1 and 2 is exemplified by the representation of the F0 contours corresponding to two real utterances. Fig. 3 shows the F0 contour for the utterance *Que terminó con lo de la banana de la chica* 'That (he/she) finished with that of the girl's banana', taken from Face (2002), and fig. 4 represents the F0 contour corresponding to the sentence *Die Mitarbeiter erfüllen ihre Aufgabe gut* 'The assistants comply well with their tasks', produced by a female native speaker of German. In Spanish, the posttonic syllable in *banana* is produced at a clearly higher pitch than the tonic one; the same is true for the syllable *con* following the oxytonic word *terminó*, which means that the posttonic bearing the higher pitch does not need to belong to the same lexical unit to which the tonic belongs. In German, *Mitarbeiter* is accented in the first syllable, which is the one bearing the peak, whereas the rest of the word shows a falling pitch. The same might be argued for the paroxytonic word *erfüllen* - the middle stressed syllable is higher than the following unstressed one - but here the voiceless onset of the middle syllable might have had a microprosodic effect on the higher tone.

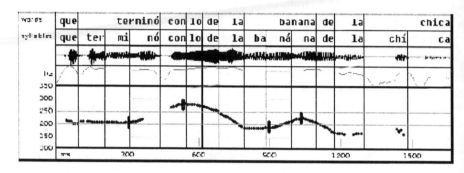

Figure 3. Example pitch tracks of broad focus sentence in target Spanish. F0 measurement points are marked with vertical black lines. (From Face, 2002)

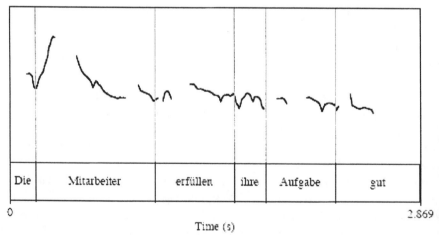

Figure 4. Example pitch tracks of broad focus sentence in target German

3. Acquisition of the two pitch accents by monolingual and bilingual children

Our first research question is: do German and Spanish monolinguals produce the two distinct pitch accents of their target languages in a target-like manner from the beginning of their production of declarative-like broad focus utterances? It should be noted that the question is meant in a phonological rather than phonetic sense. That is, as pointed out in the Introduction we would like to find out whether German children produce the relevant peaks with negative values in ms and whether Spanish children produce them with positive values. However, we will not be able to judge whether the realization of the pitch accents (i.e. the differences in Hz between Ls and Hs) have a range similar to the adult ranges, or whether the point in the syllable at which the peaks are produced exactly correspond to the points characteristic of the target languages. Although we might be able to answer these questions in the future, at this point of our knowledge, we cannot. On the one hand, it is well-known that children's voices are generally higher than the voices of adults, so that their ranges will also be larger. On the other hand, in intonation there is much individual variation in realization and we do not have clear acoustic values as regards the target languages. In Spanish Face's work provides the first concrete results in the right direction; but we are not aware of comparable work in German. We will thus try to find out whether German children produce H*L and Spanish children L*H.

Our second research question regards bilingual acquisition: assuming that the two pitch accents are acquired by the monolinguals in each language, do German-Spanish bilinguals produce the two distinct pitch accents in each target language in a target-like manner from their beginning of production of declarative-like broad focus utterances? Here, again, the question refers to phonology rather than phonetics, although the concrete acoustic values and ranges of the height in Hz and distance of the peaks from the 0 point in ms will also be ascertained. According to general predictions about the simultaneous acquisition of two languages from birth, and to our own analyses in other domains of prosodic acquisition (Kehoe 2002; Lleó 2002; Kehoe & Lleó 2003; Lleó et al. 2003), we can expect a certain interaction between the two languages. It is difficult to predict in which direction interaction might appear, that is, which language will influence the other. Our findings in previous work point to markedness of a certain grammatical phenomenon as well as to the dominance of one language over the other as predictable criteria for influence. In the present case, we have selected the most balanced bilingual children of our project, as regards their competence and performance in the two languages. This allows us to exclude dominance as a factor of influence regarding these two bilingual children. Markedness is here difficult to judge, because both pitch accents are used in many languages. However, Snow and Stoel-Gammon (1993) in their study of English children at 18 and 24 months, in which they were investigating the relationship of final lengthening and either falling or rising pitch, concluded that rising pitch should be considered as being more marked than falling pitch (see also Vihman 1996). Moreover, taking into consideration that German has the falling pattern both in nuclear and prenuclear position, whereas Spanish has the falling pattern in final position and the rising one only medially (as argued above, some authors consider that the rising pattern in Spanish broad focus declaratives occurs about 70% of the time), the frequency of H*L is much higher than L*H in the case of the bilinguals. In this sense, we can formulate the hypothesis that, on markedness considerations as well as on the basis of a frequency criterion, interaction between the two languages may lead to a certain preference for the German H*L pattern and a certain delay in the acquisition of the Spanish rising pitch pattern.

3.1. Data: Subjects and methodology

Speech samples have been selected from two longitudinal databases, a monolingual one created at the University of Hamburg in the early 1990s, and a bilingual one being collected at the present in the Research Center on Multilingualism at the same university. We have selected relatively long phrases, produced by two German children (Marion and Thomas), one Spanish monolingual child (Miguel) and two German-Spanish bilingual children (Jens and Simon) between 2;10 and 3;1 focusing on the production of trochees and non-finally stressed multisyllabic words within broad-focus declarative utterances. The goal was to collect 20 utterances for each child and language. The data of the monolingual children were recorded as part of a DFG-project (PAIDUS), and the data of the bilinguals have been recorded in recent years within the project B3/E3.[2] All data have been recorded in the children's homes, in a naturalistic setting, by interacting with the child. The relevant utterances were selected according to strict criteria: besides being high quality recordings, the utterances had to be long enough in order to include a phrase with prenuclear accent, they had to correspond to declarative sentences and not contain a focused word. That is, the utterance needed either come "out of the blue" or be the answer to a general question posed to the child, like "what is this?, what happened?", etc., but they could not themselves be questions or contain contrastive focus. All utterances were heard by two investigators; some examples that were ambiguous or differently interpreted by the two investigators were heard once more and, where necessary, re-examined with the video. Since our goal was the acoustic analysis of F0, the sound of the utterances had to be of high quality. This requirement excluded some children of the project entirely, especially in the Spanish side of the project, whose utterances were overlaid by a great deal of noise; this is why out of the Spanish group, which originally comprised 4 children, the utterances of one single child, Miguel, could be used for the acoustic analysis.

Given the strict criteria for the selection of relevant words, in some cases, e.g. the bilingual child Jens in German, the goal of 20 sentences could not be reached. Many cases had to be excluded because a) the relevant word was suspected to be focused, or b) the relevant unit was constituted by two words. In the case of (a), focused words must be excluded, because they show what can be characterized as opposite F0 contours to the ones analyzed here. That is, one way of marking focus in Spanish is manifested by the pattern that we label here as H*L (Face 2002), whereas in German, one of the possible contours to mark focus is L*H (Féry 1993). It is obvious that to include such focused words would completely alter the results. With respect to (b), in Spanish the posttonic syllable bearing the high tone of L*H can belong to a different word than the one containing the tonic syllable, or constitute a functional word (e.g. article or preposition), as in the example of Fig. 3, *terminó con* 'finished with', in which the posttonic syllable *con* constitutes a different, functional word, from the stressed verb. However, in German it is preferable to avoid the combination of more than one word, as the second (functional) one may also bear stress, as for instance the articles in *auch ein* 'also a', *haben das* 'have that' (Wiese 1996); the same is true in combinations like *das sind* 'these are', *habe hier* '(I) have here'. All of those cases, in which the posttonic syllable did not belong to the same lexical item as the tonic one, have been excluded in German, and in order to apply consistent criteria, we have also excluded those cases in Spanish.

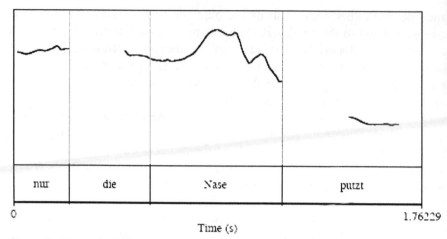

Figure 5. Example of H*L by the monolingual German child Marion

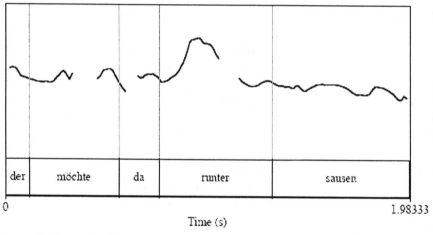

Figure 6. Example of H*L by the monolingual German child Thomas

Once the relevant utterances had been selected, they were digitized with a sampling rate of 44.1 KHz. The pitch analysis is based on accurate auto-correlation method. The pitch curves of the utterances were acoustically analyzed with Praat for MacIntosh, that is, the course of F0 was repre-sented and measured. The distance of the tone peak of the relevant word(s), corresponding to the prenuclear accent, was measured in ms, taking as the reference point the end of the stressed syllable, which counted as zero. If the posttonic syllable (the syllable following the stressed one) had a consonantal onset that was difficult to track to its exact beginning, as is sometimes the case with fricatives and glides, the middle point of the transition from the last segment of the tonic syllable to the initial consonant (of the posttonic syllable) was taken as the reference point. In problematic cases, as in some open syllables, the end of the syllable was judged to be at the end of the 2nd Formant of the vowel. The distance between the peak (highest point) and the valley (the lowest one) within the relevant word was also measured in Hz. In order to have an overview of all declarative sentences, the tone height at the beginning of the utterance was measured in Hz and compared to the tone height at the end of the utterance; this should provide the value of the final low tone and the degree of falling that has taken place at the end of the utterance, in relation to the initial tone. These additional measurements are phonetic rather than phonological, and will not be reported here.

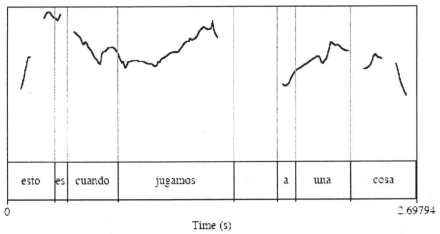

Time (s)

Figure 7. Example of L*H by the monolingual Spanish child Miguel.

Some background information about the bilingual children is to the point. As mentioned above, both Jens and Simon can be considered as balanced bilinguals. The mothers of both children are native speakers of Spanish and the children spent their first two and a half years of life with them. Besides, in the case of Simon, the parents report to usually speak Spanish at home. At the age at which the data have been analyzed, between 2;10 and 3;1, both children attended a day care center, which could give some dominance to German; the day care center, though, is a bilingual one, Spanish being used almost exclusively by the personnel and also very often among the children.

3.2. Results of the phonological analysis

The two German monolingual children produced most of the relevant words with a H*L pattern, with one single L*H exception in the case of Marion, and a few more L*H patterns in the case of Thomas. The Spanish child, Miguel, produced most of the relevant words with a L*H pattern, and a few with a H*L pattern. Figs. 5 to 7 present some typical examples of the monolingual children's productions: Figs. 5 and 6 show illustrative examples of utterances by the monolingual German Marion and Thomas, respectively, and Fig. 7 shows an example by the monolingual Spanish child, Miguel. The percentages for the two German children and one Spanish child as regards the two patterns H*L and L*H are summarized in Fig. 8, which shows H*L on the bottom half of the diagram, because it corresponds to negative values for the distance in ms from the point that we defined as zero (end of the stressed syllable) to the maximum peak of the relevant word. L*H is shown on the top half of the diagram, because it corresponds to positive values. There are some overlapping cases between the utterances produced by the two German and the one Spanish children, but the tendency is clear, as shown in Fig. 8. Fig. 9 plots the values for each individual child by means of a scatter diagram: the two groups are clearly different in their values, with a clear tendency towards the minus values in German (Marion produces 93% of the cases with minus values and Thomas 61%) and towards the plus values in Spanish (68% of the relevant cases are produced with plus values by Miguel). Fig. 9 shows also the mean value for the distance in ms for each child, calculated on the basis of all the words considered for each child: Miguel shows a mean of +47 ms, whereas the mean values for Marion and Thomas are negative, -74 ms and -28 ms respectively. Although both German children have negative values, Marion's values are higher. This can be interpreted as a clearer H*L pattern in the case of Marion. At this point, though, we cannot judge whether the difference is due to individual preferences or to a higher degree of prosodic development in the case of Marion. In order to be able to claim that the latter is the case, we would need more precise information regarding the position of the peak in the target language.

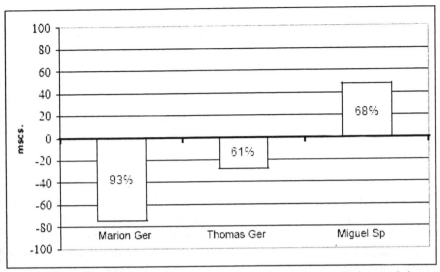

Figure 8. Mean values of peak alignment for the two German children and the one Spanish child showing negative values for German and positive for Spanish.

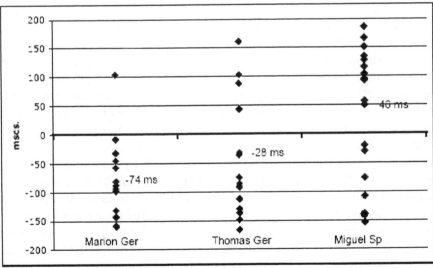

Figure 9. Scatter diagram plotting the values for each individual monolingual child (Marion, Thomas and Miguel).

These results support the conclusion that language-specific prosodic patterns are acquired also in production at a very early age; this is at least the case for intonation, especially as regards the pitch accents H*L and L*H. We now turn to German-Spanish bilinguals. Figs. 10 and 12 show one German example each for Jens and Simon, respectively, and Figs. 11 and 13 show Spanish examples for the two bilinguals, as well. Jens produces the German word *malen* 'paint' (Fig. 10) as well as the Spanish word *muchos* 'viele' (Fig. 11) with the German H*L pattern, whereas in Simon's productions the German word *Wasserflugzeug* 'hydroplane' (Fig. 12) and the Spanish word *banco* 'bench' (Fig. 13) are produced with different tones, the former with H*L in the first two syllables, corresponding to *Wasser* 'water', and the latter with the typical Spanish pattern, L*H. The percentages of production of the two patterns H*L and L*H are summarized in Fig. 14. Here, we can see that Simon has percentages similar to the monolinguals for both languages: in German 79% of the cases are minus values, corresponding to H*L, which is a value in between those of the monolinguals Marion and Thomas; in his Spanish words, he has 59% of positive values, which is a percentage close to that of Miguel, albeit a little lower. Jens' values, however, are much lower than those of the monolinguals in both languages; in fact, his 30% of positive values in Spanish resembles those of the German monolinguals (Thomas had 39% and Marion 7% of L*H). The individual values are better seen in Fig. 15, which plots the distances in ms from the end of the stressed syllable in a scatter diagram. Whereas Fig. 8 for the monolinguals exhibited very few cases of overlap, Fig. 15 shows that in the case of Jens there is a great deal of overlap: Only 55% of the German relevant cases show H*L and, as mentioned, only 30% of the Spanish cases are L*H. Fig. 15 shows the exact point in ms for each particular utterance, and it also gives the mean value for such instances for each particular child: whereas Simon's mean values are similar to the corresponding monolinguals, +65 ms in Spanish and -58 ms in German, Jens shows minus values in both languages, in fact the mean value in Spanish, -42 ms, is higher than the mean of -6 ms in German. The latter very low minus value in German is partly due to the presence of a higher percentage of positive values in German than in Spanish, which certainly affect the average. The main finding in the case of this particular child is that he does not yet control the L*H pattern of Spanish nor the H*L of German, since he seems to use both patterns indiscriminately, with a clear preference for the alignment of the peak with the stressed syllable, that is, a preference of H*L over L*H.

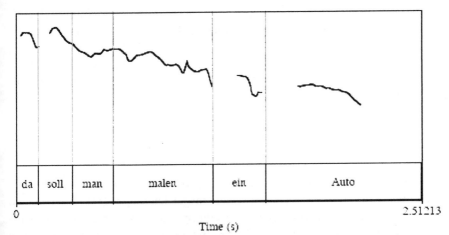

Time (s)

Figure 10. Example in German by the bilingual child Jens

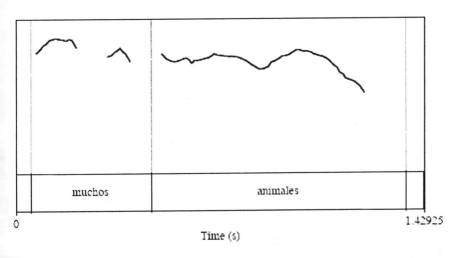

Time (s)

Figure 11. Example in Spanish by the bilingual child Jens

These results partly confirm our hypothesis: one of the bilingual children, Simon, develops like the monolinguals in each language, but the other child, Jens, has a much lower frequency of production of the rising pitch of Spanish, which he often substitutes by H*L, but he also tends to substitute the falling pitch of German more frequently than the monolingual children do.

3.3. Discussion

Our data have shown that monolingual German and Spanish children correctly produce the pitch accents of their target language, H*L for German and L*H for Spanish, from their first attempts to produce broad-focus utterances. This is not surprising given the prosodic sensitivity generally attributed to infants. Such sensitivity has been proposed as regards perception, e.g. within the prosodic bootstrapping hypothesis, which claims that it is precisely this sensitivity to the location of prominent syllables that allows the child to crack the code and set syntactic parameters (Guasti et al. 2001; Mazuka 1996).

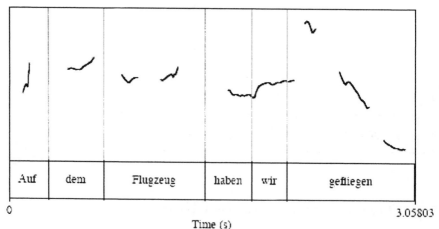

Figure 12. Example in German by the bilingual child Simon.

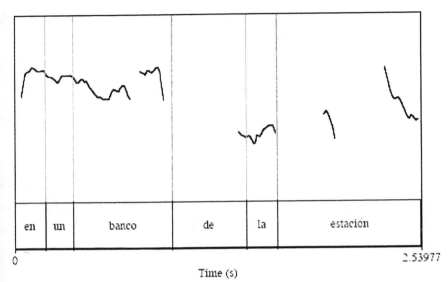

Figure 13. Example in Spanish by the bilingual child Simon

In production, results are somehow contradictory at present. Recently, though, many aspects of prosodic acquisition have been vindicated for very young infants, as well. For instance, Kehoe and Stoel-Gammon (2001) and Kehoe and Lleó (2003) have shown that the quantity opposition in vowels is acquired earlier than proposed in past work. Kehoe (1995) has also shown that children make very few stress errors in early acquisition. In Kehoe and Lleó (2004) it has also been shown that monolingual children acquiring Spanish and German produce distinct rhythmic patterns, appropriate to their target language.

In the domain of intonation, there has not been much work done, and it is thus impossible to compare our very preliminary results to previous ones.[3] Given that according to our findings both pitch accents are produced relatively target-like at the same time, depending on the ambient language of the child, there would seem to be no (un)markedness preference. In the segmental domain it has often been shown that children undertake many sound substitutions, and that the direction of the substitution may give evidence for (un)markedness. Such substitutions constitute one of the bases for the notion of markedness (Jakobson [1941] 1968), as e.g. plosives tend to be substituted for fricatives, showing that fricatives are more marked than plosives; coronals tend to be substituted for other Places, thus showing that coronal is the least marked Place of Articulation. If we look at our data from this point of view, we find the following. Although the majority of the relevant phonological phrases were produced with the expected values - negative in German and positive in Spanish - there are several substitutions both in the case of the Spanish child Miguel and the German child Thomas. The only child that practically does not substitute the pitch accent of the target language is Marion, who shows one single substitution, i.e. 7%. With such scarce data it is premature to conclude that the German H*L tone pattern is less marked than the Spanish L*H, but we may want to assume it by way of hypothesis. According to our prediction, we would expect to find more substitutions of the Spanish L*H pattern in earlier productions. We have not been able to analyze earlier productions, though, given the condition that the phrases must have prenuclear accent, that is, the child must produce more than one tone group within an utterance.

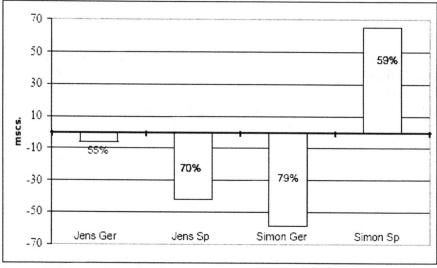

Figure 14. Mean values of peak alignment for the two bilingual children in German and Spanish

However, there is independent evidence about the (un)markedness status of H*L and L*H. Snow and Stoel-Gammon (1993) conclude that the contour L*H is more marked than H*L. The basis for this conclusion stems from data on 18 month- and 24 month-old children acquiring English, whose productions of utterances with final falling and rising tones were acoustically analyzed; the analyses focused on intonation contours and syllable lengthening. They have two reasons for their conclusion: 1) Syllable timing, i.e. final lengthening is reported to develop later than tone contours, but "final lengthening is acquired more slowly in the context of rising contours than in falling contours"; they refer to a similar finding in French by Allen (1983). 2) The rising contours are characterized by a larger standard deviation than the falling ones: at 18 months the S.D. of the rising contours amounts to 362 Hz, whereas that of the falling contours is only 139 Hz; at 24 months the S.D. of rising contours has decreased to 130 Hz, but that of the falling contours has also decreased to 91 Hz; this development leads to the claim that "the rising pattern is acquired more slowly than the falling pattern", a finding also reported in Crystal (1986).

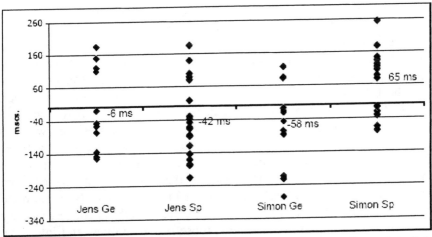

Figure 15. Scatter diagram plotting the values of peak alignment for each individual bilingual child (Jens and Simon)

This hypothesis can be put to the test with bilinguals in the following sense. Given that the Spanish-German bilinguals acquire two languages with opposite patterns appearing in the same kind of context, a rising one in Spanish and a falling one in German, the least marked of the patterns should prevail, other things being equal. Things would be unequal, if one of the languages of the bilingual dominates over the other one. As mentioned above, in Section 3.1, Jens and Simon can be considered as balanced bilinguals, given criteria for language preference (language use) as well as criteria for mastery (language competence). Our results have shown that Simon acquires both pitch accents approximately the same way as monolinguals do; however, Jens substitutes a majority of the Spanish rising pattern by the German falling one: out of 20 cases attempted in Spanish, only 6 are produced as L*H, the remaining 14 being produced as H*L. Other things being equal, Jens' findings seem thus to confirm our hypothesis that L*H is more marked than H*L, since the former is quite often submitted to substitution, i.e. 70% of the time. This would imply that as in the case of truncation (Lleó 2002) or VOT (Kehoe, Lleó, and Rakow 2004), the unmarked pattern tends to be the prevalent one. This conclusion, though, is complicated by the fact that Jens also substitutes some of the expected H*L patterns in German by the L*H pattern: 5 out of 11 analyzable cases, that is, 45% of the time. This may mean that, although the unmarked pattern prevails over the marked one, this child experiences much interaction between his two prosodic systems; that is, his prosodic systems are not kept completely separated, for which the input may bear most of the accountability.

Regarding frequency of appearance, things are not really equal for the following reasons. In Spanish and German, children are confronted with both H*L as well as L*H tones, although with different frequencies. Besides the L*H prenuclear contours which we have analyzed in this paper, Spanish has also H*L at the end of declaratives and in narrow focus. In German, H*L appears in prenuclear as well as nuclear position, whereas L*H is restricted to certain kinds of narrow focus and to interrogatives. These facts entail that in declarative sentences children are more often confronted in German with the H*L pattern than they are in Spanish confronted with L*H. Accordingly, it would be important to analyze interrogative sentences, as well, as L*H is present there in both languages, German and Spanish. Combining both results, those of declaratives and interrogatives, would allow us to disentangle the two factors discussed, markedness and input frequency.

4. Conclusions

The main findings of our study, based on two German monolinguals, one Spanish monolingual and two German-Spanish balanced bilinguals are:
1) The German monolinguals produce H*L as a prenuclear accent in broad-focus declaratives before 3;0.
2) The Spanish monolingual produces L*H as a prenuclear accent in broad-focus declaratives before 3;0.

3) One German-Spanish bilingual produces both H*L and L*H as a prenuclear accent in broad-focus declaratives before 3;0 with frequencies equivalent to those of monolinguals.

4) Another German-Spanish bilingual also produces both H*L and L*H as a prenuclear accent in broad-focus declaratives before 3;0, but he mutually substitutes many of them, especially substituting Spanish patterns with German ones.

Given the substitution patterns we have found in our data, and given previous reports for English and French, we hypothesize that L*H is more marked than H*L. Markedness can thus explain the higher frequency of substitution of H*L for L*H in Spanish. Markedness cannot explain the reverse substitution of L*H for H*L which was occasionally found in German. To explain the latter substitution pattern frequency of occurrence should also be called upon, as L*H also appears in interrogatives.

A general conclusion is warranted that children are aware of prosody not only in perception, but also in production from very early on. As regards bilinguals, they acquire the pitch accents of their target languages, too, but it may take longer for them to keep the two patterns apart, especially the most marked and/or less frequent one.

Notes

1. We are indebted to Pilar Prieto, for suggesting this means of accounting for the difference between the two languages. We also thank Michelle Steiner, who did most of the acoustic measurements.
2. We are grateful to the DFG and the University of Hamburg for their support of our project, which is carried out at the Research Center on Multilingualism.
3. Gut (2000) constitutes an exception to this claim, trying to capture the development of most phonological as well as phonetic aspects of intonation of three German-English bilingual children; but she also complains about the lack of evidence regarding monolingual acquisition of intonation.

References

Allen, George D.
    1983   Some suprasegmental contours in French two-year-old children's speech. *Phonetica* 40: 269-292.
Bosch, Laura, and Núria Sebastián-Gallés
    2001   Evidence of early language discrimination abilities in infants from bilingual environments. *Infancy* 2: 29-49.
Harold Clumeck
    1980   The acquisition of tone. In *Child Phonology, Volume 1: Production*, Grace H. Yeni-Komshian, James E. Kavanagh & Charles A. Ferguson (eds.), 257-275. New York: Academic Press.
Cruttenden, Alan
    1986   *Intonation*. Cambridge: Cambridge University Press.
Crystal, David
    1986   Prosodic development. In *Studies in First Language Development*, Paul Fletcher and Michael Garman (eds.), 174-197. New York: Cambridge University Press.
Face, Timothy L.
    2001   Focus and early peak alignment in Spanish intonation. *Probus* 13: 223-246.
    2002   Local intonational marking of Spanish contrastive focus. *Probus* 14: 71-92.
Féry, Caroline
    1993   *German Intonational Patterns*. Tübingen: Niemeyer.
Fikkert, Paula
    1994   *The Acquisition of Prosodic Structure*. The Hague: Holland Academic Graphics.
Garrido, Juan M., Joaquim Llisterri, Carme de la Mota and Antonio Ríos
    1993   Prosodic differences in reading style: Isolated vs. contextualized sentences. *Eurospeech* 93: 573-576.
Grabe, Esther
    1998   Pitch accent realization in English and German. *Journal of Phonetics* 26: 129-143.
Guasti, Maria Theresa, Anne Christophe, Brit van Ooyen, and Marina Nespor
    2001   Pre-lexical setting of the head: Complement parameter through prosody. In *Approaches to Bootstrapping: Phonological, Lexical, Syntactic and Neurophysiological Aspects of Early Language Acquisition,* Jürgen Weissenborn and Barbara Höhle (eds.), Vol. I, 231-248. Amsterdam: John Benjamins.

Gut, Ulrike
  2000   *Bilingual Acquisition of Intonation: A Study of Children Speaking German and English.* Tübingen: Niemeyer.
Hualde, José Ignacio
  2002   Intonation in Spanish and the other Ibero-Romance languages: Overview and status quaestionis. In *Romance Phonology and Variation*, Caroline R. Wiltshire and Joaquim Camps (eds.), 101-115. Amsterdam: John Benjamins.
  2003   El modelo métrico y autosegmental. In *Teorías de la entonación*, Pilar Prieto (ed.), 155-184. Barcelona: Ariel.
Jakobson, Roman
  1968   Reprint. *Child Language, Aphasia and Phonological Universals.* The Hague: Mouton. Original edition, Uppsala: Alqmvist & Wiksell, 1941.
Kehoe, Margaret
  1995   An investigation of rhythmic processes in English-speaking children's word productions. Ph.D. diss., University of Washington.
  2002   Developing vowel systems as a window to bilingual phonology. *International Journal of Bilingualism* 6: 315-334.
Kehoe, Margaret, and Carol Stoel-Gammon
  2001   Development of syllable structure in English-speaking children with particular reference to rhymes. *Journal of Child Language* 28: 393-432.
Kehoe, Margaret, and Conxita Lleó
  2003   The acquisition of phonological vowel length: A longitudinal analysis of three German-speaking children. *Journal of Child Language* 30: 527–556.
  2004   The emergence of language specific rhythm in German-Spanish bilingual children. Manuscript.
Kehoe, Margaret, Conxita Lleó, and Martin Rakow
  2004   Voice onset time in bilingual German-Spanish children. Manuscript.
Kehoe, Margaret, Cristina Trujillo, and Conxita Lleó
  2001   Bilingual phonological acquisition: An analysis of syllable structure and VOT. *Arbeiten zur Mehrsprachigkeit* 27: 38-54.
Lleó, Conxita
  2002   The role of markedness in the acquisition of complex prosodic structures by German-Spanish bilinguals. *International Journal of Bilingualism* 6: 291-313.

Lleó, Conxita, Imme Kuchenbrandt, Margaret Kehoe, and Cristina Trujillo
    2003   Syllable final consonants in Spanish and German monolingual
            and bilingual acquisition. In *(Non)Vulnerable Domains in Multi-
            lingualism*, Natascha Müller (ed.), 191-220. Amsterdam: John
            Benjamins.
Mazuka, Reiko
    1996   How can a grammatical parameter be set before the first word?
            Prosodic contributions to early setting of a grammatical parame-
            ter. In *Signal to Syntax: Bootstrapping from Speech to Grammar
            in Early Acquisition,* James L. Morgan and Katherine Demuth
            (eds.), 313-330. Mahwah, NJ: Erlbaum.
Mehler, Jacques, and Anne Christophe
    1994   Maturation and learning of language in the first year of life. In
            The Cognitive Neurosciences, Michael S. Gazzaniga (ed.), 943-
            954. Cambridge, Mass.: MIT Press.
Navarro Tomás, Tomás
    1944   *Manual de entonación española.* Madrid: Guadarrama.
Pierrehumbert, Janet
    1980   The phonology and phonetics of English intonation. Ph.D. diss.,
            Cambridge, Mass.: MIT Press.
Prieto, Pilar
    1998   The scaling of the L values in Spanish downstepping contours.
            Journal of Phonetics 26: 261-282.
Prieto, Pilar, Jan P. H. van Santen, and Julia Hirschberg
    1995   Tonal alignment patterns in Spanish. *Journal of Phonetics* 23:
            429-451.
Snow, David, and Carol Stoel-Gammon
    1993   Intonation and final lengthening in early child language. In *First
            and Second Language Phonology*, Mehmet S. Yavas (ed.), 81-
            105. San Diego, California: Singular Publishing Group.
Sosa, Juan Manuel
    1999   *La entonación del español.* Madrid: Cátedra.
Vihman, Marilyn M.
    1996   *Phonological Development: The Origins of Language in the
            Child.* Oxford, UK: Blackwell.
Vihman, Marilyn M., Rory A. DePaolis, and Barbara L. Davis
    1998   Is there a "Trochaic Bias" in early word learning? Evidence from
            infant production in English and French. *Child Development* 69:
            935-949.

Whalen, D.H. Andrea G. Levitt and Qi Wang
  1991   Intonational differences between the reduplicative babbling of French- and English-learning infants. *Journal of Child Language* 18: 501-516.
Wiese, Richard
  1996   *The Phonology of German.* Oxford: Clarendon Press.

The search for phonological targets in the tonal space: H1 scaling and alignment in five sentence-types in Peninsular Spanish

Pilar Prieto

1. Introduction

The quest for phonological and linguistic units in the F0 continuum has been and still is one of the main research questions in intonation studies. In recent years there has been accumulating evidence that LH points in the tonal space behave as phonological targets. Indeed, H peaks of both nuclear and prenuclear pitch accents are produced with an amazing degree of stability in tonal scaling and tonal alignment across languages (see Arvaniti et al. 2000; Liberman and Pierrehumbert 1984; Prieto, van Santen, and Hirschberg 1995; Prieto, Shih, and Nibert 1996; Silverman and Pierrehumbert 1990; and recent work by Xu 1999, 2002). Nowadays, a central assumption of the standard autosegmental-metrical model (and of most work on intonation) is that pitch range variation is paralinguistic, that is, it expresses exclusively differences in emphasis or prominence. This assumption relies on a version of the so-called Free Gradient Hypothesis (Ladd 1996). It is indeed clear that one of the most common effects of gradually expanding the pitch range of a given pitch accent is the pragmatic reinforcement of the utterance, that is, an increase in the degree of speaker's involvement in the speech act. Recently, though, some work within the autosegmental model has revealed that pitch range variation does not always correspond to phonetically gradient changes indicating overall emphasis/prominence (due to the speaker's implication in the speech act) but rather it can trigger categorical distinctions in meaning (Hirschberg and Ward 1992; Ward and Hirschberg 1985; Ladd 1994, 1996). Thus, steps have been taken towards the phonologization of the pitch range category such as the inclusion of a [raised peak] feature (Ladd 1994, 1996) or an upstepped accent in the tonal inventory (Beckman et al. 2002).

This work sets out to contribute to this line of research by presenting new materials from Peninsular Spanish intonation with the goal of testing the predictions of the pitch target view and the free-gradient view of intonational production on the behavior of LH pitch accents in 5 different sentence-types (statements, yes-no questions, wh-questions, commands, and exclamatory sentences). The main goal of the study is to describe the effects of sentence-type information on the scaling and alignment behavior of sentence-initial peaks (H1). In this respect, Spanish represents a particularly interesting case, as past studies on Spanish intonation have noted that the presence of higher initial peaks both in interrogative (Canellada and Kuhlmann Madsen 1987; Navarro Tomás 1944; Sosa 1992, 1999) and imperative utterances (Kvavic 1988; Navarro Tomás 1944; Willis 2002). For example, Navarro Tomás points out that "in the first accented syllable [of interrogative utterances] pitch is increased by three or four semitones over the average level." (Navarro Tomás 1944:141), while "imperative expressions such as *¡Calla!* 'Shut up!', produced with no great emphasis, are produced with a first H peak which is 7 or 8 semitones higher than statements" (Navarro Tomás 1944:186; translation mine).[1]

The data analyzed in this article reveal that F0 levels attained by L and H values are strikingly regular across repetitions of the same utterances within subjects, thus confirming the prediction of the pitch-target hypothesis (i.e., in pronouncing an intonation contour, speakers clearly aim for precise F0 targets). Utterance-initial rising accents have different LH alignment and scaling properties depending on phrasal-type information. One the one hand, while late sentence-initial peaks are typical of statements and interrogatives, early peaks characterize imperatives and exclamatory sentences. On the other hand, sentence-type has also a clear effect on H1 scaling: Statements have the lowest F0 peaks, imperatives and interrogatives are higher, and exclamatives are the highest, clearly advocating for a 2-way (or possibly a 3-way) distinction in H1 height. In sum, the results of this article clearly demonstrate that F0 scaling variation is not only a continuum that varies gradiently to express emphasis, but it can also be used to convey grammatical differences, i.e., sentence-type marking.

2. Speech materials

It has often been reported that factors like phrasal length, phrasal position and within-word position of the target accent play a crucial role in determining the phonetic realization of pitch accents. For example, Silverman and Pierrehumbert (1990) for English and Prieto, van Santen, and Hirschberg (1995) for Spanish have reported that prosodic factors like sentence-position, within-word position and distance-to-stress trigger alignment changes on pitch accent gestures. With regard to pitch scaling, several production experiments have found that peak values of prenuclear accents are quite stable within speakers and can be predicted exclusively on the basis of the value of the previous peak (Liberman and Pierrehumbert 1984 for English; Prieto, Shih, and Nibert 1996 for Spanish). The database described in this section was designed to test the effects of utterance length and within-word position on the scaling and alignment patterns of pitch accents (and especially, utterance-initial pitch accents) found in the following sentence-types:

1. Statements
2. Yes-no questions
3. Wh-questions
4. Commands
5. Exclamative sentences

The two sets of utterances below show two-accent utterances containing words with penultimate stress (left-hand column) side by side with two-accent utterances containing words with final stress (right-hand column). Stressed syllables are marked in boldface. Whenever possible, words were composed of open syllables and sonorant consonants (to avoid segmentally-induced effects on the F0 curve). For a complete set of utterances (encoded using the same notational scheme), see the Appendix.

2p1: *La **nena** **mira***	2u1: *La **mamá** **miró***
2p2: ¿*La **nena** **mira**?*	2u2: ¿*La **mamá** **miró**?*
2p3: ¿***Dónde** **mira** la **nena**?*	2u3: ¿***Qué** **miró** la **mamá**?*
2p4: (imp.) ¡***Mira** a la **nena**!*	2u4: (imp.)¡***Mirad** a la **mamá**!*
2p5: (excl.) ¡***Mira** a la **nena**!*	2u5: (excl.) ¡***Miró** a la **mamá**!*

Two speakers of Peninsular Spanish (henceforth PS) read 2 repetitions of each utterance in the database in random order, for a total of 240 utterances (60 utterances x 2 repetitions x 2 speakers = 240 utterances). Speakers were asked to read the utterances with a normal speech rate and avoiding emphatic readings and pauses. The exclamative and imperative readings (which in some instances are just the same sentence; cf. 2p4 and 2p5 in the examples above) were elicited by prompting a written message to the reader that this particular meaning was intended.[2] All of the utterances were produced in a single intonational phrase, with no prosodic breaks. The two informants were a male speaker from Lleida, Guillem

Hernández (henceforth GH), and a female speaker from Huesca, Mercedes Nasarre (henceforth MN). Even though GH is a Catalan-Spanish native bilingual speaker, the intonation patterns produced by the two speakers were very consistent across sentence-types: The differences between both subjects potentially due to dialectal differences only emerged in some isolated examples (see wh-questions in section 3.2).

The database was prosodically annotated using ToBI, and the following measurements were manually indicated in each sound file: Utterance-initial F0 value (In), utterance-final value (Fin), highest F0 peak and lowest F0 value for every pitch accent and boundary tones. To calculate the timing values of peaks and valleys, the following measurements were also marked with the help of spectrograms: Onset (On1, On2) and offset (Of) of every target syllable.

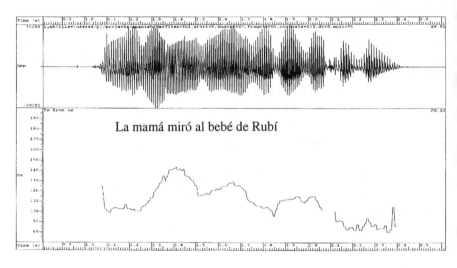

Figure 1. Waveform and F0 contour of the utterance *La mamá miró al bebé de Rubí*, produced by speaker GH.

3. Analysis of the data

3.1. Statements

Both speakers produced simple declarative sentences with a series of downstepped rising prenuclear accents and a rising nuclear accent (with very compressed pitch range). After the nuclear accent, the curve descends gradually to the bottom of the speakers' range. Figure 1 shows the waveform and the F0 contour of the 4-accent sentence *La mamá miró al bebé de Rubí* 'Mummy looked at Rubí's baby', as produced by speaker GH.

Utterance-initial and utterance-final F0 values were found to be rather constant for a given speaker, and no correlation was found between phrasal length and initial/final F0 values (with the exception of initial values in sentences with one accent, which are slightly lower than the rest for the two speakers). The two graphs in Figure 2 plot the average utterance-initial and final values (in Hz) for sentences of different lengths (1 to 4 pitch accents) for speakers GH and MN. Except for single-pitch accent sentences (e.g., *La mamá*), speakers produced the test utterances with an almost invariant utterance-initial (103 Hz for speaker GH and 225 Hz for speaker MN) and utterance-final F0 value (85 Hz for speaker GH and 184 for speaker MN). Pairwise *t*-tests comparing beginning and endpoint values in four utterance-length conditions (1 to 4 pitch accents) show that there is no statistical difference between them for the two subjects (except for utterance-initial F0 values in single-accent sentences, which are highly distinct; at $p < 0.01$). This result corroborates Liberman and Pierrehumbert's (1984) findings for English and Prieto, van Santen and Hirschberg's (1995) for Spanish.

Figure 3 plots the average absolute F0 value of the first H peak (in Hz) in utterances of different lengths (1 to 4 pitch accents) for speakers GH and MN. The height of the first accent peak is rather constant across test sentences, with the exception of initial peaks in single-accented utterances (which are substantially lower). Pairwise *t*-tests comparing H1 in 4 different sentence-length conditions reveal that differences in height are only significant for 1-accent sentences (at $p < 0.01$) for the two subjects. These results confirm previous findings on Spanish H scaling (Prieto, van Santen and Hirschberg 1995) in the sense that utterance-length does not substantially affect the control of utterance-initial H pitch range values. That is, speakers do not seem to plan out the utterance in advance and do not progressively 'adapt' the height of the first peak to the length of the sentence (thus, no evidence is found of hard preplanning in Liberman and Pierrehumbert's 1984 sense):

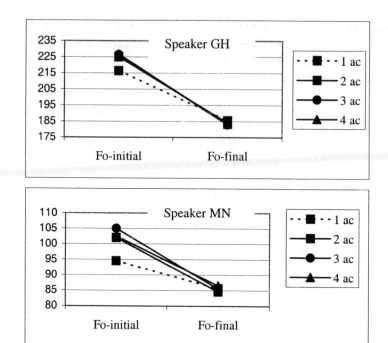

Figure 2.   Mean utterance-initial and utterance-final F0 values (in Hz) in declarative sentences of different lengths (from 1 to 4 pitch accents) for speakers GH and MN.

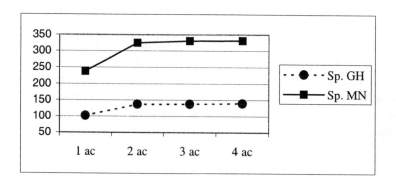

Figure 3.   Mean absolute F0 value of the first peak (in Hz) in declarative utterances of different lengths (from 1 to 4 pitch accents) for speakers GH and MN.

Previous work on Spanish intonation of statements has acknowledged that rising gestures typically start at the onset of the accented syllable, while the peak is generally placed in the posttonic syllable in prenuclear positions and within the tonic syllable in nuclear positions (Face 2001a, 2001b; Navarro Tomás 1944; Hualde 2002; Prieto, van Santen and Hirschberg 1995; Sosa 1999, among many others). One possible interpretation of these facts is that the phonological composition of both rising accents is the same and that H in nuclear position is shifted backwards by prosodic pressure from the L boundary tone (cf. Nibert 2000; Prieto, van Santen and Hirschberg 1995). By contrast, recent work has attributed the contrast in H alignment in nuclear vs. prenuclear positions to a phonological contrast between two accent-types: L+H* for early peak nuclear accents and L*+H for a late peak prenuclear accents (cf. Beckman *et al* 2002; Face 2001a, 2001b; Hualde 2002; Sosa 1999, among others). The two graphs in Figure 4 plot the mean *peak delay* of the first H peak (or distance in ms from the peak to the onset of the accented syllable) as a function of two conditions: Phrasal position (nuclear vs. non-nuclear) and within-word position (antepenultimate, penultimate and final). As expected, H peak delay is significantly shorter in nuclear than in prenuclear position, in all within-word positions. Pairwise *t*-tests comparing the values of H1 peak delay in the two phrasal conditions (nuclear vs. prenuclear) were highly significant (at $p < 0.0001$) for the two speakers. Moreover, the data in Figure 4 shows a slight effect of within-word position, that is, peaks tend to be aligned with the right edge of the word and are progressively more retracted as the distance from the peak to the end of the word decreases in non-nuclear contexts.

Table 1 shows the mean relative peak delay in parentheses (calculated by dividing the absolute peak delay by the duration of the accented syllable) in the same conditions plotted in Figure 4. Relative peak delay measures reveal peaks in nuclear position are always realized within the boundaries of the accented syllable (i.e, the proportion is always less than 1), in contrast with peaks in prenuclear positions. The relative peak delay results in Table 1 clearly advocate for a distinct phonological representation between prenuclear (delayed rise) and nuclear accents (non-delayed rise) in declaratives (as advocated by Face 2001a, 2001b; Hualde 2002; Sosa 1999, among others) and exclude a phonetic explanation for early F0 peak alignment in nuclear contexts. Indeed, the phonetic explanation would not account for the presence of early H peaks in antepenultimate positions, where the prosodic pressure from the L boundary is not active anymore.

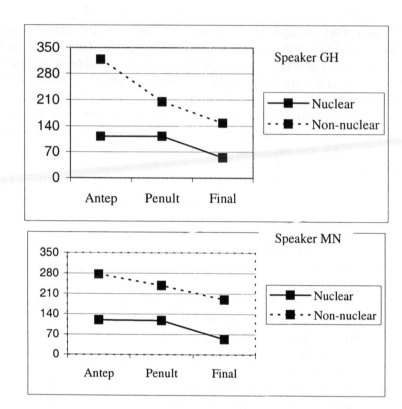

Figure 4. Mean peak delay (in ms) as a function of phrasal position (nuclear vs prenuclear) and within-word position (antepenultimate, penultimate, final) for speakers GH (top) and MN (bottom).

Table 1. Mean peak delay (in ms) in nuclear and non-nuclear positions for speakers GH (top) and MN (bottom).

Speaker GH	Prenuclear	Nuclear
antepenultimate	318.33 (2.64)	112 (0.74)
penultimate	205 (1.58)	112 (0.59)
final	148.33 (1.30)	55 (0.29)
Speaker MN	Prenuclear	Nuclear
antepenultimate	276.66 (2.15)	120 (0.70)
penultimate	238 (1.99)	118 (0.58)
final	190 (1.01)	53 (0.40)

3.2. Questions

Figures 5 and 6 illustrate the waveform and F0 contours of a yes-no question (*¿La nómada mira el número de lámina?*) and a wh-question (*¿Dónde mira la nómada el número de lámina?*) as produced by speaker GH. The two speakers used the same intonational contour for the two sentence-types (except for speaker MN, which very sporadically produced the contour in Figure 7).[3] Absolute interrogative sentences in Peninsular Spanish are characterized by an utterance-initial rising accent aligned with the first stressed syllable, followed by a continuously falling F0 gesture line over the phrase-medial accented syllables (in fact, all phrase-medial stresses were deaccented and showed a peak in our data, thus, the F0 value at the onset was always higher than at the offset). The last accent is always pronounced with a low tone followed with a final rise. Navarro Tomás (1968:226) describes the tune of a PS absolute interrogative sentence as follows: "Interrogative sentences are characterized by an utterance-initial high tone (which is higher than the normal tone), which descends gradually until it reaches the penultimate syllable in the utterance, starting to rise on the utterance-final syllable."

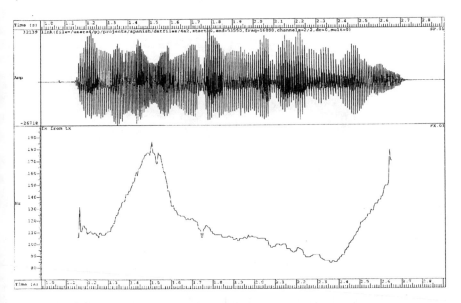

Figure 5.   Waveform and F0 contour of the utterance *¿La nómada mira el número de lámina?* produced by speaker GH.

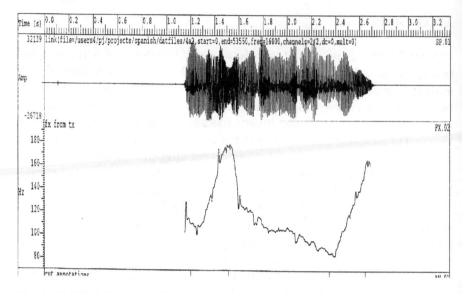

Figure 6. Waveform and F0 contour of the utterance *¿Dónde mira la nómada el número de lámina?*, produced by speaker GH.

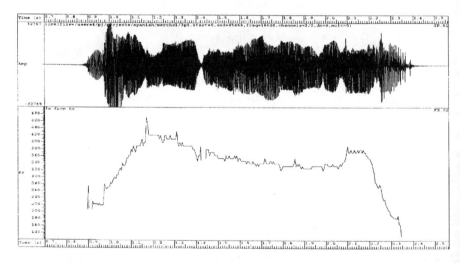

Figure 7. Waveform and F0 contour of the utterance *¿Dónde mira la nómada el número de lámina?*, produced by speaker GH.

Occasionally, speaker MN produced a different F0 contour for wh-questions, which is illustrated in Figure 7 (*¿Dónde mira la nena el loro?*). A prominent rising accent is placed on the wh-particle, and, afterwards, the pitch stays at a high level (forming a H plateau) which starts to descend drastically at the onset of the final accent. This contour is described by Navarro Tomás (1944) as one of the most common Peninsular Spanish intonational patterns for wh-questions.

Previous studies on the intonation of Peninsular Spanish (Navarro Tomás 1944, 1968; Sosa 1992, 1999; Quilis 1981) have noted that sentence-initial F0 peaks of interrogatives are significantly higher than those in statements. This phenomenon has also been noted in languages such as Danish and Swedish (Hadding and Studdert-Kennedy 1972) and in Bengali (Hayes and Lahiri 1991), but it does not occur in English or French (Mettas 1971). Navarro Tomás (1944, 1968) and Canellada and Kuhlmann Madsen (1987) claim that both utterance-initial F0 points and H1 peaks are higher in Spanish interrogatives than in statements: "Other things being equal, the melodic movement of a question is higher from the start than the same melodic movement in statements. This means that the declarative vs interrogative meaning can be perceived by the hearer from the start of the sentence." (Navarro Tomás 1944:136).[4] And "in the first accented syllable [of interrogative utterances] pitch is increased by three or four semitones over the average level characterizing the same syllable in statements." (Navarro Tomás 1944:141). By contrast, Sosa (1992, 1999) claims that it is only the first peak (and other prenuclear peaks) which is more prominent in all the Spanish dialects he analyses: "The increase in tonal height typical of interrogative contours systematically appears from the first accented syllable, not from the start of the utterance. This finding was confirmed by all of our acoustic analyses of the Spanish dialects under study, both for interrogatives ending in a final rise or a final fall." (Sosa 1999:150-154).

Let us first examine the behavior of utterance-initial and utterance-final F0 levels in interrogatives in our data. Mean utterance-initial and utterance-final values are plotted in the two graphs in Figure 8 in four length conditions (1 to 4 pitch accents) for speaker GH in both statements and questions.[5] For both sentence-types, utterance-initial and utterance-final values were almost constant across repetitions of the same contour and totally uncorrelated with sentence length for the two speakers. Moreover, utterance-initial values in questions are practically the same to those in statements: An average height of 103 Hz for statements and 104.4 Hz for interrogatives for speaker GH. *T*-tests comparing the values of utterance-initial points in statements vs. interrogatives reveal that their differences were not significant in any of the sentence-length conditions under consideration for the two speakers.

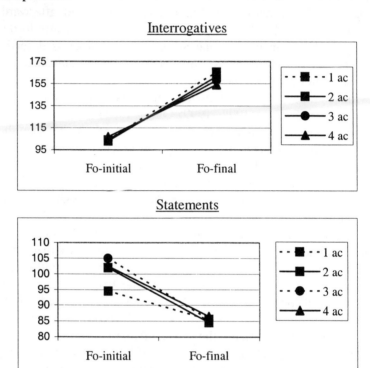

Figure 8. Mean utterance-initial and utterance-final F0 values of interrogative sentences and statements as a function of sentence-length (1 to 4 pitch accents) for speaker GH.

The two graphs in Figure 9 plot the average absolute F0 values (in Hz) of the first H peak in statements, yes-no questions, and wh-questions in utterances with different lengths (2, 3, and 4-accent utterances) for the two subjects. Most of the comparisons were performed on quasi minimal pairs of the type *La nena mira el loro, ¿La nena mira el loro?*, and *¿Dónde mira la nena el loro?* For both speakers, utterance-initial H peaks were scaled significantly higher in questions (both absolute and wh-questions) than in statements (an average difference of 20-25 Hz for the male speaker and 50-55 Hz for the female speaker). Pairwise *t*-tests comparing H1 in the three sentence-type conditions reveal that the two populations (questions vs. statements) are highly distinct (at p < 0.01) for the two subjects. As for the differences between the two types of interrogatives, only speaker MN displayed a statistically-significant tendency to pronounce higher peaks in wh-questions. MN's results confirm Navarro Tomás' claim that the first accent of a wh-question is typically more prominent than the first accent in yes-no questions. Also, the data shows a slight effect of utterance-length on the height of the first peak in questions for speaker GH: That is, 2-accent questions have a significantly lower peak than 3 and 4-accent utterances.

The plots in Figure 10 show mean peak delay values of the first H peak (or distance in ms. from the H peak to the onset of the accented syllable) in interrogatives and statements as a function of within-word position for both subjects. Clearly, there is a contrast in H1 alignment between statements and questions: While in statements H1 is generally aligned with the posttonic syllable (and, the closer the accent is to the upcoming word-boundary, the more retracted the peak is), in interrogatives the peak seems to be placed at a fixed position within the posttonic syllable (around 2/3 of the posttonic syllable; cf. Table 4) and reveal no effect of within-word position.

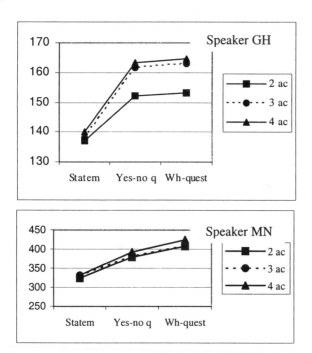

Figure 9. Mean absolute F0 value of the first peak (in Hz) as a function of sentence-type (statements, yes-no questions and wh-questions) and utterance-length (2 to 4 pitch accents) for the two speakers.

How is H1 aligned with respect to the stressed syllable in interrogative sentences? Table 2 shows the average *relative peak delay* values (calculated by dividing the absolute peak delay by the duration of the accented syllable) in different conditions (basically the same conditions plotted in Figure 10). Relative peak delay measures reveal that H1 peaks in interrogatives are realized in the posttonic syllable (within the 1.45 and the 2.14 range). Also, peaks in 2-accent sentences are placed consistently earlier than in 3 and 4-accent sentences, probably due to a clash effect with the upcoming nuclear L accent which forces H1 to shift earlier.

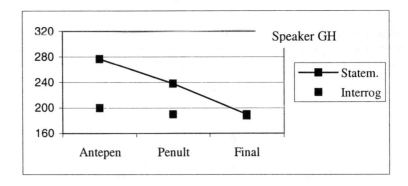

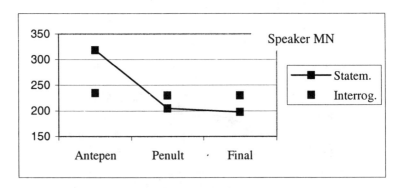

Figure 10. Mean peak delay of H1 (in ms) as a function of sentence-type (statements vs. interrogatives) and within-word position (antepenultimate, penultimate, final) for speakers GH (top) and MN (bottom).

Table 2. Mean relative peak delay of H1 interrogative sentences as a function of sentence length and within-word position.

Speaker GH	2 accents	3 accents	4 accents
antepenultimate	1.45	1.79	2.12
penultimate	1.46	1.73	1.93
final	1.38	1.62	1.64
Speaker MN	2 accents	3 accents	4 accents
antepenultimate	1.45	1.79	2.12
penultimate	1.46	1.73	1.93
final	1.38	1.62	1.64

In sum, the results presented in this section reveal that there is a clear contrast in H1 peak alignment and scaling in questions vs. statements. On the one hand, the difference between a question and a statement is conveyed by increasing the height of the first H peak (or local pitch range of the first pitch accent), even though sentence-initial F0 values are not higher in questions compared to statements (as it was claimed by Canellada and Kuhlmann-Madsen 1987 or Navarro Tomás 1944). On the other hand, H1 alignment behaves rather differently in interrogative sentences. Even though in both cases H1 is aligned with the posttonic syllable, the phonetic factors influencing its position are not the same: Specifically, H1 alignment in interrogatives is not affected by within-word position, but rather from the prosodic pressure from the upcoming L tone.

3.3. Commands and exclamatory sentences

This section investigates the tonal cues which characterize commands and exclamatory utterances. A number of studies on Spanish intonation have noted that the imperative tune is similar to the declarative one and it is mainly characterized by the use of an increased pitch range (Kvavik 1988; Navarro Tomás 1944). As Navarro Tomás (1944:186) states, "The intonation of commands, in their imperative expression, resorts to especially high and low tones. (..) Imperative expressions such as *¡Calla!* 'Shut up!', *¡Alto!* 'Stop!', *¡Fuera!* 'Get out!', produced with no great emphasis, are produced with a first H peak which is 7 or 8 semitones higher than statements and fall to the second syllable to 8 or 9 semitones lower that the reference start of the sentence (for a total fall of 16 semitones)."[6]

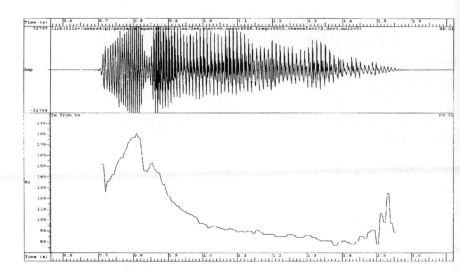

Figure 11. Waveform and F0 contour of the imperative reading of the utterance *¡Mira el loro de la nena!*, as produced by speaker GH.

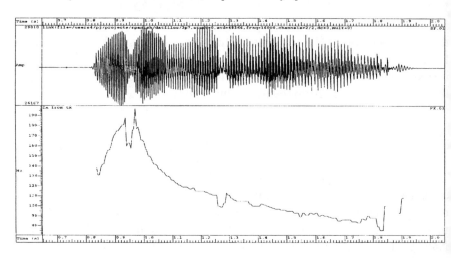

Figure 12. Waveform and F0 contour of the exclamative reading of the utterance *¡Mira a la nómada!*, as produced by speaker GH.

Figures 11 and 12 show the waveform and the F0 contours of the imperative utterance *¡Mira el loro de la nena!* and the exclamative utterance *¡Mira a la nómada!* as produced by speaker GH. Both contours, pronounced in a single intonational phrase, are characterized by a prominent sentence-initial pitch accent. The rest of the F0 contour is deaccented, looking as if the rest of the accents had been wiped out or very compressed. As can be observed below, the value of H1 height in these specific F0 contours produced by the male speaker is around 10 Hz higher in the exclamative than in the imperative utterance.

The data in Table 3 show the average utterance-initial and utterance-final F0 values for exclamative and imperative utterances. As in other sentence-types, both values are rather constant for a given speaker. *T*-tests comparing utterance-initial and utterance-final F0 values within speakers revealed that there is no statistical difference between these values in different phrasal length conditions neither in the exclamative nor in the imperative set (except for starting F0 levels of one-accent exclamatory sentences for both speakers, following the trend that starting F0 points and H peaks in utterances with one accent are lower than in longer utterances). Moreover, utterance-initial F0 values are significantly higher in both imperatives and exclamatory sentences than in statements and questions (around a 20 Hz average increase): For speaker GH, the average height of starting points for statements and interrogatives is 103 Hz and of imperative and exclamatory sentences 120 Hz; for speaker MN, 225 Hz for the former and 250 Hz for the latter).

Table 3. Mean utterance-initial and utterance-final F0 values (in Hz) of exclamative and imperative utterances for speakers GH and MN.

Speaker GH	Imperative		Exclamative	
	initial	final	initial	final
1 accent	123.24	83.25	100.6	89.4
2 accents	126.75	82.74	120.75	84.25
3 accents	121.8	84.6	115.5	88.33
4 accents	125.6	88	127.5	83.25
Speaker MN				
1 accent	268.5	190.5	231	166
2 accents	255.75	185	258.5	199.16
3 accents	258.2	184.5	262.16	197.5
4 accents	254.5	181.16	250.66	205.66

The following two graphs in Figure 13 plot the average height of the first H peak (in Hz) in exclamative and imperative utterances as a function of sentence-length (1-4 pitch accents). *T*-tests reveal that pitch scaling differences between H1 in both conditions (imperative vs. exclamative sentence-types) are statistically significant in all conditions except for the case of 3-accent sentences for speaker GH and 4-accent sentences for speaker MN.

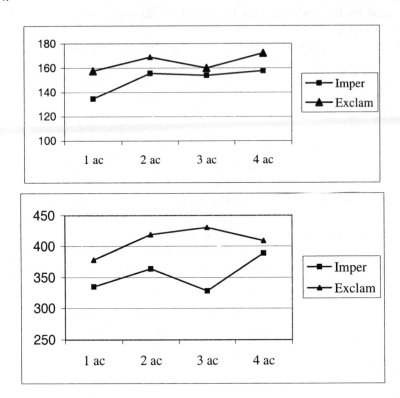

Figure 13. Mean absolute F0 value of the first peak (in Hz) as a function of sentence-type (imperative vs. exclamatory sentences) and utterance-length (1 to 4 pitch accents) for the two speakers.

How is H1 scaled in imperatives and exclamatory sentences in comparison with the rest of sentence-types? The two plots in Figure 14 show the mean absolute F0 value of the first peak (in Hz) as a function of sentence-type (statements and interrogative, imperative and exclamatory sentences) and utterance-length (1 to 4 pitch accents) for the two speakers. *T*-tests comparing H1 height differences demonstrate a significant statistical difference for H1 height between declaratives and the rest of sentence-types. In general, this lends support to Navarro Tomás' (1944) claim that pitch range of sentence-initial pitch accents were incremented by 7-8 semitones in the case of both imperatives and interrogatives. Finally, H1 is generally

higher in exclamatory sentences, even though this tendency is not completely systematic across different length conditions.

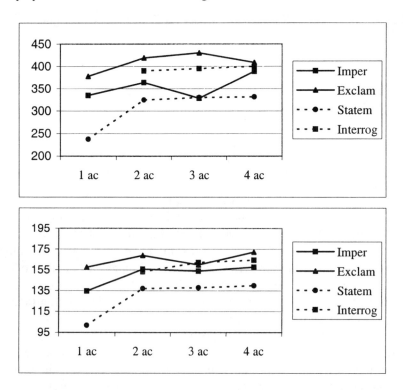

Figure 14. Mean absolute F0 value of the first peak (in Hz) as a function of sentence-type (statements and interrogative, imperative and exclamatory
sentences) and utterance-length (1 to 4 pitch accents) for the two speakers.

Table 4 shows the average *relative peak delay* values (calculated by
dividing the absolute peak delay by the duration of the accented syllable)
in imperative and exclamatory utterances of different lengths. The data in
the table reveal that the first rising pitch accent of imperative and exclamative contours is characterized by very early H alignment: The peak is
always realized within the boundaries of the accented syllable. Furthermore, no consistent effect of sentence-length is found on H1 peak placement.

Table 4. Mean relative peak delay of H1 in interrogative sentences as a function
of sentence length and within-word position for the two speakers.

Speaker GH	Imperative utterances	Exclamatory utterances
1 accent	0.66	0.75
2 accents	0.82	0.86
3 accents	0.85	0.88
4 accents	0.95	0.91
Speaker MN		
1 accent	0.80	0.77
2 accents	0.85	0.80
3 accents	0.88	0.85
4 accents	0.87	0.88

In sum, the data presented in this section clearly demonstrate that utterance-initial pitch accents of imperative and exclamative contours are characterized by a significant increase in H height, lending support to the claim
that difference between declarative vs. imperative/exclamative readings is
conveyed by tonal range differences (Navarro Tomás 1944; but see Willis
2002).[7] Moreover, H1 peaks of exclamatives tend to be higher compared to
imperatives, even though the difference is only statistically significant for
speaker MN. The data suggests that the increase in magnitude or pitch
range of the local pitch accent is not only obtained by an increase in H1
height but also of the pitch register of the whole accent gesture, as utterance-initial values are also higher in these sentences. Finally, the results in
this section show that utterance-initial pitch accents of imperative and exclamative contours are characterized by the presence of a very early peak
and that this alignment cue, together with an increase in pitch range, might
be signaling different phrase-type readings. These phonetic cues are quite
similar to the signaling of contrastive focus in Peninsular Spanish (cf. de la
Mota 1995, Face 2001a, 2001b)

4. Phonological issues

4.1. Tonal alignment

In our data, sentence-initial rising accents present two basic tonal alignment
patterns. A rise with a late H1 peak is found in statements and interrogatives and an early H1 peak is found in imperatives and exclamative utterances. As it is well-known, contrastive focus is also characterized by early

H alignment on the focused constituent (cf. de la Mota 1995, Face 2001a, 2001b). Nowadays, the standard autosegmental transcription of Spanish pitch accents with late F0 peak alignment is L*+H and for pitch accents with early F0 peak L+H* (see Sosa 1999; Face 2001a, 2001b; Beckman et al. 2002; Hualde 2002). Thus, starredness is used to express the phonetic alignment contrast properties of the H peak, following the idea that target alignment is a reflection of phonological association (Arvaniti, Ladd and Mennen 1998; Hayes and Lahiri 1991; Grice 1995, Arvaniti et al. 2000; Pierrehumbert and Beckman 1988; Pierrehumbert and Steele 1989). Indeed, such a phonological representation adequately captures the difference in H peak alignment of the pitch accents under study: Utterance-initial accents of commands, exclamatory utterances, and focused utterances are instances of L+H* and utterance-initial accents of statements and questions are instances of L*+H.

However, while this analysis easily captures the observed contrasts in H alignment, it would not account for L valley alignment contrasts like the ones reported by Willis (2003) for Dominican Spanish. This dialect displays a three-way contrast in the alignment patterns of rising accents: a) a rise with a late peak; b) a rise with an early peak; c) a posttonic rise.[8] In Dominican Spanish, the use of L*+H to express a late peak would preclude its use for a posttonic rise. In my view, if we want to provide a more comprehensive analysis of rising accents in Spanish (which can display contrasts on both H and L alignment) one must seriously reconsider using H alignment as a diagnostic for starring tones. What could be then an adequate phonological analysis able to account for contrasts in valley and peak placement? I suggest that the Spanish' representational puzzle can be resolved by resorting to Ladd's (1983, 1996:55) suggestion about separating phonetic alignment from phonological association and by using a phonological feature such as [delayed peak] as an attribute of accents, much in the same way the attribute [downstepped] and [upstepped] are used. As Ladd (1994) points out, "accents, in addition to being high or low, can be downstepped or non-downstepped, delayed or non-delayed, raised or non-raised." My proposal to account for the Dominican and Catalan facts is thus to label the three-way pitch accent contrast as follows: a) L+H*[delayed peak]: A rise with a late peak; b) L+H*: A rise with an early peak; c) L*+H post tonic rise

4.2. Tonal scaling

In their classic study about English tonal range, Liberman and Pierrehumbert (1984) found that gradual increasing in emphasis correlated with increasing tonal range of the pitch accent, without changing its phonological makeup. Nowadays, a central assumption of the standard autosegmental-metrical model (and of most work on intonation) is that pitch range variation is paralinguistic (that is, it conveys differences in emphasis or prominence). Recently, though, some work within the autosegmental model has revealed that pitch range can also display phonological categorical effects (Hirschberg and Ward 1992; Ward and Hirschberg 1985; Ladd 1994, 1996). As Ladd (1994:60) points out, "the central point of the descriptive proposals I have made here and elsewhere is that the Bruce-Pierrehumbert approach to intonational phonology must be enriched with a notion of categorical distinctions of pitch range."

The data reviewed in the preceding section has clearly shown that sentence-type information has a significant effect on H1 scaling: Exclamative contours have higher utterance-initial H peaks than imperative and interrogative contours, and, at its turn, the latter display higher H1 peaks than statements. In the recent literature, steps have been taken towards incorporating this pitch height difference in the phonological representation. In the case of Spanish, Sosa (1999) proposes the use of a sentence-initial %H boundary tone which has the effect of increasing the F0 level of the utterance-initial H peak. As he points out, "our solution is based on the claim that the utterance-initial %H boundary tone restricted to yes-no questions, has a local effect of upstep on the pitch height of the first accented syllable". We believe that Sosa's solution is not descriptively adequate, given that the height of utterance-initial positions is totally independent of the height of the first peak: 1) in imperative and exclamative contours, both the start point and H1 are produced with a higher pitch than in statements; 2) in interrogatives, the start point is produced at a normal pitch level and H1 is higher. That means that we independently need to resort to a separate phonological entity that can identify high %H boundary tones separately from high H1 peaks. Beckman et al.'s (2002) solution, on the other hand, relies on the use of a phonologically distinct upstepped accent ¡H, following Ladd's original (1983) suggestion to use an extrinsic [upstep] or [raised peak] feature assigned to pitch accents.

In my view, we need to further study the behavior or upstep phenomena and clarify what types of functions can have in a given language and what should be its phonetic interpretation. Do we have evidence for an [upstep] feature as a separate notion from [raised peak]? Do they have different properties? Recently, Truckenbrodt (2002) has shown that upstep can be found in nuclear accents of non-final intonational phrases in southern German and it is phonetically interpreted as a return to the sentence-initial F0 height and disregard of preceding downstep. In a recent Catalan experiment, Prieto (2002b) found an upstep effect on the second pitch accent of an utterance acting as a cue for a weak phrase boundary separating subjects from predicates. Figure 5 illustrates the waveform, F0 contour and labeling scheme of the utterance *El molí nét no li agrada* 'He does not like the clean mill'. Despite the fact that we are dealing with a non-descending contour, H2 height was rather constant within speakers and could be predicted quite successfully by a local upstep ratio of constant expansion from the previous' peak value.

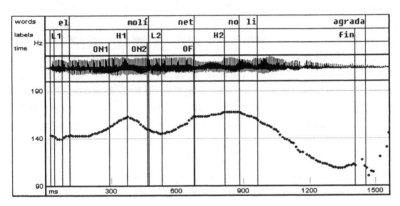

Figure 15. Waveform display, F0 contour and labels corresponding to the utterance *El molí nét no li agrada.*

I believe more work needs to be done on the characterization of upstep/raised peak features before proposing a reliable phonological interpretation of the Spanish facts. It can even be that upstep phenomena have different phonetic interpretations, like the German and Catalan cases seem to suggest.

5. Conclusions

The results of the present study clearly lend support to the target-based hypothesis of intonational production, that is, the claim that L and H points are carefully controlled by the speaker and are thus aligned and scaled in extremely consistent ways. The data shown in this article has revealed that both H1 alignment and scaling patterns are cueing sentence-type information. Most probably, Peninsular Spanish listeners rely on combinations of alignment and scaling cues of the first accent gesture to identify phrasal types from the beginning of the sentence. At its turn, speakers exploit the interplay between F0 peak alignment and F0 peak height to obtain a doubly robust cue for a phonological contrast, much in the same way contrastive focus is conveyed through early H1 peak alignment and high H1 scaling (de la Mota 1995; Face 2001a, 2001b, among others).

The analysis of the data has shown a clear constrast between late and early H1 peaks in different sentence-types: While declarative and interrogative F0 contours are characterized by a late H1 peak, imperative and exclamative contours are characterized by an early peak. The article has also addressed a recently debated issue within Spanish intonational studies about the appropiateness of a phonological analysis of these accents as L*+H vs L+H* accents. While this analysis easily captures the observed contrasts in H alignment, it is not able to capture contrasts in L valley alignment present in other Spanish dialects (contrasts such as those reported by Willis 2002 for Dominican Spanish) and in Romance languages such as Catalan. The phonological analysis proposed in this paper resorts to the extrinsic phonological notion of [delayed peak]: Accents can have the phonological property of having late or early peaks. This proposal does not directly link starredness to alignment properties and, in my view, provides a more complete analysis of rising accents in Spanish.

Finally, the article has shown that sentence-type information has a significant effect on H1 scaling: H1 peaks of interrogative, imperative and exclamatory sentences are significantly higher than peaks in corresponding statements, something which confirms previous observations on these Spanish contours (Canellada and Kuhlmann Madsen 1987; Kvavic 1988; Navarro Tomás 1944; Sosa 1992, 1999; Willis 2002). Pitch-range variability is not exclusively used in Peninsular Spanish to convey differences in emphasis or prominence (as the Free Gradient Hypothesis would contend), but rather it conveys sentence-type information. Following a suggestion by Ladd (1983), we propose to resort to an extrinsic feature [raised peak] applied to pitch accents. Even though the data seems to suggest an even further distinction in pitch height in exclamatory and wh-sentences (cf. speaker MN), we tentatively interpret this fact as a manifestation of a special degree of emphasis especially typical of these sentences.

Acknowledgments

The production experiment described in this article was recorded a few years ago with the original goal of developing a phonetically explicit F0 assignment model for the basic 5 sentence-types in Peninsular Spanish. A preliminary version of this work was presented at the conference Laboratory Approaches to Spanish Phonology and at the International Congress of Phonetic Sciences (Barcelona, 2003). I am grateful to J.M. Sosa, T. Face, J.I. Hualde, and E. Willis for helpful comments and suggestions. Thanks are due to the two speakers who read the database: Guillem Hernández, from Lleida and Mercedes Nasarre, from Huesca. This work has benefited from the participation of the author in the following research grants: "La interpretación y la combinación de los rasgos gramaticales: del léxico a la realización fonética" (BFF2000-0403-C02-02, Ministerio de Educación y Cultura), "Modelos de organización articulatoria y procesos de cambio fonético" (BFF2000-0075-C02-01, Ministerio de Educación y Cultura, Xarxa Temàtica en Gramàtica Teòrica (2000XT-00032, Generalitat de Catalunya) and Grup de Lingüística Teòrica (2001SGR 00150, Generalitat de Catalunya).

Notes

1. All translations from Spanish texts into English included in this article are the author's.
2. As the original goal of the recordings was to implement the results in a text-to-speech Spanish synthesizer, the description corresponds to intonational contours which are typical of a reading task.
3. The contours which were produced by MN with a different F0 curve were repeated during the recording session.
4. Canellada and Kuhlmann Madsen (1987) point out that "from the start of the utterance, interrogative contours are produced with a higher pitch level than statements. This is not only apparent in the strong utterance-final rise, but in each one of the utterance-initial syllables."
5. We opted not to reproduce MN's values here because the creakyness of her voice at especially high F0 levels made these F0 measurements quite unreliable.
6. Similarly, Willis (2002:347) concludes that there are also other prosodic cues which characterize imperative readings: "The local differences between imperative and declarative utterances include an increased tonal range at the local pitch-accent level, reduced intonational deaccenting, an increased use of an early H tone pitch accent associated with contrastive focus, and modifications of duration."

7. Willis (2002) argues that the increased pitch range found in Spanish imperatives presents variation and is thus not categorical. As Willis (2002:361) points out, "the data indicate there is an increased local tonal range in imperatives compared to declaratives, but it is not significant for all speakers." We believe, though, that the context used to prompt the imperative reading could have been interpreted not as a real command by Spanish participants but as an exhortative-type sentence. In my opinion, the following situation example (Willis 2002:354) does accept an ambiguous response ranging between a command and a request: Situation: "You arrive home and it smells terrible, you say to John, 'Open the door!'

8. In a closely related Romance language such as Catalan, rising pitch accents also display a three-way contrast on alignment: early accent peaks, late accent peaks and late accent peak with late accent valley (cf. Prieto 2002a).

References

Arvaniti, Amalia, Robert D. Ladd and Ineke Mennen
    1998   Stability of tonal alignment: The case of Greek prenuclear accents. *Journal of Phonetics* 26: 3-25.
Arvaniti, Amalia, D. Rober Ladd and Ineke Mennen
    2000   What is a starred tone? Evidence from Greek, In *Papers in Laboratory Phonology V: Acquisition and the Lexicon*, Michael B. Broe and Janet B. Pierrehumbert (eds.), 119-131. Cambridge: Cambridge University Press.
Beckman, Mary
    1995   Local shapes and global trends. In *Proceedings of the XIIIth International Congress of Phonetic Sciences*, Stockholm, vol. 2: 100-107.
Beckman, Mary, Manuel Díaz-Campos, Julia Tevis McGory and Terrell A. Morgan
    2002   Intonation across Spanish, in the tones and break indices framework. *Probus* 14: 9-36.
Canellada, María Josefa and John Kuhlmann Madsen
    1987   *Pronunciación del español. Lengua hablada y literaria*. Madrid: Castalia.
de la Mota, Carme
    1995   La representación gramatical de la información nueva en el discurso. Ph. D. diss., Universitat Autònoma de Barcelona.

Face, Timothy L.
  2001a   Intonational marking of contrastive focus in Madrid Spanish. Ph.D. diss., The Ohio State University. Published by Lincom Europa, 2002.
  2001b   Focus and early peak alignment in Spanish intonation. *Probus* 13: 223-246.

Grice, Martine
  1995   *The Intonation of Interrogation in Palermo Italian: Implications For Intonation Theory*. Max Niemeyer Verlag, Tübingen.

Hadding, Kerstin and Michael Studdert-Kennedy
  1972   An experimental study of some intonation contours. In *Intonation: Selected Readings*, Dwight Bolinger (ed.), 348-358. Middlesex: Penguin.

Hayes, Bruce and Aditi Lahiri
  1991   Bengali intonational phonology. *Natural Language and Linguistic Theory* 9: 253-306.

Hirschberg, Julia and Gregory Ward
  1992   The influence of pitch range, duration, amplitude and spectral features on the interpretation of the rise-fall-rise intonation contour in English. *Journal of Phonetics* 20: 241-251.

Hualde, José Ignacio
  2002   Intonation in Spanish and the other Ibero-Romance languages: Overview and status quaestionis. In *Romance Phonology and Variation. Selected Papers from the 30th Linguistic Symposium on Romance Languages* Caroline Wiltshire and Joaquim Camps (eds.), 101-116. Amsterdam: Benjamins.

Kvavik, Karen H.
  1988   Is there a Spanish imperative intonation? In *Studies in Caribbean Spanish Dialectology*, Robert M. Hammond and Melvyn Resnick (eds.), 35-49. Washington DC: Georgetown University Press.

Ladd, D. Robert
  1983   Peak features and overall slope, In *Prosody, Models and Measurements*, Anne Cutler and Robert D. Ladd (eds.), 39-52. Berlin: Springer-Verlag.
  1994   Constraints on the gradient variability of pich range, or, Pitch level 4 lives!. In *Phonological Structure and Phonetic Form: Papers in Laboratory Phonology III*, Patricia A. Keating (ed.), 43-63. Cambridge: Cambridge University Press.
  1996   *Intonational Phonology*. Cambridge: Cambridge University Press.

Liberman, Mark and Janet Pierrehumbert
1984   Intonational invariance under changes in pitch range and length.
          In *Language Sound Structure: Studies in Phonology Presented to
          Morris Halle by his Teacher and Students*, Mark Aronoff and
          Richard T. Oehrle (eds.), 157-233. Cambridge, Massachusetts:
          MIT Press.
Mettas, Odette.
1971   *Les Techniques de la phonétique instrumentale et l'intonation.*
          Brussels: Presses Universitaires de Bruxelles.
Navarro Tomás, Tomás
1944   *Manual de entonación española.* New York: Hispanic Institute in
          the United States.
1968   *Manual de pronunciación española.* Madrid: Consejo Superior
          de Investicaciones Científicas.
Nibert, Holy
2000   Phonetic and phonological evidence for intermediate phrasing in
          Spanish intonation. Ph. D. diss., University of Illinois at Urbana-
          Champaign.
Pierrehumbert, Janet
1980   The phonology and phonetics of English intonation. Ph. D. diss.,
          MIT.
Pierrehumbert, Janet and Mary Beckman
1988   *Japanese Tone Structure.* Cambridge, MA: MIT Press.
Pierrehumbert, Janet and Shirley Steele
1989   Categories of tonal alignment in english. *Phonetica* 46: 181-196.
Prieto, Pilar, Jan van Santen and Julia Hirschberg
1995   Tonal alignment patterns in Spanish. *Journal of Phonetics* 23:
          429-451.
Prieto, Pilar, Chilin Shih and Holy Nibert
1996   Pitch downtrend in Spanish. *Journal of Phonetics* 24: 445-473.
Prieto, Pilar
2001   Review of Sosa (1999). *Linguistics* 39: 1192-1199.
2002a   Entonació [Intonation], In *Gramàtica del català contemporani,
          volume 1* [Contemporary grammar of Catalan, volume 1]. Joan
          Solà, Maria Rosa Lloret, Joan Mascaró, and Manuel Pérez Sal-
          danya (eds.), 393-462. Barcelona: Editorial Empúries.
2002b   Coarticulation and stability effects in tonal clash contexts in
          Catalan. In *Proceedings of the Speech Prosody 2002 Conference*,
          Bernard Bel and Isabelle Marlien (eds.), 587-590.   Aix-en-
          Provence: Laboratoire Parole et Langage.

Quilis, Antonio
1981 *Manual de fonética acústica española*. Madrid: Editorial Gredos.
Silverman, Kim E. A. and Janet Pierrehumbert
1990 The timing of prenuclear high accents in English. In *Papers in Laboratory Phonology I: Between the Grammar and Physics of Speech*, John Kingston and Mary Beckman (eds.), 71-106. Cambridge: Cambridge University Press.
Sosa, Juan Manuel
1992 Dialectal variation and the underlying representation of Spanish intonation. In *Proceedings of the 1992 Annual Conference of the Canadian Linguistic Association*, Carrie Dyck, Jila Ghomeshi and, Tom Wilson (eds.), 301-311. Toronto Working Papers in Linguistics. Toronto: University of Toronto.
1999 *La entonación del español*. Madrid: Cátedra.
Truckenbrodt, Hubert
2002 Upstep and embedded register levels. *Phonology* 19: 77-120.
Ward, Gregory and Julia Hirschberg
1985 Implicating uncertainty: The pragmatics of fall-rise intonation. *Language* 61: 747-776.
Willis, Erik W.
2002 Is there a Spanish imperative intonation revisited: Local considerations. *Linguistics* 40: 347-374.
2003 The intonational system of Dominican Spanish: Findings and analysis. Ph.D. diss., University of Illinois at Urbana-Champaign.
Xu, Yi
1999 Effects of tone and focus on the formation and alignment of F0 contours. *Journal of Phonetics* 27: 55-105.
2002 Articulatory constraints and tonal alignment. In *Proceedings of the Speech Prosody 2002 Conference*, Bernard Bel and Isabelle Marlien, (eds.), 91-100. Aix-en-Provence: Laboratoire Parole et Langage.

Appendix

1p1: La mira.
1p2: ¿La mira?
1p3: ¿Dónde la mira?
1p4: (imperative) ¡Mira!
1p5: (exclamative) ¡La mira!

2p1: La nena mira.
2p2: ¿La nena mira?
2p3: ¿Dónde mira la nena?
2p4: (imperative) ¡Mira a la nena!
2p5: (exclamative) ¡Mira a la nena!

3p1: La nena mira el loro.
3p2: La nena mira el loro?
3p3: ¿Dónde mira la nena el loro?
3p4: (imperative) ¡Mira el loro de la nena!
3p5: (exclamative) ¡Mira el loro de la nena!

4p1: La nena mira el loro de Sara.
4p2: ¿La nena mira el loro de Sara?
4p3: ¿Dónde mira la nena el loro de Sara?
4p4: (imperative) ¡Mira el loro de la nena de Sara!
4p5: (exclamative) ¡Mira el loro de la nena de Sara!

1u1: La miró.
1u2: ¿La miró?
1u3: ¿Qué le miró?
1u4: (imperative) ¡La miró!
1u5: (exclamative) ¡La miró!

2u1: La mamá miró.
2u2: ¿La mamá miró?
2u3: ¿Qué mira la mamá?
2u4: (imperative)¡Mirad a la mamá!
2u5: (exclamative) ¡Mirad a la mamá!

3u1: La mamá miró al bebé.
3u2: ¿La mamá miró al bebé?
3u3: ¿Qué miró la mamá del bebé?
3u4: (imperative) ¡Mira al bebé de la mamá!
3u5: (exclamative) ¡Miró al bebé de la mamá!

4u1: La mamá miró al bebé de Rubí.
4u2: ¿La mamá miró al bebé de Rubí?
4u3: ¿Qué miró la mamá del bebé de Rubí?
4u4: (imperative) ¡Mirad al bebé de la mamá de Rubí!
4u5: (exclamative) ¡Miró el bebé de la mamá de Rubí!

1a1: La lámina.
1a2: ¿La lámina?
1a3: ¿Qué es una lámina?
1a4: (imperative) ¡Mírala!
1a5: (exclamative) ¡La lámina!

2a1: La nómada mira.
2a2: ¿La nómada mira?
2a3: ¿Dónde mira la nómada?
2a4: (imperative) ¡Mira a la nómada!
2a5: (exclamative) ¡Mira a la nómada!

3a1: La nómada mira el número.
3a2: ¿La nómada mira el número?
3a3: ¿Cuándo mira la nómada el número?
3a4: (imperative) ¡Mira el número de la nómada!
3a5: (exclamative) ¡Mira el número de la nómada!

4a1: La nómada mira el número de lámina.
4a2: ¿La nómada mira el número de lámina?
4a3: ¿Dónde mira la nómada el número de lámina?
4a4: (imperative) ¡Mira el número de lámina de la nómada!
4a5: (exclamative) ¡Mira el número de lámina de la nómada!

Dominican Spanish absolute interrogatives in broad focus

Erik W. Willis

1. Introduction

It is generally accepted that there are at least two categorical types of interrogatives in most languages: (1) absolute interrogatives which require a "yes/no" response, and (2) pronominal or adverbial interrogatives characterized by the use of an interrogative pronominal or adverb, such as *qué* 'what' and, *quién* 'who', etc. Both types of interrogatives have been researched in Spanish (Cid Uribe and Ortiz-Lira 2000, Dorta 2000, Navarro Tomás 1944, Prieto 2004, Quilis 1993, Sosa 1999).

Differences in the intonational contour of absolute interrogatives serve as a defining characteristic within Spanish dialectology for a distinction between Caribbean Spanish and non-Caribbean Spanish in the Americas (Quilis 1987, 1993, Sosa 1999). The widely accepted patterns for Peninsular and Caribbean Spanish in broad focus are shown in Figure 1.[1]

1a.

1b.

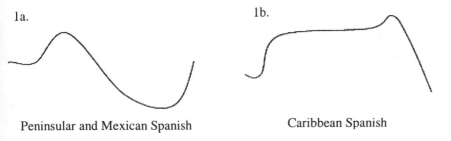

Peninsular and Mexican Spanish   Caribbean Spanish

Figure 1. Schematic of Peninsular and Caribbean Spanish absolute interrogatives.

The principal goal of this paper is to provide a description of the basic intonational contour of Dominican Spanish (DS) absolute interrogatives with broad focus through a quantitative examination of tonal values of key components of the intonational contour. Specifically, the tonal values asso-

ciated with pitch accents and boundary tones, and with initial and final tonal values are examined. The data reveal significant patterns not previously
reported for Caribbean Spanish interrogatives.

2. Caribbean Spanish absolute interrogatives: Review of literature

Navarro Tomás (1944) provides the first intonational description of Spanish absolute interrogatives in Peninsular Spanish and is illustrated in Figure
(1a) (Navarro Tomás 1944, Quilis 1987, 1993, Sosa 1999). This contour is
characterized as beginning with a comparatively higher initial tone (initial
boundary tone) followed by a rise on the first lexical item (prenuclear pitch
accent) followed by a tonal fall to the next pitch accent, which is less
prominent than the first. The lowest tonal value is a Low tone reached in
the final tonic syllable (typically the nuclear pitch accent). The final tonal
movement (boundary tone[s]) is a tonal rise that begins near the offset of
the tonic and continues until the end of phonation (Navarro Tomás 1944).[2]
This intonational pattern is found in both Peninsular and Mexican Spanish
(Sosa 1999:220 Figure 3–32).

In contrast, the standard characterizations of Caribbean Spanish absolute interrogatives report a final falling High-Low contour (see Figure
[1b]).[3] This Caribbean Spanish interrogative contour shown in Figure (1b)
and Figures (2d) and (2c) is noted in several studies (Beckman et al. 2002,
Lipski 1994, Quilis 1987, 1993, Sosa 1991, 1999), and consists of an initial
tonal rise followed by a plateau until a final boundary fall. The two characteristics of Caribbean interrogatives that serve to distinguish it from other
American dialects of Spanish include a lack of declination following the
initial tonal rise, and the aforementioned final tonal boundary fall. Quilis
reports that a final falling High-Low contour is common in the Spanish of
Puerto Rico, and the Canary Islands (1987, 1993:469–470).[4]

Based on his survey of Latin-American dialects, Sosa (1999) claims that
there are two major absolute interrogative types, (1) a type with an initial
High tone and final rise, and (2) a pattern with an initial High tone but a
final fall (see Figure [2b]). The phonological characterizations in Figures
(2a–c) correspond to variations in absolute interrogatives observed by Sosa
in non-Caribbean dialects. The distinguishing characteristic, typical of the
non-Caribbean contours, is a Low tone in the nuclear pitch accent followed
by a High edge tone.[5]

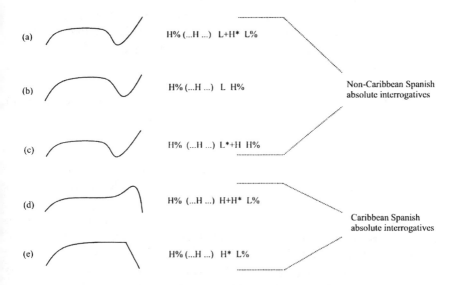

Figure 2. A reproduction of the Spanish absolute interrogative contours and tonal analysis proposed by Sosa (1999:213).

A crucial characteristic of absolute interrogatives in Caribbean dialects of Spanish is a nuclear pitch accent with a High tone followed by a Low boundary tone(s) illustrated in Figures (2d–e).[6] Beckman et al. (2002) likewise report a High-Low toneme contour for the Caribbean dialect of Caracas Spanish. In two examples from Caracas Spanish, one with broad focus and the other with narrow focus, the nuclear pitch accent is utterance prominent (Beckman et al: 2002:24 Figures (6b) and [6c]).

Spanish absolute interrogatives have also been analyzed from a pragmatic perspective; specifically based on whether or not a speaker expects a particular response. Quilis (1993) and Sosa (1999) suggest that there are differences between broad focus interrogatives and negative interrogatives (those in which a particular response is expected). Quilis and Sosa maintain that there is a pragmatic difference between the contours illustrated in Figure 2d and 2e in Puerto Rican and Maracuchan Spanish. Figure (2d) is the basic default absolute interrogative contour for the Caribbean and is used when the answer to the question can be either yes or no. The contour shown in Figure (2d) has an additional nuclear tonal rise realized immediately before the boundary fall. Sosa motivates this additional nuclear tonal rise with a H+H* pitch accent. The contour illustrated in Figure (2e) corresponds to a negative absolute interrogative, one in which the speaker expects a specific answer, either yes or no (see Sosa 1999:205). This absolute interrogative distinction is present in Puerto Rican and Maracuchon Spanish. Sosa (1999) did not find this distinction in other dialects of Caribbean Spanish (213).

Cid Uribe and Ortiz-Lira (2000) in an examination of intonation in Santiago, Chile, likewise indicate that there are differences in the intonational contour of interrogatives produced with the expectation of a particular response, and those that are produced without any expected response. Beckman et al. (2002) provide somewhat contradictory evidence for distinct contours based on utterance pragmatics (see examples 6c and 6d pages 24–25).

Integral to characterizations of Spanish interrogatives is a long-standing claim by several researchers that Spanish absolute interrogatives are produced at a higher tonal range or level in relation to the same utterances produced as declaratives (Dorta 2000, Cunningham 1983, Navarro Tomás 1944, Prieto 2004, Quilis 1987, 1993, Sosa 1999). Sosa (1999) claims that an increased initial tonal height is found in all dialects of Spanish. Willis (2003) does not find evidence to support this claim of a higher initial tone in DS absolute interrogatives with broad focus compared to identical declaratives. While this claim is not dealt with in the current study, the question of distinct tonal ranges is addressed with a comparison of identical sentences across declarative and interrogative productions in Willis (2004).

The present study reports on broad focus absolute interrogative contours in DS. The findings indicate an interrogative contour that is different from previous reports of Caribbean Spanish intonation. The DS broad focus absolute interrogative contour was consistently produced as an overall rising contour without the characteristic Caribbean tonal fall throughout the toneme (nuclear pitch accent and edge tones).

3. Procedure

Four female university students, ages 17–23, from Santiago, Dominican Republic, participated in the experiment. The informants were students at the Pontificia Universidad Católica Madre y Maestra, Santiago de los Caballeros, Dominican Republic.[7]

The informants read a series of target sentences that were preceded by a context that prompted a broad focus reading of the target sentence (see 1).

There were a total of 200 context/sentence sets produced by each informant.[8] There were eight absolute interrogative broad focus utterances repeated four times each for a total of 32 utterances per informant.

The sentences were placed on 3x5 index cards and the order of the sentences was pseudo-randomized. The interrogative corpus utterances all followed the structure V(S) O, as in *¿Miraba la luna?* 'H/She was watching the moon?' (See appendix 1).[9] An example of the prompt and target sentence is presented in (1).[10]

(1)   Example target sentence:
        ¿Alaba la mula?
        'He/she praises the mule.'

        Contexto: Ves un campesino hablando dulcemente con sus animales. No escuchaste   lo que dice y quieres saber.
        Preguntas a tu amiga: "¿Alaba la mula?"

        'Context: You see a farmer speaking sweetly with his animals. You didn't hear what he said and you want to know.
        You ask your friend: "Is he praising the mule?"'

The data were recorded into a Sony DAT recorder using an Optimus headset microphone and analyzed using Entropics Xwaves.[11] The following measurements were calculated for each sentence shown in Figure 3:
1) the initial stable tonal value at the onset of voicing for the utterance[12],
2) the tonal value of the Low tone and High tone associated with the first pitch accent,
3) the tonal value of the Low tone associated with the nuclear pitch accent,
4) the tonal values of the High tone associated with a boundary and the final F0 value of the utterance.[13]

There is also a small corpus of spontaneous speech that was examined to corroborate the findings of the experimental data. The speakers who participated in the spontaneous speech were also between the ages of 20–23 and likewise were students at the *Pontificia Universidad Católica Madre y Maestra*, Santiago de los Caballeros, Dominican Republic. There was one male speaker in the spontaneous speech corpus.

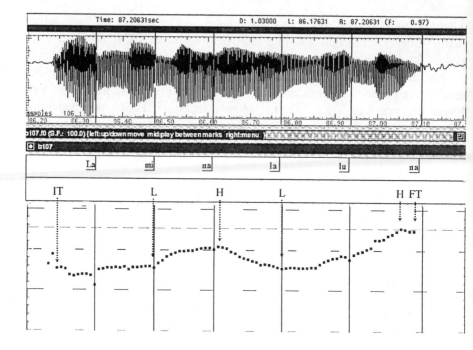

Figure 3. Speaker 1, DS absolute interrogative intonation contour. ¿Lamina la
luna? 'He/she laminates the moon?'. Absolute interrogative contour
with landmarks for quantitative analysis. IT=initial tonal value, L=Low
tone, H=High tone, FT= final tonal value.

4. DS absolute interrogatives

4.1. General description of DS absolute interrogatives

The absolute interrogatives in the experimental data were consistently realized as an overall rising intonational contour (see Figure 3 and Appendix
2). The most common contour pattern began with an initial low plateau
until a tonal rise associated with the first pitch accent. The initial tonal rise
reached a High tone or peak near the end of the first lexical word. After the
High tone, there was a slight tonal fall until reaching a Low tone or turning
point at the second (nuclear) tonic syllable. The Low tone of the second
tonal movement was produced at a higher tonal level than the first tonal
movement. Following the nuclear Low tone, there was a tonal rise that
typically reached a peak before the end of the utterance. The final 30-50 ms

of the F0 track was typically realized as a plateau or slightly falling contour (see Figure 4a).

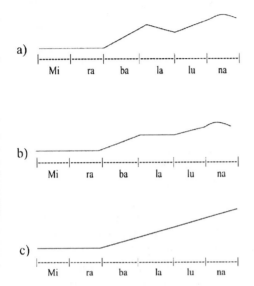

a)

| Mi | ra | ba | la | lu | na |

b)

| Mi | ra | ba | la | lu | na |

c)

| Mi | ra | ba | la | lu | na |

Figure 4. ¿Miraba la luna? 'He/she was looking at the moon? Schematic of the principal variations of broad focus absolute interrogatives in DS. The alignment of the prenuclear pitch accent reflects the unmarked Low tone alignment in DS (see Willis 2003) There was also considerable variation in the alignment of the nuclear Low tone (see appendix 2 a-d).

There were several minor variations of the principal contour just described, which are illustrated in Figures 4b and 4c. The distinction in Figure 4b is a tonal plateau following the initial tonal rise instead of a slight tonal fall as in Figure 4a, also illustrated in is a boundary plateau. This boundary plateau was not contingent on a preceding plateau. The variation shown in Figure 4c illustrates a tonal rise from the initial pitch accent through the end of the utterance that reflects an interpolation between the Low tone of the initial pitch accent and the final boundary tone. This interpolation created an essentially straight line in which the exact position(s) or surface realization of the intervening tone(s) was not discernible.

The basic DS absolute interrogative contour, illustrated in Figures 3 and 4a, is consistently and significantly different from previous characterizations of absolute interrogatives for Caribbean Spanish in several ways (see Figure 5 for a schematic of the basic Caribbean versus DS contours).[14]

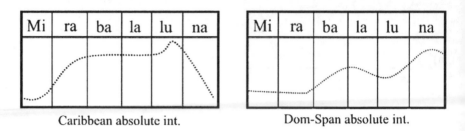

Mi	ra	ba	la	lu	na

Caribbean absolute int.

Mi	ra	ba	la	lu	na

Dom-Span absolute int.

Figure 5. Schematic comparison of Caribbean Spanish broad focus absolute interrogatives. It is currently proposed that the final rise of the DS absolute interrogative corresponds to boundary tones.

The first difference between the DS absolute interrogatives and previous characterizations of Caribbean Spanish was an overall rising contour. The second variation involved a nuclear pitch accent that is lower than the following edge tones (Low-High toneme). When there is a tonal fall at the rightmost edge, it is typically of a much lesser magnitude than the tonal fall from the nuclear High tone to a boundary Low, and in most productions there was a final suspended or plateau tone. The final tones in the experimental data did not demonstrate the characteristic Caribbean toneme with a High nuclear pitch accent followed by a Low boundary tone.

4.2. Empirical characterization

This section examines the tonal levels of the key intonational constructs in Dominican absolute interrogatives. Figure 6 is a series of boxplots of the tonal values for the principal tonal targets in the utterances previously described and illustrated in Figure 3. Each plot is based on the measurable tokens for each specified tonal value (typically between 27-32 tokens). These tonal targets include: the initial tonal value of the utterance, the Low and High of the prenuclear pitch accent (1-L and 1-H), the value of the nuclear Low tone (2-L), the High of the rising boundary tone (2-H), and the final tonal value of the utterance (FT), which was typically a distinct tonal value. The data illustrated graphically in Figure 6 serve as the basis for several additional comparisons.

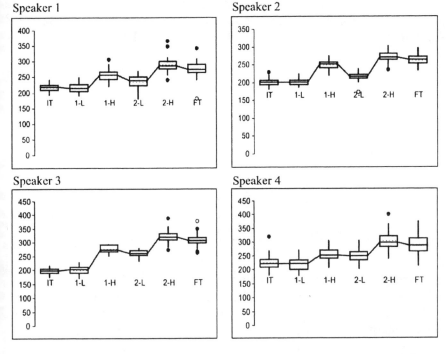

Figure 6. Boxplot of the tonal range values for all speakers (see Figure 3 for actual labelled contour). IT=initial tone, 1-L= prenuclear Low tone, 1-H=prenuclear High tone, 2-L=nuclear Low tone, 2-H=edge High tone, and FT=final tone. The tonal values for tones within a tonal interpolation contours are not included. Each boxplot is based on an average of between 27-31 tokens, except for speaker 3 who demonstrated an elevated number of interpolated contours (see appendix 2c).

4.2.1. Global tonal range

The current use of the term global tonal range refers to the total tonal difference between the lowest Low tone and the highest High tone of an utterance. One of the earliest characterizations of Spanish intonation involves a comparison of tonal range among the three basic utterance types: declaratives, absolute interrogatives, and pronominal interrogatives. Navarro Tomás (1944) reports that absolute interrogatives in Peninsular Spanish are produced with a global tonal range of 7-8 semitones (1944:101–102). I am currently unaware of any published report concerning global tonal range in Caribbean Spanish interrogatives.

The DS data exhibited a reduced global tonal range compared to the claim by Navarro Tomás for Peninsular Spanish, except for Speaker 3.[15] Conflated for all speakers, the mean tonal range for DS absolute interrogatives is 87 Hz (s.d.55).[16] The raw Hz values convert to an average range of 5.9 semitones (s.d. 2.1) for all speakers. The global tonal ranges in semitones for each speaker are presented in Table 1.

Table 1.   Semi-tone range, mean and standard deviation, for DS absolute interrogatives (the initial Low to the boundary High tone)

Speaker	1	2	3	4
N	30	30	32	32
Mean	4.9	5.1	8.1	5.3
s.d.	1.7	1.3	1.9	1.2

Clearly there is speaker variation in the global tonal range evidenced in the differing speaker ranges. Speaker 3 had the greatest magnitude of utterance tonal range variation and was also the speaker with the highest number of interpolated rising contours. There appears to be a correlation between overall tonal range and the number of interpolated contours. These two facts suggest that intermediate tones, in this case nuclear pitch accents and possibly a Low phrase tone, may be obscured by increases in tonal range within a reduced temporal space.

4.2.2. Tonal range of internal rises

As demonstrated in Figure 6, there were typically two distinct tonal rises in the majority of the interrogative utterances. The tonal range of the individual tonal rises is shown in Table 2. The first tonal excursion, the prenuclear pitch accent, is produced in connection with the first tonic syllable.

The tonal range of the toneme pitch movement, consisting of the nuclear Low tone and the edge High tone, was also consistently produced as a Low-High tonal combination. The semitone values of both tonal rises are presented in Table 2.

Table 2.   Tonal rise in semitones between the Low and High tone of the first pitch accent Low of the nuclear pitch accent and the High tone of the edge tone.

Speakers	N	1st tonal rise in semitones		2nd tonal rise in semitones	
		mean	s.d.	mean	s.d.
1	27	2.8	1.2	3.3	1.8
2	29	3.7	1.1	3.9	1.1
3	8	4.9	1.4	3.7	1.2
4	28	2.4	.7	3.5	.76

The majority of speakers produced the second pitch movement, the nuclear Low tone to the edge High tone, with a greater tonal range compared to the first tonal movement; however, the differences were not significant.[17] Previous reports of Spanish intonation indicate that the greatest tonal range is typically found on the initial pitch accents of an utterance in declarative utterances (de la Mota 1995, Prieto and Hirschberg 1995, Sosa 1999). Characterizations of tonal range, either global for the entire utterance or local with respect to individual pitch accents, have not been examined sufficiently for Spanish interrogatives. The present data provide a baseline of read speech for future comparisons and analysis.

4.2.3. Boundary range (Range between final peak and utterance final hz)

Characteristic of the DS productions of absolute interrogatives is a boundary rise-fall (High-Low) or a rise-plateau. The tonal rise from the nuclear pitch accent Low tone typically reaches a peak or High tone roughly 40 ms before the final utterance boundary as shown in Figure 7 (also illustrated in Figures 3, 8, and Appendix 2a). While there is some variation in the alignment of the boundary High tones, the majority of the productions occur within a range of 30-50 ms before the end of the utterance.

Figure 7 clearly illustrates that a tonal rise through the end of an utterance is not the most common pattern in DS absolute interrogatives in broad focus. This boundary tone peak High tone, before the end of an utterance, contrasts with published reports of Spanish rising absolute interrogatives (Quilis 1993, Sosa 1999:209–211). A non-final High tone suggests that there is an additional final tone, discrete from the High tone, which conditions the final tonal fall or tonal plateau (see Willis 2003).

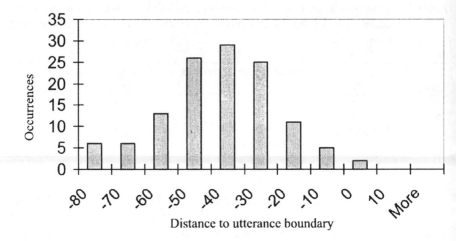

Figure 7. Alignment of the High tone preceding the utterance boundary in DS absolute interrogatives. The size of the category range was chosen arbitrarily; however, it provides an informative view into the distribution of the peak distribution of the final High tones.

In most productions, the final tonal value demonstrated a tonal fall from the boundary High tone demonstrated in the boxplots in Figure 6, while in other tokens the final tonal value occurred at essentially the same tonal level as the preceding High tone. A paired, two sample t-Test with pooled variance for each individual speaker did not indicate a significant difference for tonal levels between the boundary High tone and final tonal value of the utterance, (p > .05). With the present data, the final portion of DS absolute interrogative in broad focus is most accurately characterized as a final plateau or suspended contour. Contours from spontaneous speech also reveal a final plateau of up to 70 ms in a finished utterance (see Appendix 3b).

4.2.4. Empirical conclusions

The contour tonal ranges for the distinct measurements demonstrate an overall rising intonational contour with a final descent or plateau. There is no declination or gradual downtrend of tonal contour as reported for Peninsular Spanish interrogatives, nor is there the High-Low toneme pattern reported for Caribbean Spanish. Whereas it is always possible to produce a particular or unique contour in isolation, the repeated and consistent tonal patterns produced by the Dominican speakers indicate that this interrogative contour is a productive pattern across multiple productions and multiple speakers. The presence of a final plateau or suspended contour suggests an innovation in DS compared to other Caribbean dialects of Spanish. Future studies are required to investigate the alignment of the nuclear pitch accent tone(s).

5. DS absolute interrogatives; spontaneous speech data

An intonational contour that is significantly different from previous descriptions raises questions concerning its validity as a representative description of the natural patterns of intonation within a language. The patterns reported in the experimental corpus were also found in the corpus of spontaneous speech. Figure 8 is an example of an overall rising absolute interrogative from the spontaneous speech corpus. We can see that the nuclear pitch accent Low tone is at a higher tonal level than the Low tone of the prenuclear pitch accent, as well as the characteristic DS final plateau following the boundary rise.

The contour shown in Figure 8 was produced in response to a question concerning the identity of a friend who was to accompany Speaker 2 to a graduation ceremony. Speaker 2 first responds with the friend's name, and then asks if 1 knows the identity of the friend, Leo.

(1)   Spkr 1:   *¿Quién se graduó?*
                 'Who graduated?'
       Spkr 2:   *Leonardo, ¿tú sabe(s) quién e(s) Leo?*
                 'Leonardo, do you who Leo is?'

While Figure 8 provides evidence that an overall rise with a final plateau is a valid intonational pattern in DS, there were also examples of absolute interrogatives that had a final falling *High-Low* toneme characteristic of previous descriptions of Caribbean Spanish (see Figure 9).[18]

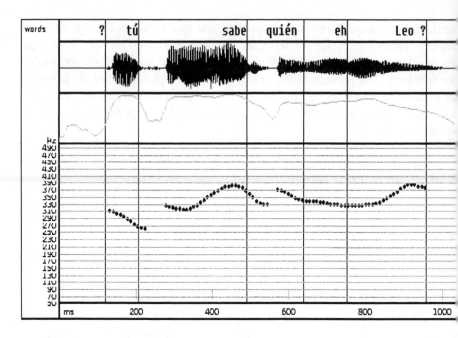

Figure 8. ¿Y tú sabe(s) quién es Leo? 'And do you know who Leo is?' Spontaneous conversation absolute interrogative intonational contour, Speaker 1.

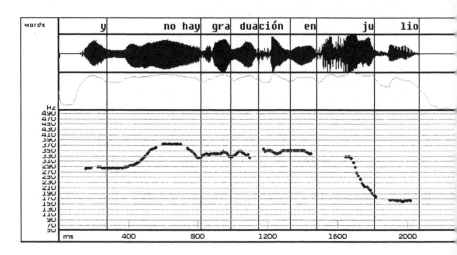

Figure 9. ¿Y no hay graduación en Julio? 'And there is no graduation [ceremony] in July? Speaker 1. Final falling absolute interrogative in DS spontaneous speech corpus.

The contour in Figure 9 is the result of an exchange in which the two speakers are discussing upcoming graduation plans, including when and where. Speaker 2 tells Speaker 1 that she will either graduate in September in the capital [Santo Domingo] or here [Santiago] in January. The F0 contour in Figure 9 illustrates an interrogative in which Speaker 1 seeks clarification about the possibility of graduating in July also. The proposition of a July graduation month is new to the discourse and was produced to convey narrow focus on the final word of the utterance, July.

(3)   Spkr 1. ...and you are going to graduate in August, right?
        Spkr 2. What do I do [unintelligible] the graduation in ah?
        Spkr 1. June, September.
        Spkr 2. No, I am going to graduate in September in the Capital, or in January here.
        Spkr 1. it's that...
        Spkr 2. Yeah?
        Spkr 1. And there is no graduation in July?[19]

The intonational contour Figure 9 has a pattern similar to previous descriptions of Caribbean absolute interrogatives (Beckman et al. 2002, Quilis 1993, Sosa 1999). In particular, the toneme (nuclear pitch accent and edge tone[s]) demonstrates the characteristic High nuclear tone with a subsequent Low boundary tone. In this final falling contour, the tonal range of the toneme is the greatest of the utterance, in contrast to the tonal range of the toneme seen in the broad focus contours.

The presence of both types of intonational contours in the spontaneous speech corpus, the *High-Low* falling toneme characteristic of Caribbean Spanish absolute interrogatives and the *Low-High* toneme seen in the DS broad focus experimental data, raises an important question: Do pragmatic issues motivate the distinct contours similar to other dialects of Spanish? The experimental data contexts were intended to elicit "out of the blue" questions in which the entire question is the focus of the query. The preceding context was included to provide a setting in which the utterance could plausibly be produced whereas the example provided in Figure 9 corresponds to an absolute interrogative with narrow focus (for additional examples see Appendix 2b and Willis 2003,).

The two examples from spontaneous speech shown in Figures 8 and 9 provide preliminary evidence for distinct contours associated with different pragmatics in DS absolute interrogatives. With a limited corpus of spontaneous speech, it is impossible to make definitive claims about the role of focus in Dominican absolute interrogatives. However, the robustness of the overall rising contour in the experimental absolute interrogatives resulting from "out of the blue" contexts, corroborated with spontaneous speech data, provides evidence for the existence of overall rising absolute interrogatives in this dialect without the characteristic toneme High-Low. The presence of absolute interrogative final falling contours with specific focus intent in the spontaneous speech corpus is similar to the distinction proposed by several researchers for other dialects of Spanish (Cid Uribe and Ortiz-Lira 2000, Quilis 1993, Sosa 1999). An initial hypothesis is that pragmatic focus plays a role in the realization of absolute interrogatives as an overall rising or falling contour in this dialect of DS.

6. Discussion of DS absolute interrogatives

6.1. Dialectal variation and global patterns

Sosa (1999) notes that a global intonational pattern used in a specific context in one dialect of Spanish may be found in another dialect with a distinct pragmatic value (also see Ladd 1996). This observation of variable pragmatics across dialects has been confirmed in the current data. The global intonational patterns observed in the three basic broad focus interrogatives of Peninsular Spanish, Caribbean Spanish (Cuba, Puerto Rico, Venezuela, and DS) occur in the other dialects with distinct pragmatic functions. For example, the default Caribbean Spanish intonational pattern for interrogatives in broad focus is used in DS for utterances with narrow focus, and the DS contour for interrogatives in broad focus is found in Peninsular Spanish in cases of exclamation or narrow focus. Pragmatically, the three basic contours shown in Figure 10 convey at least four pragmatic intents among the same three Spanish dialects.

The patterns represented in Figure 10 suggest general contour patterns and reflect exact intonational variables such as tonal alignment, tonal range, or even an identical specification of underlying pitch accents and boundary tones. However, the similarities of the patterns, despite exact phonetic and phonological differences, suggest the possibility of phonological misinterpretation among these Spanish dialects.

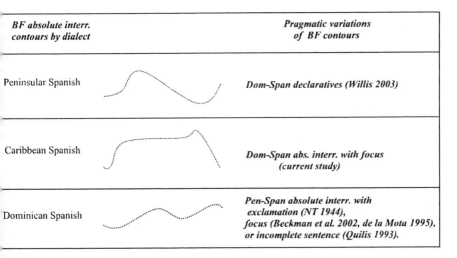

BF absolute interr. contours by dialect		Pragmatic variations of BF contours
Peninsular Spanish		*Dom-Span declaratives (Willis 2003)*
Caribbean Spanish		*Dom-Span abs. interr. with focus (current study)*
Dominican Spanish		*Pen-Span absolute interr. with exclamation (NT 1944), focus (Beckman et al. 2002, de la Mota 1995), or incomplete sentence (Quilis 1993).*

Figure 10. Variations in global intonational contours and pragmatic use in Peninsular, Caribbean and DS. Characterizations of the broad focus absolute interrogatives are provided in Navarro Tomás (1944), Quilis (1987, 1993), and Sosa (1999).

5.2. Boundary tones

There were three tonal patterns that occurred at the utterance edge in the DS broad focus absolute interrogatives. These three toneme patterns are illustrated in schematic form in Figure 11 and with actual contours in Appendix 2a.[20] The most frequent pattern involved a rise from the nuclear Low tone to a High tone followed by a tonal plateau. The second toneme configuration also involved a tonal rise to a High tone, but was followed by a slight tonal fall (8-15 Hz). The third pattern was a rising contour that began after the nuclear Low tone and continued through the end of the utterance.

It is possible that the contours schematized in Figures (a) and (b) are variations of the same underlying tones. As has been stated, the variations were produced in response to a single pragmatic context, broad focus. It is possible that the speakers applied an individual modification independent of the stated context (see Bolinger 1972).

(a)   Low rising-plateau

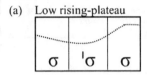

(b)   Low rising-fall

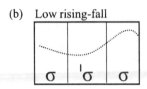

(c)   Low rise to utterance boundary

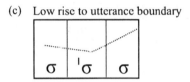

Figure 11. Schematic of the three basic final tonal configurations in DS broad fo-
    cus absolute interrogatives (see Appendix 2a).

A final suspended contour in Spanish has been noted by several researchers (Beckman et al. 2002, Cid Uribe and Ortiz-Lira 2000, Navarro
Tomás, 1944, Quilis 1987, 1993, Sosa 1999). Navarro Tomás, Quilis, and
Sosa propose that a suspended contour is used for incompleteness in Spanish. Quilis (1993) claims that a final suspension or plateau contour is produced when a speaker doubts or does not know how to end the phrase or is
interrupted (466). Sosa (1999) suggests that a suspended contour serves as
a preamble to add additional information to the discussion (129).[21]

Only recently has it been recognized that a final suspended contour
midlevel tone (Beckman et al. 2002), or a final plateau (Cid Uribe and
Ortiz-Lira 2000) in Spanish intonation is used for pragmatic reasons other
than "incompleteness". Cid Uribe and Ortiz-Lira (2000) provide evidence
of a final plateau or suspended tone in absolute interrogatives in Chilean
Spanish of Santiago. In the Santiago, Chile dialect, the presence of a final
plateau or suspended tones occurs in absolute interrogatives as a negative
question. Additionally, Beckman et al. (2002) acknowledge the possibility
of a suspended or midlevel tone in Spanish intonation and propose a tonal
specification of M% until the exact tonal behaviors are better understood.
In the initial Sp-ToBI analysis, there was a consensus to avoid rushing an
analysis of a final plateau with any of a number of possible underlying tonal specifications.[22]

In the DS experimental data, the tonic syllable with nuclear stress is the penultimate of the utterance allowing a limited space to realize the boundary tones. As noted previously, the boundary High tone occurred typically 30-50 ms before the utterance boundary. The realization of an utterance final tone, be it a Low tone or a plateau/suspended tone, was allowed a relatively small window in which to be produced. Additional experiments which manipulate this variable of unstressed syllables between the last tonic syllable and the utterance boundary are necessary before reaching a conclusion concerning the exact tonal specification of boundary tones in DS absolute interrogatives. However, at this point it is worth noting that examples from the spontaneous speech corpus illustrate a final level tone that lasts over 70 ms; ample phonetic material in which to produce a tonal fall if there were a final Low tonal target (see Appendix 2f). While a suspended contour may convey doubt in certain dialects of Spanish, it certainly does not reflect doubt in the case of absolute interrogatives in DS in either corpus.

5.3. Interrogative upstepping

One of the more interesting characteristics of the DS absolute interrogatives is the high tonal value of the nuclear Low tone compared to the preceding prenuclear pitch accent. Sosa (1999:150–154) claims that all Spanish interrogatives have an initial High boundary tone, H%, which is responsible for elevating the tonal level of the utterance, most notably on the first pitch accent and then raising the tonal level throughout the utterance until the toneme (see Ladd 1996:276–7, for additional discussion). This initial High boundary tone effect throughout the interrogative, designated *upstep* by Sosa, is reportedly productive in all dialects of Spanish. However, what is not clear from Sosa's proposal is how this *upstepping* produces different nuclear pitch accent tonal levels for absolute interrogatives with the High-Low toneme, and those dialects with the Low-High toneme. If the initial High boundary tone indeed affects all the subsequent pitch accents as claimed, why do the tonal levels of the nuclear pitch accents in the Low-High toneme dialects fall below the initial tonal level before starting the final rise as shown in the example contours? Based on Sosa's prediction of upstepping in Spanish, depending on the domain of the upstepping effect, each subsequent tone should be realized at a higher level than the previous; however, this is not the case in the DS data.

Beckman et al. (2002:23) define upstepping as the "an expansion of the pitch range that raises subsequent tones". Beckman et al. (2002) and the Sp-ToBI group found evidence for *upstepping* based on the High tone of a bitonal pitch accent, and chose to mark the distinct tonal relationship locally, on the pitch accent that exhibits the increase in pitch range.

The relationship between the prenuclear and nuclear pitch accent tonal values in the DS absolute interrogative data follows the latter upstepping prediction, and consistently demonstrates an elevated or upstepped tonal value in the nuclear pitch accent as shown in the boxplots in Figure 6. Following the upstepped nuclear pitch accent, DS absolute interrogatives in broad focus have a final boundary tonal rise in contrast to a boundary tonal fall previously reported for most Caribbean dialects of Spanish. The boundary tone rise, a common marker of interrogativity in the world's languages, simply follows the nuclear upstepping.

The proposal of a nuclear Low tone is strengthened by data from declaratives and wh interrogatives. Willis (2003) provides evidence that the DS nuclear pitch accent in declaratives and "wh" interrogatives in broad focus is typically produced as one of two possible falling tones. Based on the productivity of a falling nuclear pitch accent in other DS pragmatic types combined with clear evidence that the final rise corresponds to a boundary tone based on alignment considerations, I propose that the nuclear pitch accent is an upstepped Low tone. Until there is further data, it is tenable to suggest that DS absolute interrogatives with broad focus are characterized by an upstepped nuclear pitch accent. This upstepping of the nuclear pitch accent, in this case a Low tone, ¡L*, accounts for the significantly higher tonal value compared to the initial prenuclear tone of the same utterance.[23]

6.4. Conclusions

The DS absolute interrogatives described in this paper are different from previously described absolute interrogatives in Caribbean Spanish in three ways: (1) an absolute produced as an overall rising intonational contour, (2) the second pitch accent is "upstepped", in that it is produced at a higher tonal level than the first pitch accent, (3) a final plateau or fall from the final tonal peak to the end of the utterance. Additionally, the data reveal preliminary evidence suggesting distinct absolute interrogative tonal contours based on pragmatic intent.

The global tonal pattern seen in the range of individual tonal values demonstrated an overall rising intonational contour. The toneme in DS broad focus absolute interrogatives is phonologically distinct from other varieties of Caribbean Spanish. In previous reports, Caribbean Spanish absolute interrogatives have been described as having a High nuclear pitch accent followed by a Low edge tone. The most frequent DS absolute interrogative toneme in read speech with a context prompting broad focus is a Low nuclear tone followed by a tonal rise and fall or plateau (see Figures 5 and 11).

Whereas declination is the normal pattern in Spanish intonation, the DS absolute interrogatives in broad focus present a nuclear pitch accent that is significantly higher than the prenuclear pitch accent. I propose that this nuclear pitch accent is upstepped. This claim is addressed in more detail with corroborating evidence from identical declarative sentences in Willis (2003).

Navarro Tomás (1944) and Quilis (1987, 1993) note a suspended or plateau contour in Spanish intonation associated with incomplete utterances. The current DS data, along with corroborating data from Cid Uribe and Ortiz-Lira (2000) for Santiago, Chile, provide evidence for a final Spanish suspended or plateau tone. The inclusion of this tonal pattern in complete utterances requires a reanalysis of the tonal specifications previously allotted to Spanish intonation.

The DS absolute interrogatives in broad focus were produced with a Low-High-plateau toneme. Examples of the High-Low toneme, characteristic of absolute interrogatives in other Caribbean Spanish dialects, were found in a corpus of unscripted conversation. The examples of the final High-Low toneme found in the spontaneous speech corpus correspond to either a negative or narrow focus question.

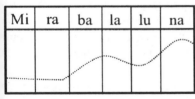

DS abs. int. with broad focus

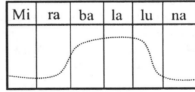

DS abs. int. with focus

Figure 12. Schematic of possible DS broad focus absolute interrogative versus a negative or narrow focus absolute interrogative. The tonal levels are not based on quantitative data, but do follow the patterns seen in the spontaneous speech corpus.

The pragmatic value of these two distinct interrogative contours suggests that focus plays a role in the use of the two contours. A preliminary hypothesis is that the Low-High toneme signals broad focus, while a High-Low toneme conveys a narrow focus or negative interrogative (see Figure 12).

This quantitative examination of DS highlights the need for empirical studies of Spanish intonation to understand better the phonological processes, such as upstepping, and their use and variation across dialects.

Acknowledgments

The data collection here was supported in part by a Tinker Grant from the University of Illinois at Urbana-Champaign and travel funds from Millikin University. I would also like to acknowledge the generous support by Dr. Ricardo Miniño of the Pontificia Universidad Católica Madre y Maestra in providing office space and access to student informants. This paper has also benefited from comments by José Ignacio Hualde and Pilar Prieto.

Notes

1. See Sosa 1999:199-201, figures 3-13 to 3-15 for actual contours similar to the schematic in (1a) for several dialects of Spanish. For example contours of schematic (1b) for Caribbean Spanish, see Sosa 1999: 204-26, Figures 3-17 and 3-18, also Beckman et al. (2002).
2. Navarro Tomás used the term *tonema* or 'toneme' to refer to the tones associated with the nuclear pitch accent and boundary tone(s) and much of his analysis revolved around the final tonal movement(s) of an utterance which he termed the *tonema* or toneme. With the long history of the toneme in Spanish intonation literature, in some instances, it is still useful to make reference to this construct for comparison with previous characterizations; in addition, some dialectal differences are more apparent in the combination of the nuclear pitch accent and boundary tone(s) manifested together.
3. Similarities of the intonational patterns of Caribbean Spanish and Canary Island Spanish have been noted by several researchers. The High-Low falling toneme typical of the Caribbean Spanish absolute interrogatives is also reported to occur in the Canary Islands (Dorta 2000, Lipski, 1994; Quilis, 1987) and Oviedo (Cunningham, 1983).
4. Quilis also provides illustrations of absolute interrogatives produced by a Puerto Rican speaker that are clearly not the characteristic falling contours

however, there is no additional discussion. Unfortunately, it is not clear if they are fundamentally different with respect to the toneme. Additionally, we do not have empirical data concerning their frequency of occurrence or a discussion concerning the implications for dialectal variation within Caribbean Spanish.

5. Sosa suggests that there are three final rising contours, each with a different phonological specification that creates slight differences in the magnitude of final rise. Arguments concerning this claim are discussed by Ladd (1996) and Willis (2003).

6. Sosa claims that a falling toneme is invariable in the Caribbean dialectal region and that that the contours of absolute interrogatives offer the clearest typological distinction of a Caribbean dialect within the Americas (1999:207).

7. The speakers are all natives of the dialectal region, educated from families in which both parents had University experience and had not traveled extensively thereby avoiding prosodic interference from other dialects or languages. The speakers were all recorded in June of 1999. The informants provided a biographical data to ensure the homogeneity of the informant population.

8. The target broad focus absolute interrogatives reported in this paper were part of a larger experiment designed to test identical sentences with varying pragmatic intents. The target utterances were interspersed among "wh" or pronominal interrogatives, imperatives and declarative utterances.

9. The current phonological structure of the utterances is somewhat restricted. Specifically, the nuclear pitch accent appears to be "crowded" with respect to the prenuclear pitch accent and final boundary tones. Additional studies are needed to permit a clearer picture of nuclear tonal alignment. For this study, it was preferred to have a larger number of comparable tokens for later comparison across pragmatic intents. In addition, I wished to avoid the insertion of potential intermediate phrase boundaries (Nibert 2000). However, the phonological structure does permit a close examination of the principal features of Spanish interrogatives, namely, initial and final boundary tones.

10. It was pointed out by a reviewer that several of the contexts potentially permitted a "reiterative" or "confirmatory" production. While this possibility does exist is some contexts, that fact that all productions followed a similar pattern suggests that the broad focus interpretation was the consistent interpretation.

11. The entire spoken corpus was digitized using Entropics Xwaves sampled at 16,000. The target sentences were removed from the digitized corpus. F0 contours and spectrograms were created for each utterance and were simultaneously aligned with the waveform. Waveforms, spectrograms, and F0 contours were produced and analyzed with Entropics ESPS/Xwaves.

12. The initial tonal value was calculated as the first stable F0 value associated with a voiced segment.

13. The tonal alignment illustrated in Figure 3 reflects the prototypical unmarked prenuclear alignment in DS, see (Willis 2003).

14. See Beckman et al. (2002) and Sosa (1999:204 Figure 3-17) for examples of the widely accepted intonational pattern for Caribbean Spanish absolute interrogatives. The magnitudes of the tonal range of the schematics do not reflect an actual comparison of tonal range.

15. The difference is reported tonal ranges should not be taken as direct evidence for dialectal differences. The DS reflects read speech, while the data for Navarro Tomás' claim is derived from direct observation and literary recordings from the *Palabra de Madrid* (Navarro Tomás 1944:11-12)

16. Specifically I used the tonal values of the first Low tone, which on average were a few Hz lower than the initial tone, and the final High tone.

17. An unpaired t-Test did not reveal a significant difference for two of the three speakers examined [$p > .05$]. I did not perform the statistical test on the data from speaker 3 because of the considerably reduced number of analyzable tokens due to the high number of interpolated contours.

18. There were additional interrogative contours in the spontaneous data that do not correspond to either the rising contour or the falling contour. These additional variations likely reflect more complex pragmatic contexts.

19. Spkr 1.   ¿. . .tú te va a graduar ahora en agosto, verdad?
    Spkr 2.   qué hago [unintelligible] la graduación en ah
    Spkr 1.   Junio, septiembre
    Spkr 2.   No, yo me voy a graduar en septiembre en la capital, o en enero aquí.
    Spkr 1.   es . . . que
    Spkr 2.   Sí
    Spkr 1.   ¿Y no hay graduación en julio?

20. I do not agree with Sosa's analysis (1999) in which he uses bitonal nuclear pitch accents to account for an increased edge tone in tonal range in absolute interrogatives in non-Caribbean dialects (see Figure 3.25, page 213). There are two reasons for this objection: 1) there is no proposed phonological contrast for the increased tonal range, and 2) in cases of an identical pitch movement defined by tonal alignment, an increase in tonal range serves as a function of emphasis (Liberman and Pierrehumbert 1984).

21. These claims by Quilis and Sosa are made in specific reference to declarative utterances; however, they do not limit them to declaratives.

22. The minutes to this meeting can be seen at http://www.ling.ohio-state.edu/~tobi/sp-tobi/minutes_formatted.html.

23. An alternative analysis is that the final rise is part of the nuclear pitch accent with an upstepped LH tonal configuration. However, this analysis contradicts repeated descriptions of Spanish rising nuclear pitch accents (LH). Typical characterizations of Spanish rising nuclear pitch accents report that the High tone of the bi-tonal pitch accent is consistently realized within the tonic boundary in cases of penult stress (Face 2002, Prieto 2004, Sosa 1999). In the DS fi-

nal tonal rises, the tonal peak is typically reached a peak 129 ms (s.d. 38) past the tonic offset, or 40-45 ms before the utterance boundary (see Willis 2003 for a complete discussion). At this point until there is further evidence, this final rise is considered part of the boundary tone configuration.

References

Alba, Orlando
   2000   *Nuevos aspectos del español en Santo Domingo.* Santo Domingo: Librería La Trinitaria.
Beckman, Mary E., Manuel Diaz-Campos, Julia Tevis McGory and Terrell A. Morgan.
   2002   Intonation across Spanish, in the Tones and Break Indices framework. *Probus* 14: 9-36.
Bolinger, Dwight
   1972   Accent is predictable (if you're a mind-reader). *Language* 48: 633–644.
Cid Uribe, Miriam, and Héctor Ortiz-Lira
   2000   La prosodia de las preguntas indagativas y no-indagativas del español culto de Santiago de Chile. *Lingüística Española Actual* 22: 23–49.
Cunningham, Una
   1983   Aspects of the intonation in Spanish. *Nottingham Linguistic Circular* 12: 21–54.
de la Mota, Carme
   1995   La representación gramatical de la información nueva en el discurso. Ph.D. diss., Universitat Autònoma de Barcelona.
Dorta, Josefa
   2000   Entonación hispánica: interrogativas no pronominales vs. interrogativas pronominales. *Lingüística Española Actual* 22: 51–77.
Face, Timothy
   2002   *Intonational Marking of Contrastive Focus in Madrid Spanish.* Munich: Lincom Europa.
Hualde, José Ignacio
   2003   El modelo métrico y autosegmental. In *Teorías de la entonación,* Pilar Prieto (ed.), 155-184. Barcelona: Ariel.
Jiménez Sabater, Max
   1975   *Más datos sobre el español en la República Dominicana.* Santo Domingo: Ediciones Intec.
Ladd, Robert D.
   1996   *Intonational Phonology.* Cambridge: Cambridge University Press.

Lipski, John
1994   *Latin American Spanish.* New York: Longman.
Navarro Tomás, Tomás
1944   *Manual de entonación española.* New York: Hispanic Institute in the United States.
Nibert, Holly
2000   Phonetic and phonological evidence for intermediate phrasing in Spanish intonation. Ph.D. diss., University of Illinois at Urbana-Champaign.
Prieto, Pilar, Jan van Santen, and Julia Hirschberg
1995   Tonal alignment patterns in Spanish. *Journal of Phonetics* 23: 429–451.
Prieto, Pilar
2004   The Search for Phonological Targets in the Tonal Space: H1 scaling and alignment in five sentence-types in Peninsular Spanish. In this volume.
Quilis, Antonio
1987   Entonación dialectal hispánica. In *Actas del I Congreso Internacional sobre el Español de América,* H. López Morales and M. Vaquero (eds.), 117–164. San Juan, Puerto Rico, Academia Puertorriqueña de la Lengua Española.
1993   *Tratado de fonología y fonética españolas.* Madrid: Gredos.
Sosa, Juan Manuel
1991   Fonética y fonología del español hispano americano. Ph.D. diss., University of Massachusetts, Amherst.
1999   *La entonación del español.* Madrid: Cátedra.
Willis, Erik W
2003   The intonational system of Dominican Spanish: Findings and analysis. Ph.D. diss., University of Illinois at Urbana-Champaign.
2004   Utterance signaling and tonal prominence relations in Dominican Spanish declaratives and interrogatives. Manuscript, New Mexico State University.

Appendix 1

Broad focus absolute interrogative context prompts and target utterances
¿Lavaba la lana?
Contexto: Un ranchero de ovejas quiere saber que hizo su trabajador el día anterior.
Pregunta: "¿Lavaba la lana?"
'Context: A sheep rancher wants to know what his worker did the previous day. He asks: "Did he wash the sheep?"'

¿Miraba la luna?
Contexto: tu mamá quiere saber qué hizo tu hermano porque no lo vió ayer.
Te pregunta: "¿Miraba la luna?"
'Context: Your mother wants to know what your brother did because she did not
    see him yesterday.
She asks, "Was he watching the moon?"'
¿Amaba a la nena?
Contexto: Ves una película con una amiga y al final el héroe deja a su novia. Te
    parece mal.
Preguntas a tu amiga: "¿Amaba a la nena?"
'Context: You see a movie with a friend and at the end the hero leaves his girl-
    friend. It seems wrong to you.
You ask your friend: 'Did he love the girl?'"
Pronominal interrogative
Contexto: Están leyendo una novela para la escuela y el profesor quiere repasar la
    historia.
El pregunta: ¿Quién amaba a la nena?
¿Alaba la mula?
Contexto: Ves un campesino hablando dulcemente con sus animales. No escuchas-
    te lo que dice y quieres saber.
Preguntas a tu amiga: "¿Alaba la mula?"
'Context: You see a farmer speaking sweetly with his animals. You didn't hear
    what he said and you want to know.
You ask your friend: "Is he praising the mule?"'
¿Emula a la niña?
Contexto: Eres una madre y notas que tu hijo se chupa el dedo.
Preguntas a tu marido: "¿Emula a la niña?"
'Context: You are a mother and notice that your child sucks his finger.
You ask your husband: "Is he imitating/emulating the girl?"'
¿Adora la mina?
Contexto: Tu padre siempre trabaja hasta muy tarde. Esto desespera a tu madre.
Hablando de tu padre ella te pregunta: "¿Adora la mina?"
'Context: Your father always works until very late. This exasperates your mother.
Referring to your father, she asks you: "Does he adore the mine?"'
¿Lamina la luna?
Contexto: Llegas a la casa y ves que tu hermano Juan está trabajando en la sala.
Preguntas a tu mamá señalando a su hermano: "¿Lamina la luna?"
'Context: You arrive home and see that your brother Juan is working in the din-
    ning room.
You ask your mother pointing to your brother, "Is he laminating the moon?"'
¿Mimaba a la niña?
Contexto: Ves a una niña que se porta muy mal y quieres saber la motivación de su
    comportamiento.
Preguntas a tu amiga: "¿Mimaba a la niña?"

'Context: You see a girl that is behaving badly and you want to know the reason
            for her behavior.
You ask your friend: "Did they spoil the girl?"'

Appendix 2

Example DS absolute interrogative intonational contours.

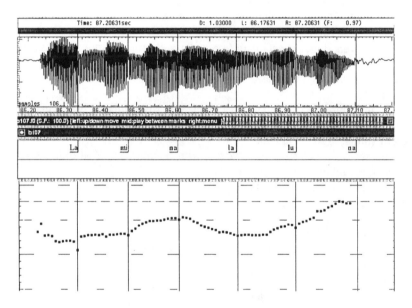

Figure A. ¿Lamina la luna? S/he laminates the moon? Late rise prenuclear pitch
            accent.

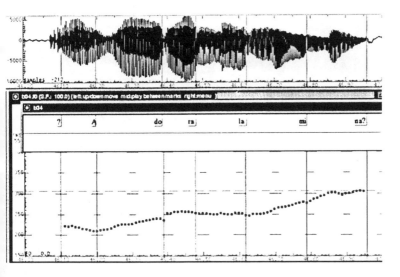

Figure B. ¿Adora la mina? Does he adore the mine? Early rise prenuclear pitch accent with a nuclear pitch accent plateau and a final boundary plateau.

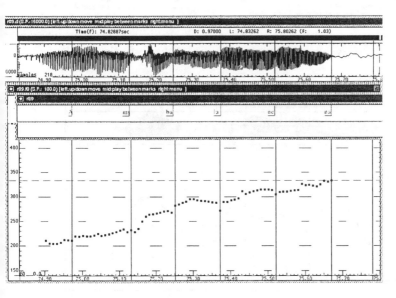

Figure C. ¿Amaba a la nena? 'He loved the [little] girl.' This contour illustrates an interpolated contour, a relatively straight line between two tonal targets, in which the overall surface manifestation obscures internal tones, perhaps due to the magnitude from the initial tonal rise to the final boundary tone.

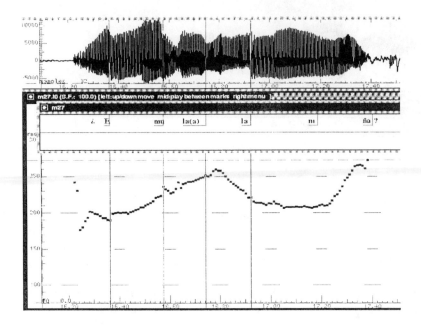

Figure D. ¿Emula a la niña? 'Does he emulate the girl? This contour provides a clearer motivation for a Low nuclear pitch accent with the subsequent boundary tone rise that plainly begins in the posttonic syllable.

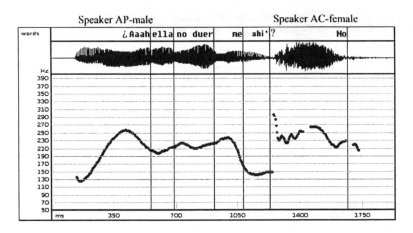

Figure E. Ah ¿Ella no duerme ahí. 'Ah, she doesn't sleep there.' An additional example of the final falling contour by a different speaker illustrated earlier in Figure 9. The context is From High-Low falling toneme in a DS absolute interrogative.

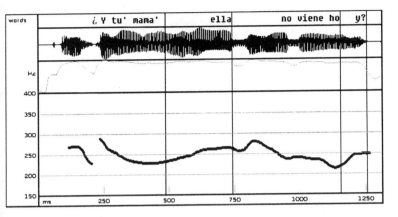

Figure F. ¿Y tu mamá, ella no viene hoy? 'And your mom, isn't she coming to-day?' An example of a final boundary plateau without the upstepped nuclear pitch accent. The final plateau has a duration of 70 ms.

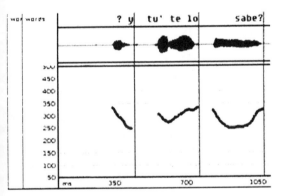

Figure G. ¿Y tú te lo sabe? 'And you [yourself] know it? Another example of a final boundary rise is spontaneous speech. The nuclear pitch accent, while not at a higher level than the prenuclear, does occur at the same level suggesting minimally a suspension of normal declination seen in other dialects of Spanish.

Part II

Syllables and stress

A computational approach to resolving certain issues in Spanish stress placement

David Eddington

1. Introduction

Spanish stress placement has been the topic of numerous linguistic analyses, especially within the generative tradition and its offshoots (e.g. Bailey 1995; Den Os and Kager 1986; Harris 1983, 1989, 1996; Hooper and Terrell 1976; Lipski 1997; Roca 1988, 1990, 1991, 1997; Saltarelli 1997; Whitley 1976). The framework within which these studies are couched, generally assumes that such accounts are relevant to the linguistic competence of an ideal speaker-hearer, and that the formal representations utilized (i.e. rules, derivations, constraints, constraint rankings) do not necessarily relate to the actual processing of language (Bradley 1980: 38; Chomsky and Halle 1968: 117; Kager 1999: 26; Kiparsky 1975: 198; 1982: 34).[1] In other words, most formal models do not purport to relate to linguistic performance but only competence, although it is not uncommon for them to be described in terms that appear performance oriented.

The present study is concerned with performance aspects of Spanish stress assignment, or in other words, models of how stress may be represented and processed in the course of language comprehension and production. I submit that language processing is largely a matter of learning and storing individual word tokens along with their inherent stress patterns. This view is consistent with empirical evidence that supports massive lexical storage of words, as well as word combinations and whole sentences (Alegre and Gordon 1999; Baayen, Dijkstra, and Schreuder 1997; Bod 1998; Butterworth 1983; Bybee 1995, 1998, 2002; Manelis and Tharp 1977; Pawley and Syder 1983; Sereno and Jongman 1997). This sort of lexicon appears to include, not only unpredictable information, but also a great deal of redundant data as well, including detailed phonetic information about individual word tokens (Brown and McNeill 1966; Bybee 1994, 2000, 2002; Frisch 1996; Goldinger 1996, 1997; Palmeri, Goldinger and Pisoni 1993; Pisoni 1997). Acquisition, in this view, entails storing and categorizing linguistic experience, rather than subconsciously gleaning generalizations from linguistic input in the form of rules, parameters, or constraints (Ellis 2002). Therefore, linguistic cognition is largely a matter of lexical access, analogy, and recombination of previous linguistic experiences which have been stored.

A number of extant models assume that language processing involves storage and analogy to stored entities (Daelemans et al. 2003; Nosofsky 1988, 1990; Pierrehumbert 2001; Skousen 1989, 1992). Such models have been applied to investigate a wide variety of linguistic phenomena such as word recognition (Goldinger 1996), Arabic and German plural formation (Nakisa, Plunkett, and Hahn 2000), linking elements in Dutch noun compounds (Krott, Schreuder, and Baayen 2002), phonological alternations in Turkish stems (Rytting 2000), Dutch stress assignment (Gillis, Daelemans, Durieux, and van den Bosch 1993), Italian verb conjugations (Eddington 2002b), and phonotactic knowledge in Arabic and English (Frisch, Large, Zawaydeh, and Pisoni 2001). The present study is a continuation of an earlier investigation into Spanish stress placement (Eddington 2000) and will be structured as follows. I begin by reviewing the findings of the previous study. In the remainder of the paper, I describe a number of simulations which were designed to determine what factors are most relevant to Spanish accentuation. Of particular interest is the role of syllable weight and the CV tier in determining word stress.

2. Previous computational findings

The database used in Eddington (2000) consisted of the 4970 most frequent Spanish words extracted from a frequency dictionary. These included inflected forms, uninflected forms, and verb plus clitic combinations. Each word was converted into a series of variables that included the phonemes of the three final syllables, as well variables indicating the person and tense of the verbal forms. Each entry was also marked to indicate which syllable was stressed. This database served as an approximation of the contents of the mental lexicon. The simulation essentially consisted of removing each word from the database, and determining its stress placement based on analogy to the stress placement of similar words in the database. The algorithm used to calculate similarities and determine stress was Analogical Modeling of Language (Skousen 1989, 1992, 1995).

The simulation was highly successful and correctly predicted stress in 94% of the cases. This demonstrates the predictive power that an explicit algorithm of analogy has in modeling linguistic phenomena. The analysis of the errors produced during the simulation is also telling because 80% of them involved regularizing irregular stress.[2] This is reminiscent of Face's (2000) nonce word study in which 64% of the errors produced by the subjects involved regularization. In other words, an analogical model of accentuation is able to recognize regular stress patterns without relying on a global generalization about the data in the form of a rule or constraint. One interesting finding is that correct assignment of words stressed on the antepenultimate syllable reached 40%. While this may not appear particularly impressive at first glance, it is important to note that this was achieved without incorporating any diacritic marking into the antepenultimately stressed words. This contrasts with the formal accounts of Spanish stress placement cited in the introduction, all of which require some sort of diacritic mark on antepenultimately stressed words in order to correctly assign stress to them.

The validity of the analogical approach is supported by other empirical data as well. In her study of stress acquisition, Hochberg (1988) elicited words with different stress patterns from preschoolers. The children performed two tasks. The first was to name various objects shown to them in a picture book. In another task, they were asked to repeat nonce words that they heard. The types of errors the children made on both tasks were tabulated. The children made fewer errors on penultimate stress followed by final stress, while the highest error rates occurred on antepenultimately stressed words. This exact hierarchy of difficulty was evident in the errors produced by the analogical simulation as well.

Hochberg also noticed that the error rate on regularly stressed words remained virtually unchanged for all of her subjects ages three to five. However, the five-year-olds produced significantly fewer errors on irregular items than did the four-year-olds. The difference between the mental lexicon of a younger versus and older child is arguably the size of the vocabulary. Therefore, in order to imitate this difference, a simulation was performed with analogs drawn from only the most frequent half of the database items. Nevertheless, stress was predicted for all 4970 original database items. When the error rates of the two simulations are compared, the percentage of errors made on regularly stressed words did not differ significantly. However, significantly fewer errors were made when the entire database was available to analogize on, compared to when only the most frequent half of the database was utilized. This again corresponds quite well with the developmental data presented by Hochberg.

3. Simulations

In the previous study (Eddington 2000), I hope to have demonstrated that from a performance perspective, accentuation may be considered an analogically governed process. However, a number of questions about the specific factors that are most relevant to stress assignment in Spanish remain unanswered. The simulations presented below are designed to address these questions.

3.1. Database and variables used in the simulations

Because the object of the present study is to determine which variables are most relevant to stress placement, the exact variables used differ in each simulation, and are specified below. Nevertheless, each simulation was based on the 4970 most frequent words from a frequency dictionary of Spanish (Alameda and Cuetos 1995). Both the test items and analogs were drawn from this database.

3.2. Analogical algorithms used in the simulations

One algorithm utilized is the Tilburg Memory-based Learner (henceforth TiMBL; Daelemans et al. 2003). TiMBL works by taking a test word and determining which items in a database of exemplars are the most similar to it — the word's nearest neighbors. During the training session, the model stores in memory series of variables which represent instances of the words in the database. These words are stored along with their stress pattern. In the case that the same word is encountered more than once in the database, a count is kept of how often each word is associated with a given behavior. During the testing phase, when a test word is presented, the model searches for it in the database and applies the behavior that it has been assigned in the majority of cases. If the word is not found in the database, a similarity algorithm is used to find the most similar words in the database. The behavior of the nearest neighbor(s) is then applied to the test word in question. If two or more words are equidistant from the word in question, the most frequent behavior of the tied database items is applied to the test word in question.

The other memory-based algorithm used is Analogical Modeling of Language (hereafter AM; Skousen 1989, 1992). AM also conducts a search of a database looking for words similar to the test word. In AM, however, the search begins with the database entries most similar to the test word whose behavior is being predicted, and then extends to less similar entries. The members of the database are grouped into sets called subcontexts whose members share similarities with the test word. For example, in determining the stress of the word *comen* 'they eat', one subcontext would be comprised of all database items ending in /n/, another would contain those that end in /en/, another all items whose final syllable begins with /m/, another all items whose final syllable begins with /m/ and ends in /n/, and so forth until all possible combinations of variables are explored.

One derived property that results from dividing the database in this manner is that of proximity. Database items that share more features with *comen* will appear in more subcontexts and will therefore have a higher likelihood of influencing the probability that *comen* will be assigned a certain stress. Gang effects also fall out of this architecture. Groups of similar words that display the same behavior will increase their chances of influencing the test word.

Heterogeneity is another important property of AM. It suggests that a word in the database cannot be chosen as an analog if there are intervening words, with a different behavior that are more similar to the test word. Calculating heterogeneity involves determining disagreements. A disagreement occurs when one member of a subcontext has a behavior that is different from the behavior of another member of the same subcontext. For example, *andén* 'platform', and *viven* 'they live', share a final /en/, but are stressed on different syllables. As a result, when they appear in the same subcontext, they disagree in terms of their stress pattern. Under certain conditions, the analogical influence of the members of a subcontext that contains disagreements will be reduced or eliminated. AM's output is given in terms of the statistical probability that one or more behaviors will apply to the test word.

3.3. Simulations 1 and 2: Syllable weights.

In Simulations 1 and 2, as in all other simulations presented below (except where noted otherwise), TiMBL was used to predict stress placement. However, TiMBL allows a number of different measures of similarity to be calculated. In the present simulations, the similarity between the values of each variable is precalculated and used to adjust the search for nearest neighbors accordingly (modified value difference metric). This precalculation permits certain values of a variable to be regarded as more similar to each other than other values. TiMBL may also calculate the outcome on the basis of one or several nearest neighbors, but in the present simulations, calculations were based on only one nearest neighbor. In a previous study (Eddington 2002a), these settings not only proved to be the most efficient, but also mirrored those produced by the AM algorithm as well.

The purpose of Simulation 1 is to test the strongest hypothesis about syllable weight, which is that the actual phonemic content of the words themselves is not important, only whether the syllables that comprise them are open or closed.[3] This sort of abstraction may be modeled by converting the final three syllables of all of the database items into three variables. The variables simply encode whether each of the three final syllables are open or closed. In the case of monosyllabic and bisyllabic words, another variable value of 'non-existent' was allowed for the antepenultimate and/or the penultimate syllable. For example, *comprenden* 'they understand', and *reloj* 'watch' appeared as shown in (1).

(1)   *Comprenden*: Penultimate stress, closed antepenultimate, closed penultimate, closed final
Reloj: Final stress, non-existent antepenultimate, open penultimate, closed final

Table 1. Success rates using different variables

	Weight Alone	Weight + Final C	CV Alone	CV + Final C	All Phonemes
A	0	0	0	0	71.1
P	95.5	96.3	95.0	98.4	94.2
F	16.9	80.4	36.6	80.0	92.9
T	72.6	87.4	76.6	88.9	91.0

A=Antepenultimate, P=Penultimate, F=Final, T=Total

In the simulation, each database item was removed one at a time, while the remaining items served as the training set from which analogs were drawn, and the stress placement of the test word was determined. The accentuation of each of the 4970 items was calculated in this manner. The second column of Table 1 indicates that syllable weights alone allow penultimate stress to be predicted with a high degree of accuracy. However, no antepenultimately stressed words were correctly stressed, and only 16.9% of the words with final stress were predicted. The overall success rate reached 72.6%. One reason that weights alone are poor predictors of stress may be because not all consonants that close a final syllable produce equal effects. For example, only 2% of the database items ending in /s/ are stressed on the final syllable. In contrast, 81.4% of the words ending in a consonant other than /s/ have final stress.

In order to address this issue, Simulation 2 was run. Simulation 2 differs from Simulation 1 in that the database contained an additional variable indicating which consonant, if any, appears in the coda of the final syllable. In column 3 of Table 1, it can be seen that the specific consonant that closes the final syllable is extremely important to the prediction of final stress in that it significantly raises the success rate from 16.9% to 80.4% ($\chi^2(1)$=8235.88, p < .0005). However, the improvement in penultimately stressed words (from 95.5% to 96.3%) is not significant ($\chi^2(1)$=0.65, p < .42). This suggests that addition of this variable is not particularly useful in predicting penultimate stress. In neither simulation is any case of antepenultimate accentuation predicted.

3.4. Simulations 3 and 4: The CV tier

In CV phonology (Clements and Keyser 1983), each consonant and vowel is assigned to a consonant or vowel slot on a tier separate from the segmental tier which contains only phonemes. Accentuation is thought to involve access to the CV tier rather than to the phonemic tier. In order to test the utility of assuming a CV tier, the database for Simulation 3 was constructed by converting all consonants and vowels into C or V respectively. The CV variables were ordered so that the onset, nucleus, and rime of each of the final three syllables belonged to the same variable in all words. An example of this can be seen in (2) with *comprenden* and *reloj*.

(2)   *Comprenden*:   Penultimate stress, C, V, C, CC, V, C, C, V, C
         Reloj: Final stress, no onset, no nucleus, no coda C, V, no coda, C, V, C

As in Simulation 1, the CV representation in Simulation 3 is unable to predict any antepenultimately accentuated words, and does a poor job of predicting final stress. Penultimate stress, on the other hand, is correctly predicted to a high degree (Table 1, column 4).

Of course, Simulation 3 suffers from the same difficulty as Simulation 1; it is unfair to consider all word final consonants on equal grounds. In the database used for Simulation 4, therefore, the words' final consonant phoneme, or lack thereof, was included as an additional variable. In this case, the addition of this phonemic information improved the predictions significantly for final stress ($\chi^2(1)$=3210.0, p < .0005), as well as for penultimate stress ($\chi^2(1)$=11.68, p < .0005), while antepenultimate stress remains completely unpredictable (Table 1).

To summarize thus far, abstractions such as syllable weight and the CV tier by themselves are able to predict stress placement in about three fourths of the cases. However, the addition of some phonetic material improves their predictive ability greatly. This is evidence that specific phonemic information plays an important role in stress placement. In fact, syl-

lable weight and CV elements are both derived from the phonemic structure of the word, while the opposite is not true. Phonemes are the more basic unit, therefore, the apparent influence of syllable weight and the CV tier
exert on accentuation may merely be epiphenomenal. That is, the phonemic
material itself rather than CV slots or syllable weights, both of which depend on the phonemic representation, are actually the most relevant factors
in accentuation. This possibility is addressed in Simulation 5.

3.5. Simulation 5: Phonemic representation

For this simulation, each database item was converted into variable vectors
which included a specification of what syllable received stress, and a phonemic representation of the final three syllables of each word. For example,
comprenden, and *reloj* as seen in (3).

(3)   Penultimate stress, k, o, m, pr, e, n, d, e, n
         Final stress, no onset, no nucleus, no coda, rr, e, no coda, l, o, x

Simulation 5 was actually run as a series of nine separate simulations. In
the first, the only variable that was included specified what consonant, if
any, appeared in the coda of the final syllable. The database for the second
simulation included the phonemes in the nucleus and coda of the final syllable. The third included all elements of the final syllable, and so on. In this
way, each step added consecutively more and more phonemic information
about the words in the database, starting from the end of each word and
working toward the left. Therefore, the ninth included all of the phonemes
in the final three syllables of each word.

As Figure 1 demonstrates, phonemic material besides the final phoneme
is important to Spanish accentuation (see also Aske 1990). Penultimate
stress is predicted at high levels of accuracy no matter how much or how
little information is provided. This corroborates the notion that penultimate
stress is the unmarked or default case in Spanish (e.g. Face 2000). The prediction of final stress shows improvement as more phonemic material is
made available. However, antepenultimate stress appears to rely very little
on elements of the final syllable, and depends more on the contents of the
penultimate and antepenultimate syllables.

The total success rate obtained in Simulation 5, when the phonemic content of all three syllables was considered reaches 91.0%. This increase, although numerically superior is not statistically significant from the success
rate of 88.9% achieved in Simulation 4 in which information from the CV
tier and the final phoneme were considered ($\chi^2(1)=1.34$, p < .25), nor is it

significantly different from the 87.4% success rate attained when syllable weights and the final phoneme were used as variables ($\chi^2(1)=2.53$, p < .11). Nevertheless, the purely phonemic representation did correctly predict the stress of 71.1% of the antepenultimately accentuated words, while the other sets of variables tested were unable to predict a single antepenultimate stress. This alone argues strongly that accentuation is phoneme-based rather than based on CV elements or syllable weights, both of which are dependent on the phonemic content anyway.

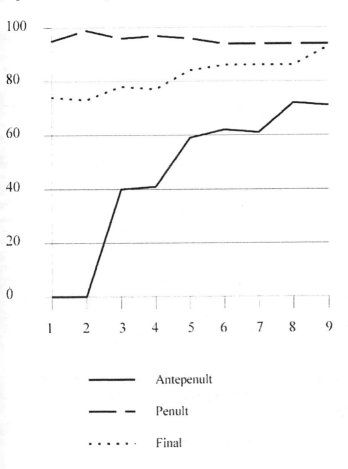

Figure 1. Success rates

This finding is reminiscent of a series of connectionist simulations designed to predict the German definite article given information about the following word (MacWhinney, Leinbach, Taraban, and McDonald 1989).

In two simulations, the variables specified the presence or absence of 38 carefully chosen pieces of morphological, semantic, and phonological information about the word the article agrees with (e.g. whether the word contains a specific morpheme, or a phoneme in a certain position). Each of these cues is thought to govern definite article usage in German. In another simulation, the only variables were the strings of phonemes that comprise the word. That is, no effort was made to include only those elements thought relevant to the task and separate them from those thought to be irrelevant. Nevertheless, the latter simulation yielded better results than the former ones that carefully eliminated cues that were considered unimportant to the task of definite article assignment. The outcome of the study of German definite articles, when coupled with the Spanish accentuation evidence suggests that speakers do not utilize the sort of generalizations and abstractions (i.e. syllable weight, CV tier) that researchers are able to glean from the data. Instead, they appear to make analogies based on surface-apparent traits such as the words' phonological content.

3.6. Simulations 6 and 7: Phonemic representation and weight or CV tier

The evidence adduced to this point suggests that syllable weight and the CV tier are simply abstract representations derived from the phonemes that comprise a word, and for this reason may be dispensed with in determining stress placement. However, one possibility that has not been explored is that accentuation does not only consider phonemic make up, but in addition, syllable weights or CV tier elements may also play a part. In order to test this hypothesis, the phonemic variables used in Simulation 5 were augmented to include the open or closed status of each of the final three syllables of each word as in Simulation 1. For example, in Simulation 6 *comprenden*, and *reloj* were encoded as in (4).

(4)   Penultimate stress, k, o, m, pr, e, n, d, e, n, closed, closed, closed
        Final stress, no onset, no nucleus, no coda, rr, e, no coda, l, o, x, empty, open, closed

In simulation 7, seen in (5), they were encoded with CV variables.

(5)   Penultimate stress, k, o, m, pr, e, n, d, e, n, C, V, C, CC, V, C, C,V, C
        Final stress, no onset, no nucleus, no coda, rr, e, no coda, l, o, x, no onset, no nucleus, no coda, C, V, no coda, C, V, C

The success rate achieved with the combination of CV and phonemic variables reached 89.8% which is a statistically equivalent to the 91.0% success rate obtained when only phonemes were considered ($\chi^2(1)=1.58$, $p < .21$). Therefore, adding syllable weights to the phonemic information does not result in more successful predictions either (89.4%; $\chi^2(1)=2.82$, $p < .09$).

3.7. Variable ranking

The data presented thus far indicate that stress placement is calculated on the basis of phonemic similarity to existing words, and not to elements of the CV tier or syllable weights. While the purpose of the present paper is to determine what phonological factors determine stress placement, this does not imply that other factors are not relevant. In fact, by adding variables indicating the person and tense of verbal forms to the phonemic variables from Simulation 5, 95.9%[4] of the words are correctly accentuated by the algorithm. TiMBL is also able to calculate how important each variable is to making predictions. As seen below, these morphological variables rank quite high. The most influential variables, in order of descending importance, are listed in (6).

(6) 1.   The consonant in the coda of the final syllable, or lack thereof.
2.   The tense of the word if it is a verb.
3.   The person of the word if it is a verb.
4.   The vowel in the nucleus of the final syllable.[5]
5.   The vowel in the nucleus of the penultimate syllable, or lack thereof.
6.   The consonant(s) in the coda of the penultimate syllable, or lack thereof.
7.   The vowel in the nucleus of the antepenultimate syllable, or lack thereof.
8.   The consonant(s) in the onset of the final syllable, or lack thereof.
9.   The consonant(s) in the onset of the antepenultimate syllable, or lack thereof.
10.   The consonant(s) in the coda of the antepenultimate syllable, or lack thereof.
11.   The consonant(s) in the onset of the penultimate syllable, or lack thereof.

The variables specifying the coda consonants of the final and penultimate syllables are among the most influential phonological variables. This lends some support to the hypothesis that syllable weight influences accentuation. However, the vowels in the nuclei of the final and penultimate syllables are also among the most influential phonological variables, yet calculation of syllable weight in Spanish does not involve syllable nuclei.

On another note, it is tempting to conclude from the above ranking that the lowest ranked variables are irrelevant to predicting stress. However, if variables 9, 10 and 11 from (6) are eliminated completely and the simulation run without them the overall success rate drops from 95.9% to 95.3%. While this difference is insignificant, $(\chi^2(1)=0.37, p < .54)$ it does demonstrate that even the least important variables play a role in assigning stress to some words.

4. Nonce word studies

As mentioned previously, one implicit supposition in an analogical analysis of stress assignment is that speakers learn and store words along with their stress pattern. Therefore, an on-line process of stress placement is generally not needed except when novel words are encountered, or in cases in which noise in the system leads to a temporary inability to remember which syllable is stressed. In the simulations discussed to this point, both the test items and the training items were drawn from the same database, which is a common practice in natural language simulations. However, if storage of characteristics such as accentuation is assumed, treating each word in the database as a novel word may be an inappropriate way to model linguistic processing (Ling and Marinov 1993). One way to avoid this potential problem is by utilizing nonce words in place of existing words.

Face (2000, 2004) and Bárkányi (2002) carried out studies in which their subjects' task was to assign stress to nonce words. Bárkányi's subjects were presented orthographic representations of invented words. She found that not every subject assigned final stress to every nonce word ending in a closed syllable, nor did they all assign penultimate stress to every word ending in a vowel. For this reason, she concludes that syllable weight is not an active factor in Spanish stress placement.

In Face (2000), subjects heard recorded nonce words which had been manipulated so that each syllable nucleus was of identical length and intensity. Their task was to determine where they perceived the stress to fall. Face submitted his results to statistical analysis and found that heavy syllables attracted stress. However, in Face (2004), the nonce words were manipulated so that each syllable, not just each syllable nucleus, was of equal length and intensity. Under these conditions, the weight of the final syllable was influential in the subjects' perception of stress placement, but the weight of other the syllables was not.

Waltermire (2004) followed up Face's experiments by presenting the same 60 nonce words from Face (2000) to 41 native Spanish speakers. The speakers were asked to indicate where they felt the words should be stressed. However, in Waltermire's study the words were presented in written rather than auditory form. Nevertheless, the outcome obtained by Waltermire mirrors that of Face quite closely; syllable weight was a significant factor in the subjects' choice of which syllable was accentuated.

Table 2. Subjects' stress preferences on nonce words

Nonce Word	% A	% P	% F	Nonce Word	% A	% P	% F
bonlandan	5	21	74	badonguel	11	18	71
dombalden	5	29	66	dalandel	13	16	71
landangon	13	0	87	comengon	5	3	92
lanlendol	21	13	66	mobalmal	16	21	63
menlembal	11	26	63	pelandon	5	3	92
bondenda	18	76	7	banenda	3	95	3
bonlamba	8	78	14	gadamba	5	95	0
dantelda	13	87	0	gobolda	9	91	0
malnanga	3	95	3	lomelda	11	86	3
mandolma	5	95	0	molanga	3	97	0
bandemel	19	19	62	dabanel	25	3	72
bondanol	8	13	79	gabadon	3	3	94
galdeman	19	11	69	mananden	11	21	68
gondabel	22	8	70	noguemol	8	39	53
naldelan	11	18	71	polanal	5	11	84
bolnala	16	68	16	beloga	33	61	6
dendana	31	67	3	dagola	89	8	3
galmeda	16	78.	5	dalona	19	81	0
ganloda	57	43	0	galema	11	89	0
landola	68	30	3	mamena	8	89	3

Using the nonce words from Face (2004), I performed a study identical to Waltermire's. These 40 nonce words were given in written form to 38 university students studying English, all of whom were natives of Spain.[6] With the exception of three participants who did not give their age, the remaining participants were between the ages of 17 and 26. The results of this study (see Table 2) were combined with those from Waltermire in order to compare them with a simulation.

The purpose of running analogical simulations with the 100 nonce words was to determine what factors most influence the subjects' choice of stressed syllable by comparing the subjects' responses with those calculated in a number of analogical simulations. To this end, the stress placement of the nonce words devised by Face (2000, 2004) was determined by analogy using the seven different sets of variables: 1) CV tier alone, 2) CV tier and final phoneme, 3) syllable weights alone, 4) syllable weights and final phonemes, 5) phonemic representation alone, 6) phonemic representation and syllable weights, 7) phonemic representation and CV elements. All 4970 database items were available as possible analogs for the nonce items. The results of the simulations were correlated with the data from Waltermire's study, and my own study that used Face's 2004 nonce words. These were used to the exclusion of the data gathered by Bárkányi and Face (2000), since the latter do not provide their subjects' responses on each individual test word, making it impossible to calculate correlations between their experimental findings and the analogical simulations.

To this point, all of the simulations reported on were carried out using TiMBL's algorithm. However, I chose to utilize AM for the nonce word simulations. This change of model deserves some justification. The first thing that should be noted is that in a previous study of Spanish stress assignment, AM and TiMBL made predictions that did not differ significantly from each other (Eddington 2002a). However, more importantly, the TiMBL algorithm used in the above simulations calculates the stress placement for a given word in absolute terms. That is, a word is predicted to have either antepenultimate, penultimate, or final stress.[7] AM, on the other hand, predicts the outcome in terms of the probability that one outcome or another will be applied (e.g. *bombilla*: antepenultimate 1%, penultimate 99%, final 0%). This sort of output has the advantage of being interpreted in two different ways. One interpretation, termed 'selection by plurality' (Skousen 1989), involves choosing the outcome with the highest probability (hence, *bombilla* receives penultimate stress). This "winner-take-all" output is the sort calculated by the TiMBL algorithm used in the above simulations, as well as by connectionist networks. With AM's 'random selection', on the other hand, one considers the degree to which two or more outcomes are predicted. This more fine-grained prediction is important when correlating the results of analogical simulations with the results of psycholinguistic experiments which usually entail some degree of variability.

AM's predictions regarding the placement of stress on the two sets of nonce items were based on analogies made on the 4970 database items. Of course, the variables used to encode each word varied in each simulation. These results were correlated with those made by Waltermire's subjects and my own subjects using Face's nonce words (see Table 3).

Table 3. Correlations to nonce words and success rates with different variable sets

	Correlation with Waltermire	Success Rates in Simulations
(1) CV Tier Alone	.503	76.6%
(2) CV Tier Plus Final Phoneme	.834	88.9%
(3) Syllable Weights Alone	.764	72.6%
(4) Syllable Weights Plus Final Phoneme	.897	87.4%
(5) Phonemic Representation	.648	91.0%
(6) Phonemic Representation Plus Syllable Weights	.695	89.4%
(7) Phonemic Representation Plus CV Tier Elements	.649	84.8%

As is evident in Table 3, the correlations that occur when CV elements and syllable weights are considered alone are greatly improved by adding the final phoneme as a variable. This demonstrates the important role that the word final phoneme plays in accentuation. However, the phonemic information itself is not a particularly good indicator of stress placement. In fact, a better correlation is obtained when syllable weights are added to the phonemic information. The best correlation occurs when the variables considered are syllable weights and the word final phoneme. Taken together, this suggests is that an abstract representation of syllable weight was indeed an influencing factor in stress assignment.

5. Conclusions

In a number of analogical simulations, test items as well as analogs were drawn from the database of 4970 items. The results of these simulations indicate that a phonemic representation of words may be what speakers use to determine stress placement. When the CV tier and syllable weights are utilized by themselves much lower success rates are attained. Only when some phonemic information is added to the more abstract CV tier and syllable weight representations are success rates achieved that rival those of the purely phonemic representation. However, syllable weights and CV tier elements are derived directly from the phonemic make up of a given word. As a result, it may be that this close relationship is responsible for the ability of these abstract representations to predict accentuation. That is, any effect of these representations may be merely epiphenomenal.

In one regard, the findings of the nonce word study mirrors the results from Simulations 1-7 quite closely; the success rates for the simulations that utilized CV and syllable weight representations alone are improved if the word-final consonants are also included as variables. However, in contrast to the database simulations, the nonce study does provide evidence that the use of abstract units such as syllable weights and CV tier elements may affect accentuation. The purely phonemic representation achieved a correlation of .648 with the subjects' determination of stress placement on the nonce words. This is much lower than the correlation of .834 that resulted when the CV tier plus the final phoneme served as variables. What is more, the highest correlation (.897) occurred when the variables included the syllable weight of the final three syllables, along with a specification of the words' final phoneme. It is this evidence that suggests that the role of CV tier and syllable weights should not be discounted. It is my hope that further psycholinguistic research will clarify the part that these abstract entities play in Spanish stress assignment.

Acknowledgments

I am particularly indebted to Timothy Face and Mark Waltermire for allowing me to use the data from their studies.

Notes

1. However, Bromberger and Halle (2000: 35) take a realist stance: "Do speakers really retrieve morphemes from their memory, invoke rules, go through all

these labours when speaking? We think they do."
2. Irregularly stressed words are those that are stressed on the antepeunultimate syllable, or that have final stress and end in a vowel or s, or that have penult stress and end in a consonant other than s.
3. The major reason given for assuming that Spanish accentuation is sensitive to syllable weight is that antepenultimate stress is not allowed if the penult syllable is heavy (Harris 1983). Hence, words such as *teléfosno are considered impossible in Spanish. However, this may be a historical relic since Alvord's (2003) subjects considered words such as *teléfosno as possible Spanish words.
4. This success rate differs insignificantly from the 94.4% found by Eddington (2000). This is due to two factors. The previous study utilized AM's algorithm and was carried out using 10 fold cross validation. The present study was done with TiML's algorithm using a 'leave-one-out' method.
5. Glides were included in the nucleus slot in these simulations. However, in a separate study, I found that whether they are placed together with the nucleic vowel, or in syllable onsets or codas does not significantly affect the outcome (Eddington 2004).
6. I am indebted to José Antonio Mompeán for administering the surveys.
7. TiMBL does have another algorithm whose output is not deterministic. However, TiMBL's predictions are made based on a small sampling of possible analogs, while AM generally allows a large number of database items to affect the outcome to varying degrees. For this reason, I believe AM's results are more similar to those produced by actual speakers.

References

Alameda, José Ramón, and Fernando Cuetos
    1995   *Diccionario de frecuencias de las unidades lingüísticas del castellano.* Oviedo, Spain: University of Oviedo Press.
Alegre, Maria, and Peter Gordon
    1999   Frequency effects and the representational status of regular inflections. *Journal of Memory and Language* 40: 41-61.
Alvord, Scott
    2003   The psychological unreality of quantity sensitivity in Spanish. *Southwest Journal of Linguistics* 22 (2): 1–12.
Aske, Jon
    1990   Disembodied rules versus patterns in the lexicon. In *Proceedings of the Sixteenth Annual Meeting of the Berkeley Linguistics Society,* Kira Hall, Jean-Pierre Koenig, Michael Meacham, Sondra Reinman, and Laurel A. Sutton (eds.), 30-45. Berkeley: Berkeley Linguistic Society.

Baayen, Harald R., Ton Dijkstra, and Robert Schreuder
1997   Singulars and plurals in Dutch: Evidence for a parallel dual-route model. *Journal of Memory and Language* 37: 94-117.
Bailey, Todd M.
1995   Nonmetrical constraints on stress. Ph.D. diss., University of Minnesota.
Bárkányi, Zsuzsanna
2002   A fresh look at quantity sensitivity in Spanish. *Linguistics* 40: 375-394.
Bod, Rens
1998   *Beyond Grammar*. Stanford, CA: Center for the Study of Language of Information.
Bradley, Diane
1980   Lexical representation of derivational relation. In *Juncture*, Mark Aronoff and Mary-Louis Keaton (eds.), 37-55. Saratoga, CA.: Anma Libri.
Bromberger, Sylvain, and Morris Halle
2000   The ontology of phonology (revised). In *Phonological Knowledge: Conceptual and Empirical Issues*, Noel Burton-Roberts, Philip Carr, and Gerard Docherty (eds.), 19-37. Oxford: Oxford University Press.
Brown, R. and D. Mc Neill
1966   The 'tip of the tongue' phenomenon. *Journal of Verbal Learning and Verbal Behavior* 5: 325-337.
Butterworth, Brian
1983   Lexical representation. In *Language Production. Vol. 2*, Brian Butterworth (ed.), 257-294. London: Academic Press.
Bybee, Joan
1988   Morphology as lexical organization. In *Theoretical Approaches to Morphology*, Michael Hammond, and Michael Noonan (eds.), 119-41. San Diego: Academic Press.
1994   A view of phonology from a cognitive and functional perspective. *Cognitive Linguistics* 5: 285-305.
1995   Regular morphology and the lexicon. *Language and Cognitive Processes* 10: 425-55.
1998   The emergent lexicon. In *CLS 34: The Panels*, M. Gruber, C. Derrick Higgins, K. S. Olson, and T. Wysocki (eds.), 421-435. Chicago: Chicago Linguistic Society.
2000   The phonology of the lexicon: Evidence from lexical difussion. In *Usage-based Models of Language*, Michael Barlow, and Suzanne Kemmer (eds.), 65-85. Stanford, CA: Center for the Study of Language of Information.

2002   *Phonology and Language Use.* Cambridge: Cambridge University Press.
Chomsky Noam, and Morris Halle
1968   *The Sound Pattern of English.* New York: Harper and Row.
Clements, George N., and Samuel Jay Keyser
1983   *CV Phonology: A Generative Theory of the Syllable.* Cambridge: MIT Press.
Daelemans, Walter, Jakub Zavrel, Ko van der Sloot and Antal van den Bosch
2003   *TiMBL: Tilburg Memory-based Learner, version 5.0, Reference Guide.* Induction of Linguistic Knowledge Technical Report, ILK 03-10. Tilburg, Netherlands: ILK Research Group, Tilburg University. Available at http://ilk.kub.nl/.
Den Os, Els, and Rene Kager
1986   Extrametricality and stress in Spanish and Italian. *Lingua* 69: 23-48.
Eddington, David
2000   Spanish stress assignment within the Analogical Modeling of Language. *Language* 76: 92-109.
2002a   A comparison of two analogical models: Tilburg Memory-based Learner verus Analogical Modeling of Language. In *Analogical Modeling: An Exemplar-based Approach to Language*, Royal Skousen, Deryle Lonsdale, and Dilworth Parkinson (eds.), 141-155. Amsterdam: John Benjamins.
2002b   Dissociation in Italian conjugations: A single-route account. *Brain and Language* 81: 291-302.
2004   Issues in modeling language processing analogically. *Lingua* 114, forthcoming
Ellis, Nick C.
2002   Frequency effects in language processing: A review with implications for theories of implicit and explicit language acquisition. *Studies in Second Language Acquisition* 24: 143-188.
Face, Timothy L.
2000   The role of syllable weight in the perception of Spanish stress. In *Hispanic Linguistics at the Turn of the Millennium*, Héctor Campos, Elena Herburger, Alfonso Morales-Front, and Thomas J. Walsh (eds.), 1-13. Somerville, MA: Cascadilla Press.
2004   Perceiving what isn't there: Non-acoustic cues for perceiving Spanish stress. In this volume.
Frisch, Stefan
1996   Similarity and frequency in phonology. Ph.D. diss., Northwestern University.

Frisch, Stefan A., Nathan R. Large, Bushra Zawaydeh, and David B. Pisoni
    2001   Emergent phonotactic generalizations in English and Arabic. In *Frequency and the Emergence of Linguistic Structure*, Joan Bybee and Paul Hooper (eds.), 159-179. Amsterdam: John Benjamins.

Gillis, Steven, Walter Daelemans, Gert Durieux, and Antal van den Bosch
    1993   Learnability and markedness: Dutch stress assignment. In *Proceedings of the Fifteenth Annual Conference of the Cognitive Science Society*, 452-457. Hillsdale, N.J.: Erlbaum.

Goldinger, Stephen D.
    1996   Words and voices: Episodic traces in spoken word identification and recognition in memory. *Journal of Experimental Psychology: Learning, Memory, and Cognition* 22: 1166-1183.

    1997   Words and voices: Perception and production in an episodic lexicon. In *Talker Variability in Speech Processing*, Keith Johnson and John W. Mullennix (eds.), 33-65. San Diego: Academic Press.

Harris, James W.
    1983   *Syllable Structure and Stress in Spanish.* Cambridge, MA.: MIT Press.

    1989   How different is verb stress in Spanish. *Probus* 1: 241-258.

    1996   Projection and edge marking in the computation of stress in Spanish. In *The Handbook of Phonological Theory*, John A. Goldsmith (ed.), 867-887. Cambridge, MA: Blackwell.

Hochberg, Judith
    1988   Learning Spanish stress: Developmental and theoretical perspectives. *Language* 64: 683-706.

Hooper, Joan B., and Tracy Terrell
    1976   Stress assignment in Spanish: A natural generative analysis. *Glossa* 10: 64-110.

Kager, René
    1999   *Optimality Theory.* Cambridge: Cambridge University Press.

Kiparsky, Paul
    1975   What are phonological theories about? In *Testing Linguistic Hypotheses*, David Cohen and Jessica R. Wirth (eds.), 187-209. Washington D. C.: Hemisphere.

Krott, Andrea, Robert Schreuder, and Harald Baayen
    2002   Analogical hierarchy: Exemplar-based modeling of linkers in Dutch noun-noun compounds. In *Analogical Modeling: An Exemplar-based Approach to Language,* Royal Skousen, Deryle Lonsdale, and Dilworth B. Parkinson (eds.), 181-208. Amsterdam: John Benjamins.

Ling, Charles X. and Marin Marinov
1993 Answering the connectionist challenge: A symbolic model of learning the past tenses of English verbs. *Cognition* 49: 235-290.
Lipski, John M.
1997 Spanish word stress: The interaction of moras and minimality. In *Issues in the Phonology and Morphology of the Major Iberian Languages*, Fernando Martínez-Gil and Alfonso Morales-Front (eds.), 559-593. Washington, DC: Georgetown University Press.
MacWhinney, Brian, Jared Leinbach, Roman Taraban, and Janet McDonald
1989 Language learning: Rules or cues? *Journal of Memory and Language* 28: 255-277.
Manelis, Leon and David A. Tharp
1977 The processing of affixed words. *Memory and Cognition* 5: 690-695.
Nakisa, Ramin C., Kim Plunkett and Ulrike Hahn
2000 A cross-linguistic comparison of single and dual-route models of inflectional morphology. In *Cognitive Models of Language Acquisition*, Peter Broeder and Jaap Murre, (eds.). Cambridge, MA: MIT Press.
Nosofsky, Robert M.
1988 Exemplar-based accounts of relations between classification, recognition, and typicality. *Journal of Experimental Psychology: Learning, Memory, and Cognition* 14: 700-708.
1990 Relations between exemplar similarity and likelihood models of classification. *Journal of Mathematical Psychology* 34: 393-418.
Palmeri, Thomas J., Stephen D. Goldinger, and David B. Pisoni
1993 Episodic encoding of voice attributes and recognition memory for spoken words. *Journal of Experimental Psychology: Learning, Memory, and Cognition* 19: 309-28.
Pawley, Andrew and Frances Hodgetts Syder
1983 Two puzzles for linguistic theory: Nativelike selection and nativelike fluency. In *Language and Communication*, Jack C. Richards and Richard W. Smith (eds.), 191-225. London: Longman.
Pierrehumbert, Janet
2001 Exemplar dynamics: Word frequency, lenition and contrast. In *Frequency and the Emergence of Linguistic Structure*, Joan Bybee and Paul Hooper (eds.), 137-158. Amsterdam: John Benjamins.
Pisoni, David
1997 Some thoughts on 'normalization' in speech perception. In *Talker Variability in Speech Processing*, Keith Johnson and John W. Mullennix (eds.), 9-32. San Diego: Academic Press.

Rytting, C. Anton
    2000   An empirical test of Analogical Modeling: The /k/ ~ Ø alterna-
            tion. In *Lacus Forum XXVI: The Lexicon*, Alan K. Melby and
            Arle R. Lommel (eds.), 73-84. Fullerton, CA: Linguistic Asso-
            ciation of Canada and the United States.
Roca, Iggy
    1988   Theoretical implications of Spanish word stress. *Linguistic In-
            quiry* 19: 393-423.
    1990   Morphology and verbal stress in Spanish. *Probus* 2: 321-350.
    1991   Stress and syllables in Spanish. In *Current Studies in Spanish
            Linguistics,* Hector Campos and Fernando Martínez-Gil (eds.),
            599-635. Washington, DC: Georgetown University Press.
    1997   On the role of accent in stress systems: Spanish evidence. In *Is-
            sues in the Phonology and Morphology of the Major Iberian
            Languages*, Fernando Martínez-Gil and Alfonso Morales-Front
            (eds.), 619-664. Washington D.C.: Georgetown University Press.
Saltarelli, Mario
    1997   Stress in Spanish and Latin: Where morphology meets prosody.
            In *Issues in the Phonology and Morphology of the Major Iberian
            Languages*, Fernando Martínez-Gil and Alfonso Morales-Front
            (eds.), 665-694. Washington D.C.: Georgetown University Press.
Sereno, Joan A., and Allard Jongman
    1997   Processing of English inflectional morphology. *Memory and
            Cognition* 25: 425-37.
Shanks, David R.
    1995   *The Psychology of Associative Learning*. Cambridge: Cambridge
            University Press.
Skousen, Royal
    1989   *Analogical Modeling of Language*. Dordrecht: Kluwer Aca-
            demic.
    1992   *Analogy and Structure.* Dordrecht: Kluwer Academic.
    1995   Analogy: A non-rule alternative to neural networks. *Rivista di
            Linguistica* 7: 213-232.
Waltermire, Mark
    2004   The influence of syllable weight in the determination of stress
            placement in Spanish. In this volume.
Whitley, Stanley
    1976   Stress in Spanish: Two approaches. *Lingua* 39: 301-332.

Perceiving what isn't there: Non-acoustic cues for perceiving Spanish stress

Timothy L. Face

1. Introduction

In studying the nature of Spanish stress, experimental studies have focused principally on the acoustic correlates of stress (i.e. pitch, duration, and intensity) both in production studies (e.g. Hochberg 1988; Quilis 1971, 1993) and perception studies (e.g. Enríquez, Casado and Santos 1989, Llisterri et al. 2003). This is only one aspect of a larger picture, however. Quilis (1971:54) states that "the sensation of a physical stimulus is channeled through the structures of a language" (translation mine). Face (2000) conducted an experiment to test whether syllable structure (specifically syllable weight) affected the perception of stress in nonsense words where a synthesized voice was controlled so as to make all syllables of equal acoustic prominence. The results indicate that different syllable weight combinations lead to a consistent agreement between native Spanish-speaking hearers as to which syllable is stressed. (See Section 3.1 for a more detailed discussion of Face's results.) The present study extends that of Face (2000) by examining other ways in which the structure of Spanish leads to the perception of a particular syllable as stressed.

In the present study, four potential non-acoustic cues to Spanish stress are considered experimentally to determine whether they affect a hearer's perception of the stressed syllable in nonsense words. The first issue considered is that of syllable weight. While the results presented by Face (2000) seem to show that syllable weight affects Spanish stress perception, certain of the results could have an explanation other than syllable weight. The present study adjusts the experimental design of the original study in order to determine whether syllable weight does indeed affect the perception of stress in Spanish or whether there is another explanation for the results reported in Face (2000). The second issue examined in the present study is the influence of the stress pattern of a similar word in the language. The third issue considered is that of subregularities in the lexicon. And the final issue investigated is the role of morphological category. Each of these issues seem to be possible factors in the perception of Spanish stress, in spite of their not being the acoustic cues to Spanish stress that have typically been investigated by phoneticians and experimental phonologists. An understanding of which of these issues affects the perception of Spanish stress will lead to a better understanding of the stress system of Spanish, and more specifically to of the ways in which the structures of Spanish are cues which aid in the perception of Spanish stress.

The remainder of this paper is organized as follows: Section 2 outlines the general issues of experimental methodology, with considerations specific to each particular issue under investigation left to the corresponding section. Section 3 reconsiders the role of syllable weight in the perception of Spanish stress. Sections 4, 5 and 6 examine the role of similar words, subregularities, and morphological categories, respectively, in the perception of Spanish stress. Section 7 presents a discussion of the implications of the experimental results reported in Sections 3-6. Finally, Section 8 offers a summary of the main points of the present paper and points to topics in need of future investigation.

2. Experimental methodology

In order to examine whether syllable weight, similar words, subregularities, and morphological category affect the perception of Spanish stress, a perception experiment was designed in which trisyllabic nonsense words, following the phonotactic patterns of Spanish, were created and synthesized. The synthesized nonsense words were presented to subjects who indicated for each the syllable that they perceived as being stressed. The nonsense words used to examine each of the issues considered in the present study were combined and randomized, with the exception of those testing the influence of morphological category. In order to test the influence of morphological category, a sentence context, rather than a single word in isolation, was required, and therefore this portion of the experiment was conducted separately. The principles guiding the creation of the nonsense words varied based on the specific issue they were meant to test, and therefore this is discussed separately in each of Sections 3-6.

Once the nonsense words to be used in the study (and their corresponding contexts in the case of those testing the influence of morphological category) were created, they were synthesized using the MBROLI speech synthesizer (Dutoit, Pagel, Pierret, Bataille, and Van de Vrecken 1996) with a Spanish voice.[1] The use of this synthesizer allowed for the fundamental frequency to be held steady throughout the production of the nonsense word and for the duration of each syllable to be identical so as to prevent either of these acoustic correlates of stress from affecting the decision of the subjects. While the MBROLI speech synthesizer does not allow for control of intensity, an investigation of the synthesized nonsense words found that intensity was consistent throughout each word. Therefore, like fundamental frequency and duration, intensity could not serve as an acoustic cue to stress in this experiment.

For each part of the experiment (i.e. words in isolation and sentences), there was a practice session so that the subjects could become acclimated to the synthetic voice and to the task of selecting the syllable of the nonsense word that was perceived as stressed. The recording of the perceived stressed syllable was done on paper. The paper answer sheet consisted of an item number (i.e. 1 for the first nonsense word presented, 2 for the second, etc.) followed by the numbers 1, 2 and 3. The subject would circle 1 if the first syllable of the word was perceived as stressed, 2 if the second was perceived as stressed, and 3 if the third syllable as perceived as stressed. Mixed with the test words in both parts of the experiment were additional cases where the nonsense word did have an acoustically stressed syllable. This was done as a control to be sure that when an acoustically stressed syllable was present, the subjects could accurately identify it. Any potential subject who did not accurately identify the acoustically stressed syllable at least 90% of the time was excluded from the study.[2]

The subjects who participated in the experiment were 10 native Spanish-speaking graduate students at the University of Minnesota who had not lived in the United States before attending graduate school. All grew up in a monolingual environment, though they came from various parts of the Spanish-speaking world. While the same three acoustic correlates of stress (i.e. pitch, duration, and intensity) are used in different dialects of Spanish, there may be dialectal differences in the importance of each. In the present study, however, this is not a factor since the experiment neutralizes these acoustic correlates of stress in order to test the role of non-acoustic factors on stress perception. The issues addressed in the present study apply equally to all varieties of Spanish. All of the subjects were naïve with respect to the purpose of the study and had no training in Spanish phonology.

3. Syllable weight

3.1 Previous research

While perception has been considered by phonologists, generally what is investigated is the role of perception in phonology rather than the role of phonology (e.g. phonological structure) in perception (Hume and Johnson 2001). Face (2000) approached this interaction from a different perspective by looking at how phonology affects perception, and specifically of how syllable weight affects the perception of Spanish stress. Bisyllabic and tri-syllabic nonsense words were created with every possible combination of heavy and light syllables. The nonsense words were synthesized, and fundamental frequency was held steady throughout the nonsense words, all vowels were of equal duration, and intensity was steady throughout the word. In this way it was assured that these acoustic factors did not influence the perception of stress. The nonsense words were then presented to subjects in a random order, and subjects selected the syllable that they perceived to be stressed (i.e. first or second in bisyllabic words; first, second or third in trisyllabic words).

Face (2000) found that there was a strong preference for the unmarked stress pattern (penultimate stress in words with a light final syllable and final stress in words with a heavy final syllable) to be perceived in the nonsense words. The overall percentage of perception of the unmarked stress pattern was 74.2%, with a percentage of 68% in words with a heavy final syllable and 80.3% in words with a light final syllable. The weight of the final syllable was highly significant in determining perceived stress. When the final syllable was heavy, final stress was generally perceived, and when the final syllable was light, penultimate stress was generally perceived. This led Face (2000) to claim that syllable weight causes perception of unmarked stress. With respect to the higher percentage of perception of the most common stress pattern when the final syllable is light, Face (2000) argues that while phonological structure may make either the penultimate syllable or the final syllable unmarked (when the final syllable is light or heavy, respectively), penultimate stress is a truly default stress pattern. This is supported by looking at cases where the phonologically unmarked stress pattern is not perceived. In cases where marked stress was perceived, in nearly 50% of the cases penultimate stress was perceived, with the remaining cases split fairly evenly between the final and antepenultimate syllables. In addition, in control words that did have acoustic prominence on one particular syllable, nearly two-thirds of the subjects' errors "corrected" the acoustic stress to the unmarked stress pattern. When acoustic stress corresponded with phonologically unmarked stress, it was perceived correctly nearly 100% of the time.

Looking beyond unmarked stress, Face (2000) notes that the rightmost heavy syllable, regardless of whether or not it is the final syllable of the word, seems to attract perceived stress. Examining those words with a light final syllable, he shows that the weight of the penultimate syllable is a factor in the perception of stress. When the penultimate syllable is heavy, it is perceived as stressed 86% of the time, and the antenpenultimate syllable is perceived as stressed only 3% of the time. When both the final and the penultimate syllables are light, the penultimate syllable is perceived as stressed 66% of the time, and the antepenultimate syllable is perceived as stressed 18% of the time. The heavy penultimate syllable attracts stress and all but prevents perception of antepenultimate stress. In addition, when both the final and penultimate syllables are light, the antepenultimate is significantly more likely to be perceived as stressed when it is heavy than when it is light.

Face (2000) takes the results of his experiment as evidence that syllable weight is important to the perception of Spanish stress. Furthermore, he states that the results provide evidence that "syllable weight is not just an abstract issue to be dealt with by phonological theory, but that it is a very real cognitive factor that influences stress perception even beyond determining unmarked stress" (11). The conclusions of Face's (2000) study are also supported by Waltermire (2004) in a study of speakers' judgments of which syllable of a nonsense word they would stress in their speech.

While the conclusions drawn by Face (2000) appear well-motivated by his experimental results, there is one potential problem. In his study, all vowels were of equal duration. This means that a coda consonant added to make a syllable heavy also increased the duration of the syllable, making heavy syllables longer than light syllables. While this is an accurate representation of what happens in real speech, for the purpose of the experiment it means that there could have been an acoustic factor leading to perceived stress. Therefore, it could be that heavy syllables were perceived as stressed not because they were heavy, but because they were longer than light syllables. The present study corrects this error of experimental design in order to investigate whether syllable weight really is a factor in the perception of Spanish stress or whether Face's (2000) results were skewed by the extra duration of heavy syllables.

3.2 Nonsense words

Forty nonsense words were created for the present study to test the effect of syllable weight on the perception of Spanish stress (see Appendix A). These forty words are all trisyllabic and include all possible combinations of heavy and light syllables. Five nonsense words were created for each of the eight possible combinations. In order to correct the potential problem in Face (2000) of heavy syllables being perceived as stressed because they are longer than light syllables rather than because they are heavy syllables, in the present study all syllables of the words testing the effect of syllable weight on stress perception were of the same length. Thus in heavy syllables the duration of the vowel and coda consonant combined was equal to the duration of the vowel alone in light syllables. An onset consonant existed in all syllables and its duration did not vary between heavy and light syllables, but was simply maintained at a constant duration. In addition, it is important that the nonsense words not resemble any real Spanish words, as the stress pattern of a real word may influence the perception of stress. For this reason, the synthesized nonsense words were played to a native Spanish speaker, and any that sounded similar to a real word were changed.

3.3 Results and discussion

In order to begin the investigation of the role of syllable weight in the perception of Spanish stress, I consider the effect of the weight of the final syllable, as it is this that determines the phonologically unmarked stress pattern. The results are shown in Table 1.

Table 1.   Perceived stress by weight of the final syllable.

Perceived Stressed Syllable	Light Final Syllable	Heavy Final Syllable
Antepenultimate	18	22
Penultimate	112	43
Final	70	135
Total:	200	200

These results confirm the finding in Face (2000) that the weight of the final syllable is a factor in the perception of Spanish stress. When the final syllable is heavy, it is generally perceived as stressed. When the final syllable is light, the penultimate syllable is generally perceived as heavy. But the overall percentage of unmarked stress perception is 61.8%, which is notably lower than the 74.2% reported in Face (2000). Also of interest is that the unmarked stress pattern is perceived more often when it is final stress than when it is penultimate stress. And combining both categories in Table 1, final stress is that which is most often perceived. Nonetheless, the phonologically unmarked stress pattern is still the most common pattern perceived in the present study.

I now consider whether heavy syllables attract perceived stress, as claimed by Face (2000). That is, when the final syllable is light, is penultimate stress perceived more often when the penultimate syllable is heavy? And when both the final and the penultimate syllables are light, is antepenultimate stress perceived more often when the antepenultimate syllable is heavy? The results for words with a light final syllable are given in Table 2, while those for words with both a light final and a light penultimate syllable are given in Table 3.

Table 2. Perceived stress in words with a light final syllable, by weight of the penultimate syllable.

Perceived Stressed Syllable	Light Penultimate Syllable	Heavy Penultimate Syllable
Antepenultimate	11	7
Penultimate	57	55
Final	32	38
Total:	100	100

Table 3. Perceived stress in words with both a light final and a light penultimate syllable, by weight of the antepenultimate syllable.

Perceived Stressed Syllable	Light Antepenultimate Syllable	Heavy Antepenultimate Syllable
Antepenultimate	6	5
Penultimate	29	28
Final	15	17
Total:	50	50

The results presented in both Table 2 and Table 3 go against the claim made by Face (2000) that a heavy syllable attracts perceived stress in Spanish. Table 2 shows than when the final syllable is light there is very little difference between the percentage of perceived penultimate stress based on the weight of the penultimate syllable. Similarly, Table 3 shows that when both the final and penultimate syllables are light there is almost no difference between the percentage of perceived antepenultimate stress based on the weight of the penultimate syllable. In fact, while the difference is by no means significant, in both cases a light syllable is perceived as stressed more often than a heavy syllable. Since a heavy syllable does not attract perceived stress in these cases, it brings into question the role of syllable weight in Spanish stress perception.

The results presented in this section show that the weight of the final syllable is a factor in the perception of Spanish stress, although not as strong of a factor as suggested in Face (2000). The most common pattern – consistent with the phonologically unmarked stress pattern of the language – is for the final syllable to be perceived as stressed when it is heavy, and the penultimate syllable to be perceived as stressed when the final syllable is light. However, when we move beyond the unmarked stress pattern, syllable weight does not play a role in the perception of Spanish stress. Contrary to the claims made in Face (2000), heavy syllables do not attract perceived stress. So how can we make sense of this mixed bag of results, where the weight of the final syllable, but of no other syllable, is a factor in Spanish stress perception?

I suggest that the lack of attraction of perceived stress by heavy syllables is an indication that syllable weight is not a factor in the perception of Spanish stress. In other words, Spanish is not quantity sensitive. This is consistent with the findings of recent experimental studies of speech production (Alvord 2003, Bárkányi 2002). If Spanish is not quantity sensitive, then there is no validity to claiming that Spanish has heavy and light syllables. But if the concepts communicated by the terms 'heavy' and 'light' are put into other words, for Spanish 'heavy' indicates a syllable with a coda consonant and 'light' indicates a syllable ending with a vowel.[3] If Spanish is not quantity sensitive, there can be no distinction between heavy and light syllables. But speaker/hearers are certainly aware of the presence of a consonant. Thus I propose that the most common pattern of perceived stress is not the result of syllable weight (as there is evidence against the role of syllable weight as a factor in the perception of Spanish stress as discussed above), but rather is the result of the nature of the final segment of the word. Speaker/hearers of Spanish know that the majority of words ending in a vowel have penultimate stress while the majority of words ending in a consonant have final stress. This knowledge is accessible by speaker/hearers, and can be used actively in both the production and perception of Spanish. Since it is segmental information at the end of the word that determines the most common stress patterns, this explanation also accounts for why coda consonants in non-final syllables do not affect stress perception, a fact that could not be accounted for by a syllable weight explanation.[4]

4. Similar words

4.1 Nonsense words

In order to test whether the stress pattern of a similar word has an effect on the perception of Spanish stress, ten real trisyllabic Spanish words ending in a consonant and having final stress (e.g. *hospital* 'hospital') were chosen. These were the similar words that could have an influence on the perception of stress in a segmentally similar nonsense word. In order to create nonsense words similar to the real words but which should have a different stress pattern if there were no influence of the similar word, nonsense words were synthesized which were segmentally identical to the real words except that they lacked the final consonant of the real word (see Appendix B). Since the nonsense words are vowel final, they should generally be perceived as having penultimate stress if the similar real word is not an influence. However, if a similar real word does influence stress perception, then the nonsense words should generally be perceived as having final stress. Care was taken to be sure that the nonsense word was not the beginning of multiple real words, since this could lead to the conflicting influence of different stress patterns from different real words.[5]

While eliminating the final consonant of a real word with final stress sets up a clear prediction of what the results should look like if real words do have an influence on stress perception and if they do not, there is something else to consider. Since the nonsense words are segmentally identical to real words except for the lack of the final consonant, processing of the nonsense word matches the real word up until the nonsense word ends, which should clearly activate the real word for the subject (see Luce and Pisoni 1998 and Pisoni et al. 1985 for information on word recognition and activation). In order to test whether a similar word could have an influence on stress perception without the possibility of being processed as identical to the real word, a second set of nonsense words was created. The second set of nonsense words was identical to the first set except that a final [s] was added to the end of each. Since words ending in [s] generally have penultimate stress, there should again be a difference between perceived penultimate stress if the real word is not an influence and perceived final stress if the real word is an influence. The predictions, then, are the same as with the first set of nonsense words. The difference is that the addition of the final [s] should prevent the nonsense word from being perceived as actually being the similar real word.

4.2 Results and discussion

The results of the stress perception experiment for the nonsense words testing the effect of a similar word on stress perception are given in Table 4.

Table 4.   Perceived stress in nonsense words with a similar real word.

Perceived Stressed Syllable	Vowel-final	s-final
Antepenultimate	12	18
Penultimate	29	45
Final	59	37
Total:	100	100

The results for vowel-final nonsense words, which are segmentally identical to a real word except that the real word has a final consonant, show that final stress is perceived 59% of the time. Since a vowel-final word would be expected to have penultimate stress, which is perceived only 29% of the time in these cases, 59% is a very high percentage of cases of perceived final stress. This is confirmed when this 59% is compared to the cases in Table 1 in Section 3.3, where words with a final light syllable (i.e. vowel-final words) are perceived to have final stress only 35% of the time. The much higher percentage of perceived final stress in vowel-final words in Table 4, then, can be attributed to the influence of the similar real words, which all have final stress. The question could be raised as to why the percentage is not even higher than 59%. The answer is that the stress pattern of the similar real word is one of probably many factors than influence stress perception. In this case the vowel-final nature of the word likely is an influence that counters final stress perception, as vowel-final words generally have penultimate stress.

While the high percentage of perceived word-final stress in the vowel-final words in Table 4 appears to indicate that the similar real words do have an effect on the which syllable is perceived as stress in the nonsense words, there exists the possibility that some of these nonsense words were mistakenly heard by the subjects as actually being the similar real word. In order to maintain a similar nonsense word and eliminate (or at least highly reduce) the possibility of the nonsense word being mistaken for the real word, which would all but certainly lead to perceived final stress, the s-final nonsense words were included, as discussed above. Since s-final words generally have penultimate stress, if the real word is not an influence, a percentage of penultimate stress similar to the 56% found for vowel-final words (which also generally have penultimate stress) in Table 1, where there were no similar real words, would be expected. Likewise a percentage of perceived final stress should be similar to the 35% in Table 1. As can be seen in Table 4, in the s-final nonsense words, penultimate stress is perceived 45% of the time and final stress is perceived 37% of the time. While 37% final stress seems still to be a relatively high percentage when penultimate stress is expected, it is nearly identical to the 35% for vowel-final words. Thus it must be concluded that the final [s] distinguishes the nonsense word sufficiently from the similar real word and does not invoke the influence of the stress pattern found on the real word.

5. Subregularities in the lexicon

5.1 Previous research

Aske (1990) conducted an experiment to test the psychological reality of general stress rules in Spanish. In doing so, one of the issues he considered was the presence of a subregularity in the lexicon. Specifically, he noted that while the general (and overwhelming) pattern is for non-verbs ending in [n] to have final stress, non-verbs ending in [en] are split fairly evenly between penultimate and final stress. Aske (1990) pointed out that this is a good set of words to use in a test of the psychological reality of Spanish stress rules. If a general stress rule is employed by speakers, a new word ending in [n] should be produced with final stress. If, on the other hand, stress is stored in the lexicon, speakers should access the lexicon and use the surface patterns found there in assigning stress. If this is the case, new words ending in [en] should be produced with a mix of penultimate and final stress, reflecting the distribution of stress in known words ending in [en]. New words ending in any vowel except [e], and followed by [n], should be produced almost exclusively with final stress, again representing the distribution of stress in known words ending in these segmental strings.

Aske (1990) created 12 nonsense words ending in [n], with six preceded by [e] and the other six preceded by other vowels. These were then embedded in contextualizing sentences so that each was interpreted as either a noun or an adjective. Subjects read the sentences, which were written in all capital letters since accent marks are commonly not marked on capital letters. The results were that for words ending in [en], final stress was produced 55.6% of the time and penultimate stress was produced 43.5% of the time. In contrast, words ending in an [n] preceded by any vowel except [e] were produced with final stress 96.8% of the time and penultimate stress only 3.2% of the time. Aske (1990) argues that these results support a model in which speakers access actual patterns in the lexicon and that they are not compatible with a model in which general stress rules are employed. In addition, he notes that an attempt at incorporation of these results into a rule-based account would be problematic since the subregularity (i.e. penultimate stress in words ending in [en]) is variable rather than categorical.

Aske's (1990) results for stress production on words ending in [n] are rather convincing. It is worth noting, however, that these results were obtained from a production study. The same lexical subregularity was tested in a perception experiment for the present study. This experiment is the subject of Sections 5.2 and 5.3.

5.2 Nonsense words

The nonsense words were designed to test the subregularity noted by Aske (1990) that non-verb words ending in [n] overwhelmingly have final stress, except for those where the vowel preceding the [n] is [e]. In this latter case there is a fairly even split between penultimate and final stress. Three sets of nonsense words were created, with each set containing ten nonsense words (see Appendix C). One set contained words ending in [an], one set words ending in [en], and one set words ending in [on]. While Aske (1990) makes a distinction between words ending in [en] and all other words ending in [n], the present study required one further distinction due to the nature of the experimental design. Aske (1990) had all of the words contextualized in sentences where the only interpretation was as a noun. However, since the present study presented individual nonsense words in isolation to the subjects, it would be possible for words ending in [en] to be interpreted as the third person plural present tense form of a verb, and these forms have penultimate stress. Therefore a higher percentage of perceived penultimate stress could be the result of the existence of verb forms with this stress pattern, in contrast to forms ending in [on], where the nonexistence of present tense verb forms ending in this segmental sequence prohibits a verbal influence toward perceived penultimate stress.[6] The [an] and [on] sets were both included so that the influence of verb forms could be noted. Since some third present plural present tense verb forms end in [an], comparing this set with the [en] set will show whether the [en] set leads to perceived penultimate stress more than the [an] set. If so, then the lexical subregularity is likely the reason. On the other hand, a close similarity between the [en] and [an] set, but with both having a higher percentage of perceived penultimate stress than the [on] set, would indicate that verb forms, rather than a lexical subregularity, explain the perceived penultimate stress in the [en] forms.

5.3 Results and discussion

The results of the stress perception experiment for the nonsense words testing the effect of a lexical subregularity on stress perception are given in Table 5.

Table 5.   Perceived stress in nonsense words ending in [n].

Perceived Stressed Syllable	[en] words	[an] words	[on] words
Antepenultimate	12	13	13
Penultimate	29	19	12
Final	59	68	75
Total:	100	100	100

These results show that final stress is perceived in 75% of the cases in [on] words, 68% of the cases in [an] words, and 59% of the cases in [en] words. While the effect of the set of nonsense words on stress perception is not statistically significant as determined by a Chi-square test (p=.05), the pattern is of interest. The two sets (i.e. [en] and [an]) where the nonsense words could be interpreted as a verb form have a higher percentage of perceived penultimate stress (and a corresponding lower percentage of perceived final stress) than the set (i.e. [on]) where the nonsense words could not be interpreted as a verb form.[7] Since the [an] set, as well as the [en] set, has a higher percentage of perceived penultimate stress than the [on] set, it appears that the possibility of these forms being verbs did have some effect on stress perception (although the difference between possible verb form and not possible verb form is still not a statistically significant factor on the perception of stress – a Chi-square test shows p=.04). While this pattern is of interest, it is also interesting that there is a notable difference in perceived stress between the [en] and [an] sets, indicating that being a possible verb form is not the only explanation needed. Notably, it is the [en] set that has a higher percentage of perceived penultimate stress (though again a comparison of only the [en] set and the [an] set as they affect perceived stress shows a difference that is not statistically significant – a Chi-square test shows p=.25). The difference between the [en] and [an] sets, then, could be the result of the lexical subregularity discussed by Aske (1990) – nouns ending in [en] are largely split between penultimate and final stress, while other nouns ending in [n] typically have final stress.

The results obtained in the present study are less dramatic than those obtained by Aske (1990) with regard to the influence of a lexical subregularity on stress. Nonetheless, the patterns discussed above show that the lexical subregularity is a factor in the perception of Spanish stress, although its influence appears to be smaller than indicated by Aske (1990).

6. Morphological category

6.1 Previous research

In addition to the subregularity of penultimate stress on words ending in [en], Aske (1990) considers another subregularity based on the morphological category of the word. He notes that the majority of words ending in [iko] or [ika] have antepenultimate stress due to the unstressed (in rule terms, stress retracting) nature of the adjective-forming suffix [ik]. Of the words ending in [iko] or [ika] that have antepenultimate stress, 76% are adjectives, and another 19% are both adjectives and nouns. Only 5% are nouns only. And in the adjectives, nearly half are not analyzable, or only partially analyzable, as consisting of a stem plus [iko] or [ika]. Aske (1990) predicts that if speakers follow a general stress rule, they will produce new words in [iko] or [ika] with penultimate stress since there is not evidence for a stress-retracting suffix and morphological category is not relevant for stress assignment. On the other hand, he predicts that if speakers consult the lexicon and search for similar words, morphological category may be one of the factors used in determining stress placement.

Aske (1990) created 12 nonsense words ending in [iko] or [ika] and place them into sentences so that six were only interpretable as nouns and six were only interpretable as adjectives. As with the study of words ending in [n], the sentences were written in capital letters, since accent marks are often not used on capital letters. The results were that for the adjectives antepenultimate stress was produced 83.3% of the time and penultimate stress 16.7% of the time. For the nouns antepenultimate stress was produced 63.4% of the time and penultimate stress 36.6% of the time. While these results point in the direction of speakers treating nouns and adjectives ending in [iko] and [ika] differently, the results are not statistically significant, and there is still a large percentage of antepenultimate stress produced on nouns. While the results are much less convincing than those found for words ending in [n], Aske (1990) notes that the results do show that speakers treat words ending in [iko] and [ika] differently from other words ending in a vowel, and that this supports a model where speakers consult existing patterns in the lexicon.

Aske's (1990) results for words ending in [iko] or [ika] do not provide motivation that morphological category is a factor in stress placement. However, this distinction between antepenultimate and penultimate stress in words ending in [iko] and [ika] may not be a very salient distinction, especially as determined by morphological category. Using Bosque and Pérez Fernández's (1987) reverse dictionary, he finds a total of 3580 words ending in [iko] or [ika] with antepenultimate stress and only 121 with penultimate stress (of which only 19 he considers to be familiar to him). Of those with antepenultimate stress, he finds that about 19% are both nouns and adjectives, and only 5% are nouns only. That means that 24% can be nouns. 24% of the 3580 words with antepenultimate stress is 859. That means that 859 nouns have antepenultimate stress while only 121 have penultimate stress. So it should have been expected that nouns would also be produced with antepenultimate stress in the majority of cases. While these results support Aske's (1990) claim that speakers access the lexicon rather than general stress rules, they offer no insight as to whether or not morphological category is one of the factors used in determining stress placement. Interestingly, Eddington (2004) finds in a computer simulation of Spanish stress placement that morphological variables are among the most influential in determining stress placement. It is yet to be seen, however, whether actual human performance data support Eddington's finding. Sections 6.2 and 6.3 describe an experiment carried out for the present study to determine if morphological category is a factor in the perception of Spanish stress.

6.2 Nonsense words

In order for the present study to test whether or not morphological category affects the perception of Spanish stress, a salient stress difference between words in different morphological categories, but sharing the same terminal segmental string, had to be found. Such a difference exists between nouns and third person plural present tense verb forms ending in [n]. Nouns ending in [n] generally have final stress, and the third person plural present tense verb forms always have penultimate stress (except when monosyllabic). These verb forms end in either [an] or [en], but forms ending in [an] were chosen for the present study. In this way it could be assured that there would be a clear difference between stress patterns, since nouns ending in [en] often have penultimate stress.[8]

The 10 nonsense words ending in [an] that were used in the experiment testing the effect of a lexical subregularity on the perception of Spanish stress were used to test the effect of morphological category on Spanish stress perception as well. Each of these ten nonsense words was inserted into two contextualizing sentences. In one sentence (i.e. *María quiere un _____*. 'María wants a _____.'), the nonsense word could only be interpreted as a noun, and in the other (i.e. *Los alumnus _____ en la clase*. 'The students _____ in class.') it could only be interpreted as a verb. The contextualizing sentence was synthesized to sound as natural as possible, while the nonsense word inserted, in following with the other experiments in the present study, had no syllable that was acoustically more prominent than the others.

If morphological category does influence the perception of Spanish stress, then those cases in which the nonsense words can only be interpreted as a noun should show a strong preference for perceived final stress, and those cases in which the nonsense word can only be interpreted as a verb should show a strong preference for perceived penultimate stress. Since this distinction based on morphological category is so extreme in real words, it is expected that the results of the present study should be quite clear if indeed morphological category has an effect on the perception of Spanish stress. Any results that do not clearly show a difference in perceived stress based on morphological category would likely mean that morphological category does not have an effect on Spanish stress perception.

6.3 Results and discussion

The results of the stress perception experiment for the nonsense words testing the effect of morphological category on stress perception are given in Table 6.

Table 6.   Perceived stress by morphological category.

Perceived Stressed Syllable	Nouns	Verbs
Antepenultimate	4	3
Penultimate	15	86
Final	81	11
Total:	100	100

These results show a highly significant and very convincing difference between perceived stress on nouns and on verbs. Nouns ending in [an] are expected to have final stress, and final stress is perceived 81% of the time. Third person plural present tense verb forms always have penultimate stress when they are polysyllabic, and penultimate stress is perceived 86% of the time. These results show quite clearly that morphological category does have a very significant effect on the perception of Spanish stress. These results also provide concrete performance data that support the finding of Eddington's (2004) computer simulation of stress assignment, where he finds that morphological variables are among the most influential variables in predicting the placement of Spanish stress.

7. General discussion

The experiments reported on in the preceding sections have given us new insight into what non-acoustic factors affect the perception of Spanish stress. In Section 3 the role of syllable weight was reconsidered. The results showed that a previous study which had claimed that syllable weight plays a role in the perception of Spanish stress was in error. A flaw in the experimental design of Face's (2000) study on this topic led to heavy syllables also being longer than light syllables. When this design flaw was corrected in the present study, the results were different. Heavy syllables were found not to attract perceived stress, which is evidence against syllable weight and quantity sensitivity in Spanish. Whether or not the final syllable is open (i.e. ends with the nuclear vowel) or closed (i.e. has a coda consonant) is an important factor in the perception of Spanish stress, but this seems more adequately explained by the nature of the terminal segment than by syllable weight. In Section 4 the effect of a similar word on stress perception was examined, and it was found that stress perception is affected by the stress pattern of a similar word, at least until the segmental composition of the (nonsense) word in question becomes such that it can no longer be processed as a potential instantiation of the similar word. In Section 5 it was found that there is an effect of lexical subregularities on the perception of Spanish stress. The results were not as convincing, however, as in a previous production study (Aske 1990). Finally, in Section 6 the role of morphological category on Spanish stress perception was considered, and it was shown that morphological category has a highly significant effect. But what are the larger implications of these experimental results?

Although syllable weight was found not to play a role in the perception of Spanish stress, the segmental nature of the final syllable does. If the word ends in a vowel, it is most likely to be perceived as having penultimate stress, and if it ends in a consonant, it is most likely to be perceived as having final stress. Such a segmental effect on stress does not tell us much about how stress works for speakers of Spanish. If Spanish speakers have general stress rules (whether actually rules, the result of ranked constraints, or otherwise), they could include reference to such segmental factors.[9] And if Spanish speakers refer to real words stored in the lexicon, they will find in the lexicon that the majority of words ending in a vowel have penultimate stress and the majority of words ending in a consonant have final stress. Therefore, consulting the lexicon produces the correct results as well.

The results for the influence of the stress pattern of a similar word, on the other hand, have much more to tell us about how stress works. When nonsense words were created that were similar to real words, but where the nonsense word – based solely on the terminal segment – should have penultimate stress and the similar word has final stress, it was found that the similar word had an effect on the perception of stress. The nonsense words included in the experiment ended in a vowel, yet were perceived as having final stress in 59% of the cases. This is a much higher percentage of perceived final stress than is found in vowel-final words that are not similar to a real word. These results cause difficulty for any model which includes general stress rules. The present study shows that speaker/listeners in the majority of cases do not perceive the most common stress pattern when the word in question is similar to another word with a different stress pattern. Rather the stress pattern of the similar word is imposed upon the word in question. No phonological model which incorporates general stress rules can account for this finding, even by complicating the stress rules with sub-generalizations, since any word stored in the lexicon could serve as a model for the stress pattern of a segmentally similar new word. The findings for the influence of similar words on Spanish stress perception provide strong evidence that Spanish speakers access the lexicon and use whole words stored in the lexicon as analogical models.

The results for the influence of lexical subregularities on the perception of Spanish stress indicate that there is a minor influence. While the results do not achieve statistical significance, the pattern is clear. There is a clear preference for perceived final stress when the word ends in [on], less preference for final stress when the word ends in [an], and even less when the word ends in [en]. Recall that this experiment tests the effect on stress perception of the subregularity that non-verbs ending in [en] are split between penultimate and final stress while other non-verbs ending in [n] generally have final stress. The words ending in [on] are the clearest case of non-verbs, since there segmental composition does not allow them to be interpreted as a verb. Any word ending in [an] or [en] could be interpreted as a verb form, so both were included to see if there was a difference between them. Both of these groups of words showed less final stress perception and more penultimate stress perception, which is likely due to the fact that they could be verbs. However, the difference between the [an] and [en] groups is not attributable to the category of the word, and appears to result from the frequency difference of final stress between these categories in real words. The only way in which such a lexical subregularity can be explained, as Aske (1990) has argued, is through a model in which speaker/hearers have access to whole words stored in the lexicon. Therefore, while in the present study the results for this lexical subregularity are not as strong as those for similar words, the fact that some effect of the lexical subregularity was found points to the same conclusion.

Morphological category was shown to be a very significant factor in the perception of Spanish stress. When words ending in [an] were placed in a context in which they had to be interpreted as a noun, they overwhelmingly had perceived final stress. When they were place in a context in which they had to be interpreted as a third person plural present tense verb form, they overwhelmingly had perceived penultimate stress. Speaker/hearers, then, are able to make use of the context in which the word occurs, and use this information in determining the stressed syllable. This requires the speaker/hearer to have a knowledge that nouns ending in [an] generally have final stress while third person plural present tense verb forms have penultimate stress. This knowledge is available by consulting the lexicon.[10]

The cumulative effect of the experimental results of the present study is that they support a phonological model in which the lexicon plays a large role. The results show that speaker/hearers must consult the lexicon and that they use the information there in determining stress placement. This finding provides difficulties for any generative model which generates stress through rules or ranked constraints. However, it provides evidence in favor of usage-based models (e.g. Bybee 2001; Johnson 1997a, 1997b) where tokens of language use are stored in the lexicon in full phonetic detail and with contextual information, and then are consulted by the speaker/hearer and used actively in language production and perception. This adds to the growing number of studies on Spanish that argue that usage-based models in which the lexicon plays a large and active role are able to best explain various phonological and morphological phenomena (e.g. Eddington 2000, 2002, 2004; Face 2003, in press; Hualde 2000).

8. Conclusion

The present study considered four different factors as possible influences on the perception of Spanish stress: syllable weight, similar words, lexical subregularities, and morphological category. It was found that syllable weight is not an influence on Spanish stress perception, contrary to the finding of Face (2000). All of the other three factors, though, do influence stress perception, with similar words and morphological category having a strong influence and lexical subregularities having a weaker influence. The present study expands our knowledge of Spanish stress perception by showing that there are various non-acoustic factors that influence it. Furthermore, the results of the present study lend support to usage-based models of phonology in which speaker/hearers consult the lexicon and make use of patterns stored there in language production and perception.

In addition to making a contribution to our knowledge of Spanish stress, the present study also raises some questions for future investigations. One very broad question to be addressed is how these non-acoustic factors interact with acoustic correlates of stress. Face (2000) noted that in words where an acoustically stressed syllable was present, errors tended to be in the direction of perceiving the most common stress pattern rather than perceiving acoustic stress. What other similar interactions are there? Also, what differences are there in the effect of the factors considered here on perception and production. Aske (1990) found a strong effect of the lexical subregularity of penultimate stress on nouns ending in [en], while the present study found a weaker effect. Could it be that this is attributable to Aske's (1990) study being a production study while the present study is a perception study? Little work has been done on the non-acoustic factors involved in either stress production or stress perception. And certainly one of the interesting topics to be investigated is whether these factors have different effects on production and on perception. So while the present study has taken a step forward and offered new insight into the perception of Spanish stress, these issues and many more remain to be investigated by future studies.

Notes

1. The MBROLI synthesizer has voices for many different languages, with each created through the compilation of a diphone database.
2. While all speaker/hearers of Spanish are exposed to the acoustic correlates of Spanish stress on a daily basis, explicit identification of them and their function (i.e. as markers of stress) is not a natural use of their knowledge of the Spanish language. While most speaker/hearers are able to accurately identify an acoustically stressed syllable in a nonsense word, some do struggle with such a task. In the present study 3 potential subjects were eliminated because they perceived stress correctly less than 90% of the time.
3. It is worth noting that while this is the common use of these terms in Spanish (though simplified, as post-nuclear glides are not included in a definition such as this), this is not a universal definition. Languages with a vowel length distinction may consider an open syllable containing a long vowel to be heavy even though not containing a coda consonant.
4. While it is the presence or absence of a word-final consonant that determines the most common stress pattern in Spanish, it has been suggested that speakers take into account more segmental information than just the final consonant (Aske 1990, Eddington 2000).
5. One of the nonsense words, *capita*, was the beginning of both *capital* 'capital' and *capitán* 'captain'. This is not a problem, however, since both words involve the addition of just one final consonant to the nonsense word and both have final stress. Therefore, regardless of the fact that some speakers may take *capita* as similar to *capital* and others may take it as similar to *capitán*, the results would be identical.
6. There are verb forms that end in [on], but these are always preceded by [r]. In order to avoid a potential interpretation as such a verb form, none of the nonsense words had [r] preceding the final vowel-[n] sequence.
7. It is worth noting, however, that even the [en] and [an] sets were much more often perceived as having final stress than as having penultimate stress, indicating that they were most commonly interpreted as not being verbs.

8. While this subregularity was not found to be a significant factor in the perception of Spanish stress in Section 5, there was some indication of a minor influence. And since there is a clear difference in stress patterns in real words between nouns ending in [en] and those ending in [an], it is preferable to maximize the difference from the verb forms by employing forms ending in [an] in the present study.
9. It must be pointed out, however, that even these "general" Spanish stress rules include diacritics to account for exceptions. These diacritics are no different than lexical marking of stress and raise serious questions as to just how general the Spanish stress rules are to begin with.
10. It should be noted that different stress rules have sometimes been proposed for verbs and for non-verbs (e.g. Harris 1987). But these have the same difficulty of diacritic use as was mentioned in footnote 9.

References

Alvord, Scott
    2003   The psychological unreality of quantity sensitivity in Spanish. *Southwest Journal of Linguistics* 22(2): 1–12.
Aske, Jon
    1990   Disembodied rules versus patterns in the lexicon: Testing the psychological reality of Spanish stress rules. In *Proceedings of the Sixteenth Annual Meeting of the Berkeley Linguistics Society*, Kira Hall, Jean-Pierre Koenig, Michael Meacham, Sondra Reinman and Laurel A. Sutton (eds.), 30-45. Berkeley: Berkeley Linguistics Society.
Bárkányi, Zsuzsanna
    2002   A fresh look at quantity sensitivity in Spanish. *Linguistics* 40: 375-394.
Bosque, Ignacio and Manuel Pérez Fernández
    1987   *Diccionario inverso de la lengua española*. Madrid: Gredos.
Bybee, Joan
    2001   *Phonology and Language Use*. Cambridge: Cambridge University Press.
Dutoit, T., V. Pagel, N. Pierret, F. Bataille and O. Van der Vrecken
    1996   The MBROLA project: Toward a set of high-quality speech synthesizers free of use for non-commercial purposes. *Proceedings of ICSLP'96*: 1393-1396.
Eddington, David
    2000   Spanish stress assignment within the analogical modeling of language. *Language* 76: 92-109.

2002   Spanish diminutive formation without rules or constraints. *Linguistics* 40: 395-419.

2004   A computational approach to resolving certain issues in Spanish stress placement. In this volume.

Enríquez, Emilia V., Celia Casado and Andrés Santos
1989   La percepción del acento en español. *Lingüística Española Actual* 11: 241-269.

Face, Timothy L
2000   The role of syllable weight in the perception of Spanish stress. In *Hispanic Linguistics at the Turn of the Millennium*, Héctor Campos, Elena Herburger, Alfonso Morales-Front and Thomas J. Walsh (eds.), 1-13. Somerville, MA: Cascadilla.

2003   Consonant strength innovations across the Spanish-speaking world: Evidence and implications for a usage-based model of phonology. In *LACUS Forum XXIX: Linguistics and the Real World*, Douglas W. Coleman, William J. Sullivan, and Arle Lommel (eds.), 25–35. Houston: LACUS.

in press Theoretical implications of double morphological marking. In *CLS 38: The 38th Meeting of the Chicago Linguistics Society*. Chicago: Chicago Linguistics Society.

Harris, James W.
1987   The accentual patterns of verb paradigms in Spanish. *Natural Language and Linguistic Theory* 5: 61-90.

Hochberg, Judith G.
1988   Learning Spanish stress: Developmental and theoretical perspectives. *Language* 64: 683-706.

Hualde, José Ignacio
2000   How general are linguistic generalizations? In *CLS 36: The 36th Meeting of the Chicago Linguistic Society*, Arika Okrent and John P. Boyle (eds.), 167-177. Chicago: Chicago Linguistic Society.

Hume, Elizabeth V. and Keith Johnson (eds.)
2001   *The Role of Speech Perception in Phonology*. San Diego: Academic Press.

Johnson, Keith
1997a   Speech perception without speaker normalization: An exemplar model. In *Talker Variability in Speech Processing*, Keith Johnson and John W. Mullennix (eds.), 145-165. San Diego: Academic Press.

1997b   The auditory/perceptual basis for speech segmentation. *OSU Working Papers in Linguistics* 50: 101-113.

Llisterri, Joaquim, María Jesús Machuca, Carme de la Mota, Montserrat Riera
        and Antonio Ríos
    2003   Algunas cuestiones en torno al desplazamiento acentual en espa-
            ñol. In *La tonía: Dimensiones fonéticas y fonológicas*, Ester
            Herrera Z. and Pedro Martín Butragueño (eds.), 163–185. Mexi-
            co City: El Colegio de México.
Luce, Paul A. and David B. Pisoni
    1998   Recognizing spoken words: The neighborhood activation model.
            Ear & Hearing 19: 1-36.
Pisoni, David B., Howard C. Nusbaum, Paul A. Luce and Louisa M. Slowiac-
        zek
    1985   Speech perception, word recognition and the structure of the lexi-
            con. *Speech Communication* 4: 75-95.
Quilis, Antonio
    1971   Caracterización fonética del acento español. *Travaux de Linguis-
            tique et de Littérature* 9: 53-72.
    1993   *Tratado de fonología y fonética españolas*. Madrid: Gredos.
Waltermire, Mark
    2004   The influence of syllable weight in the determination of stress
            placement in Spanish. In this volume.

Appendix A

List of nonsense words used to test the role of syllable weight in Spanish stress perception. Syllable structure is indicated by H (heavy syllable) and L (light syllable).

HHH	HHL	HLH	HLL
bonlandan	bondenda	bandemel	bolnala
dombalden	bonlamba	bondanol	dendana
landangon	dantelda	galdeman	galmeda
lanlendol	malnanga	gondabel	ganloda
menlembal	mandolma	naldelan	landola

LHH	LHL	LLH	LLL
badonguel	banenda	dabonel	beloga
comengon	gadamba	gabadon	dagola
dalandel	gobolda	manaden	dalona
mobalmal	lomeada	Noguerol	galema
pelandon	molanga	polanal	mamena

Appendix B

List of nonsense words and corresponding real words used to test the role of a similar word in Spanish stress perception. In each nonsense word the final *s* is in parentheses, as one nonsense word included the *s* and another did not.

Nonsense word	Corresponding real word
arsena(s)	arsenal
calama(s)	calamar
capita(s)	capital/capitán
champiño(s)	champiñón
corazo(s)	corazón
ecuado(s)	Ecuador
funera(s)	funeral
huraca(s)	huracán
hospita(s)	hospital
tenedo(s)	tenedor

Appendix C

List of nonsense words used to test the role of a lexical subregularity on Spanish stress perception. The *–an* group was also used to test the role of morphological category.

-an	-en	-on
balendan	balenden	balendon
cameldan	camelden	cameldon
gamoltan	gamolten	gamolton
gobelman	gobelmen	gobelmon
logolnan	logolnen	logolnon
malamban	malamben	malambon
medolman	medolmen	medolmon
tabonlan	tabonlen	tabonlon
tagandan	taganden	tagandon

Another look at effects of environment on L2 epenthesis: Evidence for transfer of ranked constraints

Sharon Gerlach

1. Introduction

Research in second language (L2) phonological acquisition has discussed influence of native language transfer as well as influence of universal markedness (e.g. Tarone 1987; Hodne 1985; Broselow 1992, among others). Recently it has been suggested by several researchers (Hancin-Bhatt and Bhatt 1997 for syllable structure and Broselow, Chen, and Wang 1998 for metricality) that Optimality Theory (Prince and Smolensky 1993; McCarthy and Prince 1995; henceforth OT) provides a phonological framework that unites the two influences, given its language-specific ranking of universal markedness and faithfulness constraints. Although originally conceived as a general theory of phonology applying to a speaker's native language, it implies that a second language learner brings to the learning process a set of universal constraints with a language-specific ranking. In order to acquire the L2 phonology, the learner must attempt to re-rank the relevant constraints to match the target language rankings.

The present study brings new data to and proposes an OT analysis for a problem that has not been adequately explained by previous analyses—that of patterns of vowel epenthesis in L2 acquisition by native speakers of Spanish. It is well known that Spanish speakers tend to epenthesize before word-initial clusters of the type sC(C) in a language such as English which permits such clusters, e.g. *school* [eskul]. Since in native Spanish words such as *escuela* this word-initial vowel is predictable in this environment, it has often been assumed in generative phonology to be generated by a rule of epenthesis. However, other scholars have suggested that it is simply stored in the lexicon of native speakers, since it is always present in Spanish #*esC(C)* words (e.g. Hooper 1976; Eddington 2001). In contrast, the epenthetic nature of this vowel is clearer in second language acquisition, since learners never hear the vowel in the input they receive from native speakers of the target language and would therefore have no reason to include it in their lexicon. Its presence, then, must be explained by an active process of epenthesis.

2. Previous findings for effects of environment

Two major patterns concerning L2 vowel epenthesis in Spanish speakers have emerged in previous research conducted by Carlisle (1997) and later Abrahamsson (1999) which inform the present study. First, vowel epenthesis is somewhat more frequent before three-member sCC onsets (e.g. *spring*) than for two-member sC onsets (e.g. *spot*). Carlisle found an average frequency of 48% versus 38% in his study of 11 native Spanish speakers learning English, while Abrahamsson found an average rate of 77% versus 59% in his longitudinal study of a native Spanish speaker learning Swedish. They attribute this to the fact that longer onsets are universally more marked.

The second finding is that despite the influence of onset length, preceding environment was the most important factor determining frequency of epenthesis. Carlisle compared the influence of a preceding vowel versus a consonant, while Abrahamsson added the category of silence (after a pause). Their results are summarized in Table 1.

Table 1.   Summary of previous results: Frequency of epenthesis by context

Environment	Carlisle 1997	Abrahamsson 1999	Example
Preceding vowel	35%	34%	He [e]spoke
Preceding pause	---	62%	# [e]spoke
Preceding consonant	51%	94%	Mike [e]spoke

Previous analyses of these results have relied largely on a rule-based approach. Carlisle presumes that the predictable /e/ in Spanish is not in the underlying form but rather generated by a rule. He suggests that Spanish native speakers transfer both an epenthesis rule and a prosodic resyllabification rule (e.g. *las alas* [la.sa.las]) into the interlanguage. He is reluctant to conclude, however, that speakers would resyllabify the string *He spoke* as [his.pok] because the rule characterizing Spanish resyllabification applies only to a word-final consonant resyllabifying with a following vowel, not the reverse; e.g. *la escuela* with a presumed input /la skwela/ does not become *[las.kwe.la].[1] Instead, he suggests that epenthesis is more likely after a consonant because it serves to feed the resyllabification rule, producing *Mike spoke* as [maj.kes.pok] after both epenthesis and resyllabification. He considers universal markedness as part of his overall analysis, noting that epenthesis occurred less frequently both after open (less marked) syllables and before shorter (less marked) onsets, but comments that "...these findings still do not explain why environment has consistently been the first-order variable constraint. This question awaits a principled linguistic explanation" (Carlisle 1997: 353).

Abrahamsson's analysis differs somewhat from Carlisle in that he is cautious not to assume that Spanish speakers have an active rule of epenthesis in their grammars. Rather, he appeals to native syllable structure constraints to account for the creation of an epenthesis rule in the interlanguage. In his discussion of effect of preceding environment, he notes the conflicting forces of native syllable structure and target-like output, suggesting that a preceding vowel allows for resyllabification and avoidance of epenthesis. He concludes that "...Spanish learners resyllabify in accordance with principles that are neither transferred native principles nor acquired target language principles, but rather typical interlanguage principles/strategies" (Abrahamsson 1999: 497). He further suggests that a preceding consonant may increase likelihood of epenthesis because the consonant needs to resyllabify, although the motivation for resyllabification is not clear in his analysis.

An area in which there have been conflicting findings is the effect of sonority of the second member of the onset. While Carlisle noted that the onset /sl/ was modified less often than /st/, the learner in Abrahamsson's study epenthesized before /sl/ more frequently than any other onset. The focus of the present study will be preceding environment, not onset sonority, but its potential to influence the rate of epenthesis indicates that it is a factor that should be controlled for.

3. Motivation for the present study

This paper considers the possibility that OT provides the "principled linguistic explanation" sought by Carlisle for the fact that preceding environment is the most important influence on frequency of epenthesis in the interlanguage of native Spanish speakers. In order to pursue this question, however, more information is needed. While previous studies considered the categories of preceding vowel, consonant, and pause, they did not consider the specific quality of the consonant. There is evidence, however, that the place of articulation of a particular consonant may be a factor in native language syllable structure constraints. In her presentation of syllable structure constraints of Spanish in an OT framework Colina (1995) proposes a Coda Condition[2] constraint that disfavors non-Coronal coda consonants in word-final position. In addition, the importance of sonority in syllable structure has long been recognized. Yet previous studies did not examine the segmental properties of the preceding consonant.

This motivates the present study, which elicits data in a similar fashion to Carlisle, but controls more specifically for preceding consonant. The purpose of the study is two-fold:

1) To confirm previous results on rate of epenthesis after a consonant, vowel, and pause, since the latter environment was only examined in one subject; and
2) To determine what effect the sonority or place of articulation of the preceding consonant may have on rate of epenthesis.

It was hypothesized based on Colina's Coda Condition that the rate of epenthesis might be somewhat higher after consonants such as /p/ and /k/ (and perhaps /t/) which do not occur natively in word-final position, and that the sonority of the preceding consonant might have an effect on whether it may be resyllabified with the following /s/ in lieu of epenthesis. Details of how these factors were controlled for are provided in the section below on methods, which will be followed by a presentation of the results of the study and finally a formal account of the data within an OT framework.

4. Methods

4.1. Subjects

Eight native speakers of Spanish ages 20-38 from a variety of Spanish-speaking countries (Spain, Argentina, Bolivia, Chile, Ecuador, and Peru)[3] participated in the study. Five participants were students in an ESL course at the University of Minnesota and three were graduate students employed as teaching assistants in Spanish. All had at least a high intermediate proficiency level in English (based on placement in the ESL course or ability to meet ESL standards for teaching assistants), since it was thought that a lower level of proficiency would interfere too greatly with the fluent reading of English sentences. Length of time in the United States ranged from three weeks to nearly three years. Participants of varying levels of proficiency were included in the study in order to capture all relevant epenthesis patterns. As an incentive to participate, each participant was entered in a drawing for a gift certificate at the university bookstore.

4.2. Instrument

Participants were recorded reading a list of 54 sentences containing 64 target onset clusters in various environments. Since previous studies have found a somewhat higher rate of epenthesis before triliteral onsets and the focus of this study is preceding environment, only biliteral /sC/ onsets were included. Furthermore, since both Carlisle and Abrahamsson also found the sonority of the onset to be a factor in rate of epenthesis, the present study included only /s/ + stop onsets. Preceding environment was controlled by including approximately equal numbers of four different segmental categories: stops, fricatives, nasals, and liquids. Only four pauses were built into the list (i.e. /sC/ onset at the beginning of a sentence), since it was anticipated that subjects would hesitate elsewhere in the course of reading aloud.

4.3. Procedure

As they read the sentences out loud, participants were asked to perform a grammaticality judgment task. This was incorporated into the study in order to encourage participants to concentrate on the meaning of the sentences and less on careful pronunciation. The sentences were presented in pairs in which the only difference was the verb form, as in (1).

(1) a. *Most Americans are eating steak twice a week.*
     b. *Most Americans eat steak twice a week.*

After reading the sentences, they checked off one of three choices: sentence (1a) is unacceptable; sentence (1b) is unacceptable, or both sentences are acceptable. Participants were instructed to read each pair out loud twice while reflecting on the grammaticality of the sentences, effectively doubling the number of tokens recorded of each target cluster for a total of 128 potential tokens.[4] Their speech was recorded digitally in a language laboratory with a headset microphone using the DAVID (Digital Audio-Video Interactive Device) speech recording program.

5. Results

The eight participants in the study fell into two main groups: four who epenthesized rather frequently, and four who rarely epenthesized. It is worth noting that rate of epenthesis did not necessarily correlate with proficiency or previous instruction in English or length of time spent in the United States, nor was this the focus of the study. Among the epenthesizers, three were ESL students, but one was a graduate student who had spent nearly three years in the United States. The group of non-epenthesizers included two of the ESL students. The individual differences in background are illustrated in Table 2, with the non-epenthesizers shaded in gray. Status refers to whether the subject was a student in an ESL class (ESL) or a graduate student teaching Spanish (Grad).

Turning to the patterns of epenthesis found in the two groups, the first goal of this study was to confirm the frequency of epenthesis found by Abrahamsson for preceding vowel, consonant, and pause, so we first look at these three broad categories. In determining rate of epenthesis by preceding environment, it is only useful to consider the epenthesizing group, as displayed in Table 3.

Contrary to expectations, Abrahamsson's results were not confirmed. Instead of consistently finding the highest rate of epenthesis after a consonant, epenthesis was most frequent after a pause for three out of four speakers. Despite the small sample size, a blocked ANOVA showed that the results were statistically significant, given $F(2, 6) = 9.145$, $p = .015$. A Tukey's post-hoc test revealed, however, that while preceding vowel differed significantly from both consonant and pause, the latter two categories did not differ significantly from one another. This is probably due to the anomalous rate of epenthesis after a pause for S-2 (highlighted in italics), since otherwise the rates of epenthesis for each speaker are very similar.

Table 2.   Background of subjects in epenthesizing and non-epenthesizing groups

Epenthesizers	Status	Country of Origin	Previous Study of English	Length of time in U.S.
S-2	Grad	Argentina	5 years HS; 2 years private	2.75 years
S-3	ESL	Spain	12 years public schools; 2 summers in London	3 weeks
S-9	ESL	Peru	1 year	5 months
S-8	ESL	Ecuador	1 year	1.5 years
Non-epenthesizers	Status	Country of Origin	Previous Study of English	Length of time in U.S.
S-4	ESL	Bolivia	2 years middle school; immersion setting	3 weeks
S-5	ESL	Spain	4 years HS	7 months
S-6	Grad	Chile	10 years public schools	2.75 years
S-7	Grad	Spain	12 years public schools; 10 months in Ireland	9 months

Table 3.   Epenthesizers: Rate of epenthesis by broad segmental categories

Subject	Vowel	Consonant	Pause
S-2	3/33 or 9%	42/73 or 58%	*5/18 or 27%*
S-3	9/30 or 30%	36/59 or 61%	30/34 or 88%
S-9	3/31 or 10%	32/67 or 48%	10/24 or 71%
S-8[5]	2/7 or 29%	18/28 or 64%	21/21 or 100%
Mean Percent	19%	58%	64%

This somewhat surprising result for rate of epenthesis after a consonant makes the second question posed by the study even more intriguing. Are all consonants created equal, or do the segmental properties of the consonant make a difference? An interesting result was found for the four sonority categories controlled for in the study, illustrated in Table 4. The number of tokens for each type varies for each speaker due to differences in where each speaker paused during the reading.

Table 4. Epenthesizers: Rate of epenthesis after consonants, by segment type

Subject	Stop	Fricative	Nasal	Liquid
S-2	15/29 or 52%	14/21 or 67%	10/13 or 77%	3/7 or 43%
S-3	20/22 or 91%	14/18 or 78%	1/11 or 9%	1/6 or 17%
S-9	12/20 or 60%	12/23 or 52%	7/13 or 54%	1/10 or 10%
S-8	7/7 or 100%	8/8 or 100%	3/10 or 30%	0/3 or 0%
Mean Percent	76%	74%	43%	17%

Once again, S-2 shows a somewhat different pattern than the other three subjects; yet epenthesis is least frequent for all subjects after a liquid. A blocked ANOVA confirms a significant difference for the results, where F (3, 9) = 4.833 and p < .05 (p = .029). A post-hoc Tukey's test shows that the rate of epenthesis after either a stop or fricative differs significantly from that found after a liquid. The rate of epenthesis after a nasal, on the other hand, does not differ significantly from any other group due to the large variance.

Table 5. Non-Epenthesizers: Tokens of epenthesis after consonants, by segment type

Subject	Stop	Fricative /f,v/	/s,z/	Nasal	Liquid
S-4	0	0	3	0	0
S-5	0	1	2	0	0
S-6	0	2	7	1	0
S-7	0	0	2	0	0

An additional pattern of interest emerged somewhat unexpectedly when examining the data from the non-epenthesizers. These subjects never epenthesized after a vowel or a pause, and only occasionally after a consonant. There was one peculiar environment, however, where nearly everyone epenthesized. To illustrate, Table 5 shows the precise environment in which each token of epenthesis occurred, with fricatives broken down by place of articulation.

In other words, the primary environment in which these speakers still epenthesized was after a fricative with the same place of articulation as the following /s/: e.g. *is* [e]*staying*. The same trend was evident in the epenthesizing group, if we again subcategorize fricatives by place of articulation, as in Table 6.

Table 6.   Epenthesizers: Epenthesis after fricatives only

Subject	/f,v/	/s,z/
S-2	3/6 or 50%	11/15 or 73%
S-3	3/6 or 50%	11/12 or 92%
S-9	4/8 or 50%	8/15 or 53%
S-8	3/3 or 100%	5/5 or 100%
Mean	63%	80%

Again, when the fricative had the same place of articulation as the following /s/ in the target onsets (e.g. *his skis*), epenthesis was more likely than for other places of articulation (although for S-8, epenthesis could not be any more frequent for /s,z/ than for other fricatives since it was already at 100% for all obstruents).

Although not the focus of this study, deletion of coda consonants was also noted since in a few instances they altered the preceding environment of the target cluster (e.g. *Unite<d> States*, a simplification observed in all four epenthesizers). Singleton codas were rarely deleted, even those having a disfavored place of articulation (i.e. in violation of Colina's Coda Condition), except by subject S-8. Complex codas such as /st/, /nd/, /ld/, /vz/, however, were frequently simplified, in all instances by deleting the final consonant. A summary of deletions and reductions made by the epenthesizing group is shown in Table 7. (Only one coda simplification, [nd] --> [n], occurred among the non-epenthesizers.)

Table 7.   Coda deletions and simplifications among epenthesizers

Simple coda deletions		
Subject	Codas deleted	Examples
S-2	s, t, d	*has, stories, great, United*
S-3	d, k	*United, exercise*
S-9	D	*United*
S-8	t, d, k; ts→Ø	*right, night, United, lake, States*

Complex coda simplifications		
S-2	st, ns, nd, ld, rs, lt, vz	*most, last, placed, found, spilled, stairs, difficult, spoiled, lives*
S-3	st, nd, ld, rd, d͡ʒd; kst	*placed, found, spilled, start, changed, next*
S-9	st, rs, d͡ʒd; kst	*most, last, years, changed, next*
S-8	st, ŋk, nd, rt, vz, d͡ʒd; rts, kst	*most, placed, past, last, shirt, skirt, think, pink, found, York, lives, sports, spends, next*

Summarizing the trends in the data, it was found that:

   1) Epenthesis tends to be less likely after a liquid
   2) Epenthesis tends to be more likely after a stop or fricative
   3) Epenthesis is most likely after a fricative with the same place of articulation as the following /sC/ onset, i.e. after /s/ and /z/

4) Non-native codas did not trigger epenthesis, but complex codas frequently underwent deletion of the final consonant.

The following section presents an OT analysis of the patterns of epenthesis in the data.

6. Analysis

Conflicting forces in the speaker are modeled in OT by Faithfulness constraints and Markedness constraints. If OT is an effective model for representing phonological transfer, the likelihood of epenthesis should be explained by the interaction of constraints related to syllable structure in Spanish. Before outlining the constraints involved, a general overview of Spanish syllable structure is in order. The following summary is based primarily on Hualde (1991):

1) Onset clusters are limited to stop + liquid (e.g. /pl, pr, tr, kr, kl, dr, bl, br, gr, gl/) or /f/ plus liquid (/fr, fl/). Most dialects exclude /dl/ or /tl/ clusters.[6]
2) Codas: a single consonant is permitted, though word-final stops are rare (normally avoided by final vowel, e.g. *parte, nube*). Complex codas are rare; word-internally /rs/ is attested (e.g. *pers.pec.ti.va*) and /ns/ may be heard in the most careful styles (*trans.por.tar*, but often deleted producing [tras.por.tar]).
3) Syllabification: Onsets are normally maximized within a word (e.g. *co.pla*) but not across word boundaries (e.g. *clu.b#abierto* but *club.#latino*).

Let us turn to the relevant OT constraints, beginning with Spanish resyllabification, since this particular process and how it is transferred to the speaker's interlanguage was of particular interest in both previous analyses of the effect of preceding environment. The basic markedness constraints, seen in (2),are used by Colina (1995) in her account of resyllabification in Spanish.[7]

(2)   a.   Onset: A syllable must have an onset.
       b.   NoCoda: A syllable must not have a coda.
       c.   *Complex Onset: Complex onsets are disallowed.
       d.   Align ([Stem, [σ): Align every initial stem-edge to an initial
             syllable edge (*i.e. syllables should not cross word bounda-
             ries*).

The rankings that Colina proposes for Spanish are seen in (3) and are
illustrated in Tableau 1.[8] The ranking of NoCoda above *Complex Onset
motivates the maximization of onsets within a word.

(3)   Onset >>Align ([Stem, [σ) >> NoCoda >> *Complex Onset

Tableau 1.   Allowable onsets are maximized within a word to satisfy NoCoda:
               hablar 'to speak'

/ablar/	Onset	Align([Stem, [σ)	NoCoda	*Complex Onset
ab.lar	*		**!	
☞ a.blar [9]	*		*	*

Onset, which is highly ranked among the markedness constraints, serves
to motivate classic resyllabification in Spanish, in which a preceding consonant provides an onset to a vowel-initial word. An example of this is seen
in Tableau 2.

Tableau 2.   Align is violated to satisfy Onset
               las alas 'wings'

/lasalas/	Onset	Align([Stem, [σ)	NoCoda
las.#a.las	*!		**
☞ la.s#a.las		*	*

Resyllabification does not occur with a consonant-initial word, however—even if doing so would create an allowable complex onset—because
ONSET is already satisfied, as seen in Tableau 3.

Tableau 3.   No maximization of onsets across word boundaries
pub lindo 'nice pub'

/publindo/	Onset	Align([Stem, [σ)	NoCoda
pu.b#lin.do		*!	*
☞ pub.#lin.do			**

The basic faithfulness constraints relevant to the present discussion are seen in (4) (as formulated in McCarthy and Prince 1995).

(4)   a.   Max I-O: Maximize segments from the input in the output. (No phonological deletion.)

b.   Dep I-O: Segments in the output are dependent on segments in the input . (No epenthesis.)

We infer that these faithfulness constraints outrank the above-mentioned markedness constraints, since Spanish does not insert epenthetic consonants to satisfy Onset (given onsetless words in isolation, e.g. *aquí*), nor are onsetless vowels deleted.

Finally, Colina proposes the following highly ranked constraint in (5) regarding onset clusters, which she holds primarily responsible for epenthesis in Spanish (Colina 1995: 63).[10]

(5)   Onset Sonority (O.Son): For two segments to be parsed in an onset, a certain distance in the sonority scale must be maintained. In Spanish, it is the maximum distance, the least sonorous onset and the most sonorous, an obstruent and a liquid.

Colina further notes that it is preferable in Spanish to epenthesize than to delete segments or violate sonority, which leads to the ranking in (6).

(6)   O.Son >> Max I-O >> Dep I-O

We now apply these rankings to the patterns in the epenthesis data. In fact, several different patterns of epenthesis emerged, which appear to represent different stages in the learning process. The learners who epenthesized most frequently (S-3, S-9, and S-8) apparently represent an early stage in phonological acquisition, one in which the native language rankings remain essentially unchanged. These three subjects strongly favored epenthesis after a pause, disfavored it after a vowel, and varied in their rates of epenthesis after consonants. Each of these environments will be considered in turn.

6.1. Epenthesis after a pause (favored)

A preceding pause is the most neutral environment for epenthesis, since there is no preceding segment to take into consideration. The speaker's behavior in this environment therefore primarily represents whether or not he or she has overcome the high ranking of Onset Sonority in Spanish. In the sample of epenthesizers in this study, three out of four subjects had an epenthesis rate of over 70% after a pause, indicating that the ranking of this constraint is still quite high in their grammars. The relevant ranking is illustrated in Tableau 4.

Tableau 4.   Preceding silence (average frequency of epenthesis = 68%).

'speak' /spik/	O.Son	Dep I-O	Onset	NoCoda
#spik	*!			*
☞ #es.pik		*	*	**

Due to the high ranking of O.Son, epenthesis is the preferred solution in the speaker's interlanguage, despite the violations of Dep I-O, Onset, and NoCoda that are incurred as a result. The same constraint ranking, however, may have a different result when we add a preceding vowel to the input.

6.2. Epenthesis after a vowel (disfavored)

As in the two previous studies by Carlisle and Abrahamsson, the present study showed that epenthesis is less likely after a vowel. It turns out that this is the expected result given the constraint rankings for Spanish, as illustrated in Tableau 5. The now relevant Align constraint is included since two words are involved in the input.

Tableau 5.   Preceding vowel (average rate of epenthesis = 17%).

'to school' /tu skul/	O.Son	Dep I-O	Onset	Align([Stem, [σ)
tu.#es.kul		*!	*	
tu.#skul	*!			
☞ tu#s.kul				*

The same constraint ranking proposed by Colina to account for regular Spanish syllable structure predicts no epenthesis in this L2 environment in favor of resyllabification, since it provides an alternative to violating highly-ranked O.Son through violation of lower-ranked Align([Stem, [σ). As Abrahamsson observed, the speaker is able to produce target-like output while still respecting native language syllable structure constraints. However, one objection might be raised: shouldn't this ranking also predict resyllabification and avoidance of epenthesis in vocalic environments in Spanish, e.g. *la escuela* *[las.kwe.la]?[11] Why should we find a difference in the way the constraints play out in the L2 as opposed to the L1?

One possibility lies in the nature of the input. Unlike a rule-based approach, OT does not require that predictable phonological material such as the /e/ before sC(C) onsets be generated rather than stored in the input. Regardless of whether the /e/ is in the input, the native speaker of Spanish learns that Onset Sonority is highly ranked since it is never violated. Within OT, the principle of Lexicon Optimization (Prince and Smolensky 1993; Itô, Mester, and Padgett 1995) suggests that the learner will choose as the real input the one which most closely resembles the output. In the case of Spanish words such as *escuela*, this would result in the learner positing an underlying /e/. Therein may lie the difference between the L1 output and the L2 output. If the so-called epenthetic /e/ in Spanish is synchronically stored in the lexicon of native speakers, they retain this vowel in the output because it is present in the Spanish input. This is clearly not the case in the L2 words. Faithfulness constraints can thus account for the difference.

6.3. Epenthesis after a consonant (varies)

We turn now to the final environment for epenthesis: a preceding consonant. One of the predictions that failed to be strongly supported in the data was that learners would be more likely to epenthesize after stop codas like /p, k/, which are disfavored in Spanish, though allowed in certain word-internal environments. Colina highlights the data in (7).

(7)   a.   *abstracto*   [as.trak.to]
       b.   *ex-alumno*   [ek.sa.lum.no]
       <u>but</u>

       c.   *ex-presidente*   [es.pre.si.den.te]   (deletion)
       d.   *nube*   (final epenthesis?)
       <u>but</u>

       e.   *apto*   [ap.to]   (no epenthesis or deletion)

Recall that Colina had proposed the constraint on codas in Spanish, seen in (8), which is evident word-finally due to higher ranked constraints prohibiting epenthesis within a morpheme.

(8)   Coda Condition: Only Coronal point of articulation in a coda.[12]

If Coda Condition were a motivating factor in epenthesis, we should see its effects in other environments, but there is very little evidence that the learners had difficulty with this constraint. These so-called disallowed codas never triggered epenthesis in the absence of a following /sC/ onset, although they were occasionally deleted phrase-finally (particularly by speaker S-8). One possibility is that this particular constraint on Spanish syllable structure, which governs only the position of an otherwise viable consonant, is easier to overcome than other constraints, and thus one of the first to be re-ranked. Note that the learner who shows the most evidence of this constraint in her grammar (S-8) is also the one who epenthesized 100% of /sC/ onsets after a pause, suggesting that she is in an earlier stage of acquisition.

In some cases, however, the presence of a consonant clearly did affect the likelihood of epenthesis. For a true picture of when epenthesis is likely after a consonant, this broad category must be broken down into subcategories based on segmental features which may either increase or decrease the likelihood of epenthesis. In the group that rarely epenthesized, it is evident that these learners have already re-ranked O.Son in their grammars (or they would continue to epenthesize after a pause). As illustrated in Table 5, however, epenthesis still occurred after alveolar fricatives. If the constraint primarily responsible for epenthesis has been re-ranked, why do these learners continue to epenthesize after /s,z/? One possible explanation is that the effects of another constraint, previously masked by highly ranked O.Son, have become evident in the output. This constraint is related to the Obligatory Contour Principle (OCP) (Leben 1973; Goldsmith 1976). Although originally formulated to rule out sequences of identical tones (e.g.

HH), this principle has been extended to explain why in many languages, sequences of segments identical in one or more features are disallowed. In the L2 situation, speakers trying to be faithful to the /sC/ onset run into a problem when the preceding consonant is /s/ or /z/–a sequence of consonants identical in both place and manner of articulation. This constraint is formalized in (9).

(9)   OCP [Place, Manner]: Adjacent segments identical in Place/ Manner are disallowed.[13]

In fact, evidence of an OCP constraint for [Coronal] alone is arguably found in the coda simplifications in Table 5. The complex codas /st, ns, nd, ld, lt, ld, rs, rt/ and /dʒd/ (as in *changed*), in which the second consonant was deleted, accounted for 23 of the 28 simplifications of biliteral codas in the data for epenthesizers. Four of the five remaining simplifications occurred in consonant clusters that also violated OCP type constraints; e.g. OCP[Dorsal] (*pink, think*) and OCP[cont] (*lives*).[14] While these types of codas were frequently deleted, dissimilar codas were left intact (e.g. /ft/ in *gift*, /mz/ in *comes*, /rk/ in *York*).[15]

The constraint ranking for these learners would be as indicated in Tableau 6, where Onset Sonority has already been re-ranked below Dep I-O to suppress epenthesis after a pause. Resyllabification does not improve the situation in this environment, since it does not break up the disallowed sequence of adjacent segments.

Tableau 6.   Preceding /s,z/

his skis /hɪz skis/	OCP [Place, Manner]	DEP I-O	O.SON
hɪz.skis	*!		*
☞ hɪ.zes.kis		*	

One might wonder whether the existence of Spanish cognates for target words in the reading instrument (e.g. *eskis* for English *skis*) may have had an influence on the presence of the epenthetic vowel in the data. In general, the reading instrument was designed to include a variety of English words containing /s+stop/ onsets without resorting to rare vocabulary that might not be familiar to the speakers, but was not rigorously screened for cognates. Fortunately, we have some indication that cognates had no appreciable effect. First, there are very few known cognates in the data (see the Appendix for a complete list of sentences used). More importantly, the list happened to include the lexical item *skis* in two different environments: once following /z/ (*his skis*, sentence pair #9) and once following a nasal (*on skis*, sentence pair #18). An examination of the tokens of epenthesis produced by the non-epenthesizing group reveals that three out of the four epenthesized at least twice in the phrase *his skis*, but never in the phrase *on skis*. The fourth subject epenthesized only in the phrases *was skating* and *thanks Stephanie*. It is clear that the cognate status of *skis* had no bearing on the likelihood of epenthesis.

The OCP constraint can therefore account for the somewhat higher rate of epenthesis after /s,z/ in both groups. Turning to the patterns in the epenthesizing group, recall that the subjects in the epenthesizing group still had trouble with the high ranking of Onset Sonority, but epenthesized less frequently after liquids (only 19% on average). It has already been shown that epenthesis was disfavored after a vowel (17% frequency) due to the alternative presented by resyllabification. Might this be an option after some consonants as well? Given the relatively low ranking of the Align constraint presented above, resyllabification should be an option unless another higher ranked constraint (or constraints) prohibits it. We need to look more closely at constraints on complex codas in Spanish.

As noted in the syllable structure summary earlier, complex codas are typically avoided in Spanish, the only common exception being /rs/ (e.g. *pers.pec.ti.va*). In addition to the Coda Condition cited in (8), Colina proposed the constraint, in (10), which she ranked above the constraints against deletion and epenthesis.

(10)   *Complex Coda: Only single consonants allowed in codas.

The high ranking of this constraint as formulated above would predict that resyllabification would only help if accompanied by epenthesis. The question mark, *?*, in Tableau 7 indicates that this candidate, though optimal in the tableau, is not borne out in the data.

Tableau 7.   Preceding liquid (average rate of epenthesis = 19%); incorrect optimal candidate.

veal special /vil spɛʃəl/	O.Son	*Complex Coda	Dep I-O	Align([Stem, [σ)
vil.#spɛ.ʃəl	*!			
vil#s.pɛ.ʃəl		*!		*
? vi.l#espɛ.ʃəl			*	*

Since the learners in question have not yet re-ranked Onset Sonority, leaving the /sp/ onset intact is not an option. Resyllabification of the /s/ with the preceding /l/ would apparently violate *Complex Coda. Yet in the data, we find that epenthesis is rare in this environment.

The problem may lie in the formulation of this constraint, which does not explain the permissible complex coda /rs/ nor exceptional codas in borrowings such as *vals, biceps, fraks, clubs,* etc. in which there is no epenthesis in the plural. Colina simply stipulates that irregular plurals are marked in the lexicon as foreign terms, re-ranking *Complex Coda under the constraint against epenthesis. A more likely explanation for the fact that this constraint can be violated in foreign borrowings is that it may not be a strongly active constraint in the language synchronically. As seen above, many complex codas are already ruled out by OCP constraints, possibly eliminating the need for a separate *Complex Coda constraint.

If this is the case, then resyllabification may indeed be an option for learners of a second language. However, the ease with which a preceding consonant may be resyllabified may very well depend on its sonority. Elsewhere in her dissertation, Colina makes reference to the constraint in (11), capturing a well-known principle of syllable structure.

(11)   Margin Sonority: Sonority must increase toward the nucleus and decrease when moving away from it.

It should not be surprising to find that a speaker would find it easier to resyllabify when the resulting coda respects Margin Sonority, and that the greater the distance in sonority, the easier (and thus more likely) the task will be. Liquids would thus be most likely to be eligible for resyllabification over epenthesis. This seems to be a case in which universal markedness constraints become visible in the interlanguage, even when they may not be crucially ranked in the native language, similar to the "emergence of the unmarked" proposed by Broselow, Chen, and Wang (1998).

One final note is in order regarding the rate of epenthesis after nasals, which varied greatly by learner. Recall that /ns/ as a coda in Spanish was said to be possible word-internally in more careful speaking styles and word-finally in plurals of foreign borrowings such as *yens*. Whether or not resyllabification after a nasal is an option for an individual learner may depend on factors such as the acceptability of /ns/ as a coda in their particular dialect of Spanish or how far the learner has progressed in re-ranking of sonority constraints.

An objection that might be raised to the OT analysis is that the proposed rankings point to only one optimal candidate, yet most speakers exhibited some degree of variation in a given environment. This variation is not all that surprising, however, if we consider the learning process from an OT perspective. As the speaker attempts to acquire the rankings of the second language, we would expect some variation in their constraint rankings. A similar observation is made by Broselow, Chen, and Wang (1998: 274), who refer to constraint rankings in the L2 learner as being "in flux." We can view the re-ranking of syllable structure constraints as the learner's ability to overcome the limits placed on their native syllable structure. Presumably this would require some attention to phonological output, which may not be continuously sustainable depending on the learner's mindset at the time. As a result, although the tableaux predict a single optimal pronunciation, we do not expect that the learner would consistently produce this output 100% of the time in this or any other context. Rather, the constraints represent the opposing forces in effect most of the time in the speaker's evolving grammar. An additional factor which might contribute to variation is the fluency of the learner's speech at any given moment, which may affect the length of the phrase being treated as a prosodic unit. This could account for the fact the fact that speakers do not always take advantage of the resyllabification option in the environment of a preceding vowel.

7. Summary

It has been suggested that the native language constraint ranking found in Spanish, along with universal markedness constraints, predict the patterns in the L2 data for /sC/ onsets as follows:

1) Epenthesis after a pause is likely due to high ranking of Onset Sonority.
2) No epenthesis is predicted after a vowel due to ranking of Align below Onset (resyllabification option is available).
3) Epenthesis after /s,z/ is expected even for learners who have re-ranked Onset Sonority, due to OCP constraints against sequences of identical elements.
4) Epenthesis is less likely after high-sonority consonants such as liquids and possibly nasals, depending on the individual, due to the possibility of resyllabification.

8. Conclusions

The data presented here bear on questions of interest for phonological theory in general, as well as Spanish phonology in particular. The differing outputs after a vowel in Spanish (presence of /e/) versus the L2 (absence of epenthetic /e/) provide indirect evidence that the so-called epenthetic /e/ in native Spanish words such as *escuela* is actually stored lexically and not generated by a rule of epenthesis. The results add to the growing body of evidence questioning the active role of epenthesis in Spanish, though it is an undeniable reality in interlanguage.

The new data presented here provide a more complete picture of the effect of preceding environment. The somewhat different patterns seen in the learners in this study highlight the fact that the stage of acquisition of the learner must be taken into consideration when making generalizations. While previous studies suggested that a preceding consonant increased the likelihood of epenthesis while a preceding pause was a neutral environment, the current study shows that epenthesis can be just as likely after a pause as after a consonant, if the learner has not yet begun to re-rank the Onset Sonority constraint. Rather, it is the resyllabification option presented by a preceding vowel that is primarily responsible for the statistically significant differences in likelihood of epenthesis.

The constraint-based analysis proposed for the data in this study also suggest an answer to the question posed by previous researchers: Why has preceding environment been found to be the first-order variable influencing rate of epenthesis in previous studies, more important than length of onset? The answer is found in the fact that preceding environment will always affect the interaction of the constraints that favor resyllabification over epenthesis, regardless of the length of the following onset. The low ranking of the Align constraint that permits standard Spanish resyllabification across word boundaries (i.e. a coda consonant as the onset of a following vowel-initial syllable) will also allow for resyllabification as an alternative to epenthesis in the environment of a preceding vowel. As for the effect of length of onset, it appears that there is no strict ranking of syllable structure constraints that would make epenthesis before a triliteral onset more optimal than when a biliteral onset is involved (e.g. resyllabification of the phrase *to spray* [tus.prej] still provides a viable alternative to epenthesis, assuming the biliteral onset left after epenthesis is an allowable one in Spanish). The explanation for this effect must lie elsewhere. It may be that the longer onset indirectly affects the interaction of the constraints by increasing the processing load for the learner and slightly increasing the chance of pausing before the onset. If the speaker breaks up the phrase with a pause, resyllabification is no longer an option. This hypothesis could be tested in a future study.

The analysis presented here shows that OT can be an effective model for representing L2 phonological transfer as it relates to epenthesis, lending support to its viability as a general phonological theory. It is superior to a rule-based approach, in that it does not require the transfer of existing rules in Spanish, nor does it require us to posit "typical interlanguage principles/strategies" as suggested by Abrahamsson (1999: 497). Instead, the transfer of the universal constraints and their ranking from the L1 accounts for the primary trends in the data. These conclusions are similar to those presented by Yip (1993) within an early OT framework for Cantonese loanword phonology. Rather than requiring a special component in the grammar, the new inputs are merely subject to the ranked constraints present in the native grammar. In the case of an L2, the native language constraint ranking applies until such time as the learner begins to acquire aspects of the L2 phonology via re-ranking of constraints, as was seen in the group of subjects who rarely epenthesized in the present study. While a usage-based approach (e.g. Bybee 2001 generally; Eddington 2001 specifically for Spanish) accounts for a variety of issues related to frequency of use, it is difficult to see how it would predict the patterns of epenthesis observed here and the status of preceding environment as the first-order variable in frequency of epenthesis.

Acknowledgments

Thanks are due to Timothy Face for guidance during the research process and to an anonymous reviewer for helpful suggestions on organization and areas that needed clarification. Any errors are, of course, my own.

Notes

1. A native speaker has observed that the string la escuela may indeed be perceived in fast speech as [laskwela], but this appears to be due to coalescence of adjacent vowels. In careful speech, the /e/ would always be present.
2. The condition as formulated by Colina did not fully account for disallowed word-final codas, given the nonexistence of /t/ in native Spanish codas.

3. Two of the ten Spanish speakers originally recorded were excluded from the study because they never modified the target onset clusters in the reading instrument (no tokens of epenthesis).
4. Despite explicit instructions, not all students remembered to read every sentence twice, and thus the total number of tokens varied by individual.
5. S-8 read sentences only once, but paused frequently
6. Dialects which allow /tl/ onsets, as in Mexican Spanish, may well be influenced by indigenous languages.
7. The present analysis assumes the Correspondence Theory version of OT (McCarthy and Prince 1995); as a result constraint names may differ slightly from those in Colina's analysis.
8. As is standard in OT analyses, the highest ranked constraint is listed farthest to the left. An asterisk indicates violation of a constraint, an exclamation mark indicates a fatal violation, and the pointing finger indicates the optimal or winning candidate in the speaker's output.
9. Spirantization of /b/ is ignored for ease of presentation since we are concerned with syllable structure.
10. Colina assumes that obstruents may be grouped together as the least sonorous segments on the sonority scale (an assumption which is supported by the results in Table 4). She notes that the fricative /f/ is allowed in complex onsets (e.g. flor 'flower') but that "more needs to be known about the status of /f/ to determine whether its acceptability in an onset cluster answers to sonority or featural specifications" (p. 46).
11. Colina did not specifically address a preceding vocalic environment in her analysis of Spanish syllable structure.
12. See note 3.
13. A similar but more specific OCP constraint on place of articulation (anterior Coronals) may account for the permissibility of /fl/ in Spanish onsets while /sl/ is prohibited (as well as /tl/ in most dialects), a fact that was left unexplained in Colina's analysis (see footnote 10). Such a constraint would allow attested /tr/ onsets since the trill is not anterior.
14. An example of this constraint in child acquisition comes from the author's son, who produced [lajbz] lives and [wejbz] waves for many months from age two to age three.
15. One might wonder why such codas triggered deletion instead of epenthesis, which is ostensibly the preferred solution in Spanish. This is likely due to a type of positional faithfulness (see Beckman 1997), though it is beyond the scope of this paper to explore this in detail.

References

Abrahamsson, Niclas
   1999   Vowel epenthesis of /sC(C)/ onsets in Spanish/Swedish inter-
           phonology: A longitudinal case study. *Language Learning* 49:
           473-508.
Beckman, Jill
   1997   Positional faithfulness. Ph.D. diss., University of Pennsylvania.
Broselow, Ellen
   1992   Transfer and universals in second language epenthesis. In, *Lan-
           guage Transfer in Language Learning*, Susan M. Gass and Larry
           Selinker (eds.), 71-86. Philadelphia: John Benjamins Publishing
           Company.
Broselow, Ellen, Su-I Chen and Chilin Wang
   1998   The emergence of the unmarked in second language phonology.
           Studies in Second Language Acquisition 20: 261-280.
Bybee, Joan
   2001   *Phonology and Language Use*. New York: Cambridge University
           Press.
Carlisle, Robert
   1997   The modification of onsets in a markedness relationship: Testing
           the interlanguage structural conformity hypothesis. *Language
           Learning* 47: 327-361.
Colina, Sonia
   1995   A constraint-based analysis of syllabification in Spanish, Cata-
           lan, and Galician. Ph.D. diss., University of Illinois at Urbana-
           Champaign.
Eckman, Fred and Gregory Iverson
   1993   Sonority and markedness among onset clusters in the interlan-
           guage of ESL learners. *Second Language Research* 9: 234-252.
Eddington, David
   2001   Spanish epenthesis: Formal and performance perspectives. *Stud-
           ies in the Linguistic Sciences* 31: 33-53.
Goldsmith, John
   1976   Autosegmental phonology. Ph.D. diss., MIT.
Hancin-Bhatt, Barbara and Rakesh Bhatt
   1997   Optimal L2 syllables: Interactions of transfer and developmental
           effects. *Studies in Second Language Acquisition* 19: 331-378.
Hodne, Barbara
   1985   Yet another look at interlanguage phonology: The modification
           of English syllable structure by native speakers of Polish. *Lan-
           guage Learning* 35: 404-422.

Hooper, Joan Bybee
1976   *An Introduction to Natural Generative Phonology.* New York: Academic Press.
Hualde, José Ignacio
1991   On Spanish syllabification. In *Current Studies in Spanish Linguistics,* Hector Campos and Fernando Martínez-Gil (eds.), 475-493. Washington, DC: Georgetown University Press.
Itô, Junko, Armin Mester and Jaye Padgett
1995   Licensing and underspecification in Optimality Theory. *Linguistic Inquiry* 26: 571-613.
Leben, William
1973   Suprasegmental phonology. Ph.D. diss., MIT.
McCarthy, John and Alan Prince
1995   Faithfulness and reduplicative identity. In *University of Massachusetts Occasional Papers in Linguistics 18: Papers in Optimality Theory,* Jill Beckman, Laura Walsh Dickey and Suzanne Urbanczyk (eds.), 249-384. Amherst, MA: Graduate Linguistic Student Association.
Prince, Alan and Paul Smolensky
1993   Optimality Theory: Constraint interaction in generative grammar. Manuscript., Rutgers University, New Brunswick, New Jersey, and University of Colorado, Boulder, Colorado.
Tarone, Elaine
1987   Some influences on the syllable structure of interlanguage phonology. In *Interlanguage Phonology: The Acquisition of a Second Language Sound System,* Georgette Ioup and Steven H. Weinberger (eds.), 232-247. Cambridge, Mass: Newbury House Publishers.
Yip, Moira
1993   Cantonese loanword phonology and optimality theory. *Journal of East Asian Linguistics* 2: 261-291.

Appendix

Sentence Pairs in Reading Instrument

1. a. I go to school three days a week.
   b. I am going to school three days a week.
2. a. I enjoy to participate in sports.
   b. I enjoy participating in sports.

3. a.   Most Americans are eating steak twice a week.
   b.   Most Americans eat steak twice a week.
4. a.   She placed the vases on a sturdy table.
   b.   She has placed the vases on a sturdy table.
5. a.   I think I will skip my math class next Friday.
   b.   I think I will be skipping my math class next Friday.
6. a.   We walked to Steve's house after the party.
   b.   We have walked to Steve's house after the party.
7. a.   Skating is a popular winter sport in Minnesota.
   b.   Skating is being a popular winter sport in Minnesota.
8. a.   I have found a great spot for a picnic.
   b.   I found a great spot for a picnic.
9. a.   Did he take his skis with him?
   b.   Did he takes his skis with him?
10. a. Are you liking this pink skirt?
    b. Do you like this pink skirt?
11. a. Yesterday I spilled my coffee all over my shirt.
    b. Yesterday I have spilled my coffee all over my shirt.
12. a. You'd better start studying more for your chemistry class.
    b. You'd better starting studying more for your chemistry class.
13. a. The American life style has changed greatly over the past fifty years.
    b. The American life style changed greatly over the past fifty years.
14. a. I am speaking to my boss on the phone right now.
    b. I speak to my boss on the phone right now.
15. a. The hot soup has scalded him when he tasted it.
    b. The hot soup scalded him when he tasted it.
16. a. Luisa is coming from Brazil, but she lives in the United States.
    b. Luisa comes from Brazil, but she lives in the United States.
17. a. Did he thanks Stephanie for the gift?
    b. Did he thank Stephanie for the gift?
18. a. Have you ever been on skis before?
    b. Were you ever on skis before?
19. a. Last Halloween we read scary stories all night long.
    b. Last Halloween we have read scary stories all night long.
20. a. When I was a little girl, I skated on this lake in the winter.
    b. When I was a little girl, I was skating on this lake in the winter.
21. a. Speaking in public was always difficult for me.
    b. Speaking in public has always been difficult for me.
22. a. The pope stays in Rome most of the year.
    b. The pope is staying in Rome most of the year.
23. a. Walking up stairs is good exercise.
    b. To walk up stairs is good exercise.
24. a. The chef has spoiled the meal last night by adding too much pepper.
    b. The chef spoiled the meal last night by adding too much pepper.

25. a. Did she wear the black skirt or the blue skirt?
    b. Was she wearing the black skirt or the blue skirt?
26. a. Bill spends every Monday night studying French.
    b. Bill is spending every Monday night studying
27. a. My favorite meal at the Italian restaurant in New York was the veal special.
    b. My favorite meal at the Italian restaurant in New York has been the veal special.

The effect of syllable weight on the determination of spoken stress in Spanish

Mark Waltermire

1. Introduction

1.1. The issue of stress placement

Spanish stress is overwhelmingly penultimate due to a strong tendency toward open syllables (i.e. those ending in a vowel) in this language. Out of a list of 33,105 non-verbs containing at least three syllables that were taken from the Dictionary of the Spanish Academy (DRAE), Bárkányi (2002) found that 27,211 of these words (82.2%) end in a vowel. The basic stress pattern for Spanish is that words ending in a vowel receive penultimate stress. However, as Bárkányi's data show, only 23,940 vowel-final words actually receive penultimate stress (88.0%) while the remainders receive antepenultimate stress (10.8%) or final stress (1.2%). A possible reason for this variability is that stress placement may not only be contingent on the weight of the final syllable of a word but also on the weights of the penultimate and antepenultimate syllables. According to Face (2000: 8), "when the penultimate syllable is light, it greatly increases the possibility of the antepenultimate syllable being perceived as stressed. In these cases a heavy antepenultimate syllable attracts perceived stress while a light antepenultimate syllable does not."

1.2. Generative accounts of Spanish stress placement

The role of syllable weight in the assignment of stress has been studied exhaustively within the rule-based generative tradition by a number of linguists (Dunlap 1991; Harris 1983, 1992; Hooper and Terrell 1976; Whitley 1976). Accounts of stress such as these typically explain exceptions to regular stress patterns through the use of abstract underlying segments and/or lexical diacritics. There are two major difficulties with rule-based accounts of stress placement. First, they are not variable. In other words, these analyses do not adequately account for the variety of stress occurrence that is evident among the three possible stress positions for Spanish words. Rules quite simply are not capable of correctly predicting spoken stress one hundred percent of the time. Recognizing that rules cannot account for all instances of stress assignment in Spanish, generative phonologists have devised algorithms based on underlying forms in order to account for exceptional words. All rule-based accounts within this tradition have depended on a variety of abstract rules and/or ways of marking exceptional instances. These include extrametrical segments (Harris 1983), redundancy rules (Whitley 1976), and lexical diacritics (Hooper and Terrell 1976) that manage to shift accent in order to achieve the correct results. Second, these kinds of procedures are exceedingly abstract and must be questioned with regard to their psychological validity. Are we to believe that speakers process words in an on-line fashion through the use of rules for regular words while resorting to even further rules to account for exceptional words? Even though generative phonologists do not purport to directly explain the cognitive processes that guide language use,

> Rules are often spoken of as if they were algorithmic operations or mental processes. If this were true then they would be candidates for attaining [psychological] reality in the strong sense. However, though they are often spoken of in this way, they are usually defined in terms of speakers' intuitions, tacit knowledge or underlying representations, and not in terms of mental processes. Since they are defined in these terms, they cannot be considered psychologically valid in the strong sense. As a result, one must speak of the psychological reality of a rule or representation in Cutler's weak sense.[1] (Eddington 1996a: 18)

I follow Eddington (1996a: 18) in his assertion that "what is potentially real in an analysis is not the formal notation with its derivations, rules and orderings" but rather the function that these rules serve in better explaining the knowledge that we have with regards to language processing and use.

1.3. Psychological approaches to language processing and use

More recent approaches to stress placement in Spanish have focused on the psychological reality that certain phonological phenomena have within human cognition. Many analyses have abandoned recourse to rules altogether given the preponderance of evidence that supports the hypothesis that phonological elements are stored for individual lexical entries in the mental lexicon and can be directly retrieved from memory (see Bybee

1985, 1988, 2001; Jackendoff 1975; Stemberger 1994). Others, however, still assert that language processing is the result of the application of rules at the moment of speech production (see Taft 1979, 1981, 1985, 1994). Some analyses have tried to bridge the gap between these two types of language processing. These analyses claim that separate mechanisms exist for the retrieval of regular versus irregular forms. For example, in the model proposed in Schreuder and Baayen (1995), it is proposed that the most time-efficient mechanism (either the use of rules or direct retrieval of a form) will apply to a given word. The model espoused by Pinker (see Pinker and Prince 1994; Pinker 1991, 1997; Prasada and Pinker 1993) suggests that rules are applied to regularly inflected words whereas irregular inflections are stored individually in the mental lexicon and therefore do not require the application of rules during processing.

1.4. The importance of experimental approaches to phonology

The failure of rules to explain the relationship between psychological reality and language use has instigated the use of experimental methods in phonology. Through experiments, linguists have gained insight into the psychological reality that certain phonological phenomena have for speakers. A wide variety of phonological phenomena in Spanish have been studied through the use of experimental methods, including diminutive formation (Eddington 2002), diphthongization in derivational morphology (Eddington 1996b), vowel perception (Figueroa 2000), palatal allomorphy in derivational morphology (Pensado 1997), diphthongization in inflectional morphology (Bybee and Pardo 1981), and perception of syllable boundaries (Sebastián-Gallés 1996).

These experiments have incorporated a variety of methods in order to ascertain the psychological reality that these phenomena have for speakers of Spanish. The most common methods incorporate nonce word probes and/or computer models of language. Nonce word probes are ideal in that speakers do not have direct access to the words in question. In other words, they do not know the phonological properties of the nonce words and must make inferences about these properties based on something other than previously stored information. Due to the fact that certain patterns emerge for nonce words that parallel those of actual forms in the mental lexicon, it can be reasonably claimed that speakers process phonological elements through analogy. Other experimental methods used in testing the existence of analogical processing employ computer models (such as Analogical Modeling

of Language, or AML [Skousen 1989], and the Tilburg Memory Based
Learner, or TiMBL [Daelemans, Zavrel, van der Sloot and van den Bosch
2003]). These computer-generated simulations of small-sized mental lexi-
cons select forms based on similarity to existing forms in a database.

1.5. Experimental approaches to Spanish stress assignment

1.5.1. Eddington's 2000 study (Analogical Modeling of Language)

Several studies of Spanish stress placement have been conducted using experimental methods. Eddington (2000) used AML in order to determine
whether this analogical model would correctly predict the stress of already-
existing words in Spanish given several variables (including the attack, nucleus, and coda for each syllable, tense, and grammatical person).[2] Using a
database of 4,970 of the most frequent Spanish words as a simulation of a
human mental lexicon, AML assigned stress correctly for the majority of
examples. The percentages with which the model assigned stress correctly
are shown below in Table 1.

Table 1.   AML predictions of Spanish stress assignment (N=4,970) (Eddington
2000)

Syllable	Percentage correct
Penultimate	98.9%
Final	93.6%
Antepenultimate	40.1%

AML did well in predicting stress for the majority of words which receive penultimate and final stress in the database. The fact that only 40.1%
of words receiving antepenultimate stress in Spanish were correctly assigned this type of stress by AML reflects the fact that there are no general
tendencies for assigning antepenultimate stress in Spanish. These results
support the claim that stress placement is determined on the basis of already existing words in the mental lexicon. In other words, when the need
arises for an unknown word to be stressed, the mental lexicon is accessed
for words that are structurally similar to the word in question and assigned
that stress by analogy.

1.5.2. Face's 2000 study (nonce probes)

Face (2000) also supports the theory that stress placement is based on analogy to existing forms. In his experiment, ten native Spanish speakers were presented 60 nonce words (five examples for each of the twelve possible combinations of heavy and light syllables for disyllabic and trisyllabic words). These nonce forms were manipulated by an MBROLI speech synthesizer (Dutoit, et al. 1996) to eliminate acoustic stress cues that normally indicate which syllable carries word stress.[3] The speakers seem to have chosen the unmarked forms (i.e. those adhering to the most frequent patterns of the language) based on whether the final syllable was closed or open. More specifically, "of the 600 responses, 445 (74.2%) chose the unmarked stress pattern" (Face 2000: 3). The selection of unmarked stress according to the phonological nature of the final syllable for the nonce words in his study is evident in Table 2.

Table 2.   Selection of unmarked stress in neutrally pronounced forms (Face 2000)

Weight of final syllable	N(=300)	%
Heavy	204	68
Light	241	80.3

As shown in Table 2, when a nonce word ending in a consonant (that is to say, a heavy final syllable) was presented to the subjects, they assigned final (unmarked) stress to the word 68% of the time. When presented a nonce word ending in a vowel (or, light final syllable), they assigned penultimate (unmarked) stress 80.3% of the time. Since the unmarked stress was not assigned consistently, especially when the final syllable was heavy, rules for assigning stress based on syllable weight cannot be seen as operative. However, since the percentages do show a tendency toward assigning unmarked stress, Face (2000) performed a statistical analysis to determine whether the weights of the penultimate and final syllables are significant factors in the choice of stress assignment. His analysis found that the weight of the final syllable is statistically significant in determining both final and penultimate stress. The statistical analysis did not, however, reveal any significant effect of the weight of the penultimate syllable on the perception of final or penultimate stress. Therefore, Face (2000) asserts that the determining factor in the perception of stress is the weight of the final syllable alone for words with penultimate and final stress. The analysis reveals that the influence of the weights of the penultimate and antepenultimate syllables is also statistically significant when the final syllable is light. Therefore, Face (2000: 8) concludes that:

> When the final syllable is light, it greatly increases the possibility of the penultimate syllable being perceived as stressed. When the penultimate syllable is light, it greatly increases the possibility of the antepenultimate syllable being perceived as stressed. In these cases a heavy antepenultimate syllable attracts perceived stress while a light antepenultimate syllable does not. In other words, syllable weight has a very real cognitive effect: A heavy syllable is far more likely to be perceived as stressed, even when there is no acoustic stress present, than is a light syllable. Furthermore, it is the rightmost heavy syllable in a word that is significant.

1.6. Purpose of the current study

The purpose of the current study is to further explore and test these claims. Since the conclusions reached by Face (2000) were based on the responses of only ten speakers, there is a need to put these claims to test with a much wider sample of speakers in order to ascertain with absolute certainty that heavy syllables have a real cognitive effect for speakers in the assignment of stress to Spanish words. In order to replicate this study in a consistent manner, I used the same list of nonce words used in Face (2000). In this way, I have been able to control the experiment for the same factors deemed important in the creation of this type of nonce word probe.[4] By reproducing a previous study, our understanding of stress placement in Spanish and the cognitive effect of heavy syllables will be furthered. It should be noted, however, that certain changes have been made in this study which differ slightly from Face (2000). These will be discussed in the next section.

2. Methodology used in the experiment

2.1. Procedure

In order to determine whether native Spanish speakers are psychologically cognizant of stress placement based on syllable weight as predicted in Face (2000), a written questionnaire of 60 nonce words was given to 41 subjects, all native speakers of Spanish.[5] This questionnaire made use of the nonce words used in Face (2000). The subjects indicated spoken stress with a written accent mark for each nonce form following their native intuitions regarding stress. In other words, they marked stress according to how they would pronounce the word were it an actual word in Spanish. The decision to use a written questionnaire was based on two factors. First, there was a problem with Face's original procedure, which could be avoided by using a written questionnaire. Face (2000) made use of nonce words which were acoustically neutralized based on vowel duration alone. Therefore, syllable duration might have altered the choices made by his subjects (see this volume for a detailed analysis of the corrected experiment). Second, the use of a written questionnaire was more effective in the willful participation of the 41 subjects, given the short amount of time needed to complete the questionnaire (only about ten minutes). Subjects were not given any sort of time limit, either. I feel that this aspect of the experiment reduced anxiety and allowed subjects enough time to think about how they would pronounce the nonce words were they actual words in their native language.

2.2. Subjects

The experiment was conducted with the cooperation of 41 native Spanish speakers who are currently studying English as a second language at the Universidad de Murcia in Murcia, Spain. Out of the 41 subjects, 40 range in age from 17 to 26. One of the speakers is older than 26. No linguists, of course, were given the questionnaire, as they are much more conscious of the information being solicited by this type of study.

2.3. Materials

The same group of nonce words used in Face (2000) was used in the current study. This set of words comprises all possible combinations of heavy and light syllables for disyllabic and trisyllabic words, with five examples each for the twelve combinations. Heavy syllables for words used in the experiment have one of the following consonants in the coda: /d/, /l/, /m/, /n/, or /r/. Light syllables are characterized by their lack of a coda and end in one of the following vowels: /i/, /e/, /a/, /o/, or /u/. It should be noted that the only word-final vowel for any of the nonce forms was /a/. This is important due to the morphological function of stressed word-final /i/, /e/, and /o/, which are the preterit tense endings for regular verbs in Spanish for first person singular (–/é/ for first conjugation verbs and –/í/ for second and

third conjugation verbs) and third person singular (all of which end in –/ó/).
Words with the following syllable weight combinations appeared in random order on the questionnaire (H=heavy, L=light: HH, HL, LL, LH,
HHH, HHL, HLH, HLL, LHH, LHL, LLH, and LLL). The words were
randomized so that no effects of priming for the same stress patterns for
certain syllable weight combinations would skew the results. Note also that
none of the nonce words ended in –/ar/, –/er/, or –/ir/ given that these are
the infinitival endings for the three verb conjugations in Spanish and cate-
gorically receive final stress. The word final rhymes
    –/an/ and –/en/ were also avoided for the nonce forms since these could
potentially be construed as third person plural inflectional endings for the
present indicative, present subjunctive, or imperative tenses, which cate-
gorically receive penultimate stress. The questionnaire appears in its en-
tirety as Appendix A.

3. Results

In order to better control for the interaction of syllable weights for each
possible weight combination for the 60 words, the words were separated
into disyllabic and trisyllabic categories. A total of 2,439 tokens resulted
from the approximately 60 responses for each of the 41 subjects.[6] Of these
2,439 tokens, 815 were disyllabic words. These could be assigned either
final or penultimate stress (see Table 3). The percentages of stress assigned
to each of the individual nonce words used in this experiment can be seen
in Appendix B.

Table 3.   Distribution of syllable stress for disyllabic words according to possible
syllable weight combinations (H=heavy, L=light)

Weight combinations	Penult. stress	Final stress
HH	66/202 (32.7%)	136/202 (67.3%)
HL	204/205 (99.5%)	1/205 (0.5%)
LL	197/204 (96.6%)	7/204 (3.4%)
LH	52/204 (25.5%)	152/204 (74.5%)

It is not surprising that the majority of nonce words ending in a consonant were assigned final stress by the subjects. This was the most frequent
choice of stress despite the weight of the penultimate syllable. Therefore, a
word such as 'ban.sil' was assigned final stress almost equally as often as a
word such as 'pa.ton' (67.3% compared to 74.5%). Likewise, words ending

in light syllables were most often assigned penultimate stress. The assignment of stress to these words seems to not have been contingent upon the weight of the penultimate syllable. Words ending in a vowel were assigned penultimate stress in 401 out of 409 instances (or 98% of the time) regardless of the weight of the penultimate syllable.

The interaction of syllable weights is largely deterministic for words comprised of two syllables. This interaction is much more difficult to see, however, when a word has three syllables. For trisyllabic words, stress may be based upon the weight of not only the final syllable but also on the weights of the penultimate and antepenultimate syllables (following Face 2000). For example, words such as 'com.bal.tur' or 'bor.da.nor' are predicted to receive final stress since they have heavy final syllables, whereas words ending in a vowel (such as 'bir.san.ca' or 'fan.du.la') are expected to receive penultimate stress. However, what types of syllable weight combinations (if any) favor antepenultimate stress? The interaction of syllable weights for all three syllables is crucial in understanding whether syllable weight affects stress placement on the antepenultimate syllable. A total of 1,624 trisyllabic words were assigned stress by the subjects. Table 4 shows the distribution of syllable stress for all possible syllable weight combinations for trisyllabic words. For a more detailed account of the type of stress assigned to individual words in this study, see Appendix B.

Table 4. Distribution of syllable stress for trisyllabic words according to possible syllable weight combinations (H=heavy, L=light)

Weight combinations	Antepenult. stress	Penult. stress	Final stress
HHH	34/203 (16.8%)	24/203 (11.8%)	145/203 (71.4%)
HHL	16/204 (7.8%)	186/204 (91.2%)	2/204 (1%)
HLH	28/202 (13.9%)	34/202 (16.8%)	140/202 (69.3%)
HLL	53/203 (26.1%)	150/203 (73.9%)	0/203 (0%)
LHH	23/203 (11.3%)	35/203 (17.3%)	145/203 (71.4%)
LHL	17/204 (8.3%)	186/204 (91.2%)	1/204 (0.5%)
LLH	12/203 (5.9%)	18/203 (8.9%)	173/203 (85.2%)
LLL	19/202 (9.4%)	183/202 (90.6%)	0/202 (0%)

As shown in Table 4, there is a strong tendency to avoid antepenultimate stress. Only 202 trisyllabic words were assigned antepenultimate stress (12.4%). The only type of syllable combination that shows any signs of favoring antepenultimate stress is when the antepenultimate syllable is heavy while the final and penultimate syllables are light. The tendency against assigning antepenultimate stress may be interpreted as a result of two possible factors. First, words with antepenultimate stress are not exceedingly common in Spanish. Out of a total of 33,105 nouns taken from the 21st edition of the Dictionary of the Spanish Academy (DRAE), Bárkányi (2002) shows that only 3,126 (9.4%) receive antepenultimate stress. This percentage is very similar to that found in this study (12.4%). Second, the assignment of stress to the antepenultimate syllable seems to be favored when both final and penultimate syllables are light. This means that the choice of antepenultimate stress depends on two syllable weight requirements (instead of one), therefore greatly reducing the frequency of this type of stress in Spanish. This requirement is reflected in Table 4 and also in the DRAE corpus. Out of the 3,126 words with antepenultimate stress found in the DRAE corpus, 2,938 (94%) have a light final and a light penultimate syllable (either HLL or LLL).

The distribution of stress placement for these nonce words conforms largely to the predictions made in Face (2000). The rightmost heavy syllable favors stress placement for all possible syllable weight combinations with the exception of one. Notice that HLL syllable combinations favor penultimate stress. The subjects for the current study chose penultimate stress for these combinations 73.9% of the time. Though they also chose antepenultimate stress more frequently for this type of combination than any other (at 26.1%), why did they still overwhelmingly place penultimate stress on these words? Perhaps due to such infrequent occurrence of antepenultimate stress in Spanish, the weight of this syllable is not extremely influential in the assignment of stress to trisyllabic words. Even when the antepenultimate syllable is heavy, the subjects prefer assigning penultimate stress to words ending in vowels. This choice supports the idea that the most frequently occurring stress patterns for actual Spanish nouns are accessed by speakers, who then assign like stress to novel forms through the process of analogy.

4. Analysis

To test whether the distribution of stress placement is actually significantly affected by syllable weight, syllable weights and the stress chosen by the consultants for the disyllabic and trisyllabic words were entered into VARBRUL (Pintzuk 1988; Rand and Sankoff 1990). VARBRUL is a statistical analysis program that generates probability weights that correspond to observed frequencies in a corpus. This program converts frequencies of occurrence of a variable (for example, stress position) according to certain linguistic factors into probability weights. This weight index reflects the effect that these factors have on the occurrence of the dependent variable. VARBRUL also gives the statistical significance of the established correlations. For a correlation to be statistically significant, the probability of error must be less than five cases out of 100 (p < 0.05).

Disyllabic and trisyllabic words were analyzed separately. The dependent variables used were stress position (final and penultimate for disyllabic words and final, penultimate, and antepenultimate for trisyllabic words). The independent variables used were syllable weight (light and heavy) for each of the possible syllables. These results are shown in Tables 5-8.

Table 5 shows the probability with which a word received final stress according to the weight of the final and penultimate syllables. Contrary to the findings presented in Face (2000), both the weights of the final syllable and penultimate syllable were determined by VARBRUL to be statistically significant in the determination of stress placement for disyllabic words. When two or more factors are determined to be significant in the choice of the dependent variable, it is extremely important to determine the range within each factor group. The group that has a greater range is more powerful in the co-occurrence of factors and the dependent variable. Therefore, it is highly probable that a disyllabic word ending in a heavy final syllable will receive final stress. The weight of the penultimate syllable, though significant, is not as strong a determiner of final stress placement for disyllabic words.

Table 5. Variable rule analysis of the contribution of syllable weight to the probability of final stress placement for disyllabic words (p<.05)

Syllable position	Syllable weight	Factor weight
Final		
	Heavy	.92
	Light	.08
		Range 84
Penultimate		
	Light	.56
	Heavy	.44
		Range 12

This type of analysis was perfectly suited for disyllabic words in that VARBRUL can only compare two dependent variables given all of the independent variables. It does not work so easily, however, with trisyllabic words since three dependent variables must be accounted for in the analysis. This aspect of the program was overcome by running three separate analyses. The results of the first analysis are shown in Table 6. The dependent variables used in this analysis were final stress versus other stress (penultimate or antepenultimate). The weights of both the final syllable and the antepenultimate syllable were selected by VARBRUL as statistically significant in the determination of final stress placement for trisyllabic words.

Table 6.   Variable rule analysis of the contribution of syllable weight to the probability of final stress placement for trisyllabic words (p<.05)

Syllable position	Syllable weight	Factor weight
Final		
	Heavy	.97
	Light	.03
		Range 94
Antepenultimate		
	Light	.55
	Heavy	.45
		Range 10

As with disyllabic words, the weight of the final syllable for trisyllabic words is the most powerful determiner of final stress. The probability with which a trisyllabic word ending in a consonant will be given final stress is extremely high. These findings further support the claim made in Face (2000) that the weight of the final syllable seems to be a psychologically real factor for speakers during the assignment of stress. Contrary to Face's findings, however, the weight of the antepenultimate syllable is also significant in the assignment of final stress to nonce words. When this syllable is light, the probability that the word will receive final stress is increased. The subjects' choice of stress placement is clearly based on the combination of these syllable weights, not merely on the weight of the final syllable.

For the second statistical analysis of trisyllabic words, the probability of co-occurrence of syllable weight factors with penultimate stress was generated. The dependent variables were, therefore, penultimate stress versus other stress (final or antepenultimate). The results of this analysis are shown below in Table 7.

Table 7. Variable rule analysis of the contribution of syllable weight to the probability of penultimate stress placement for trisyllabic words (p<.05)

Syllable position	Syllable weight	Factor weight
Final		
	Light	.87
	Heavy	.13
		Range 74
Penultimate		
	Heavy	.56
	Light	.44
		Range 12
Antepenultimate		
	Light	.54
	Heavy	.46
		Range 8

Table 7 clearly indicates that even though all three syllable weights are significant in the determination of penultimate stress, the weight of the final syllable is the most powerful factor. Though this analysis supports the conclusion proposed in Face (2000) that the rightmost heavy syllable favors stress, it also shows that the weight of the antepenultimate syllable is significant in the determination of stress placement. Given this evidence, it can now be proposed that there is a much more subtle interplay of syllable weight factors in the determination of stress placement for nonce words than that originally proposed in Face (2000).

Considering that there is a significant interaction between all syllable weights in the determination of penultimate stress placement for trisyllabic nonce words, a third analysis using VARBRUL was conducted to determine whether the weights of all syllables also affect the determination of antepenultimate stress placement. In this analysis, the dependent variables were antepenultimate stress versus other stress (final or penultimate). The results are shown in Table 8.

Table 8. Variable rule analysis of the contribution of syllable weight to the probability of antepenultimate stress placement for trisyllabic words (p<.05)

Weight of antepenultimate syllable	Factor weight
Heavy	.59
Light	.41

Only the weight of the antepenultimate syllable was determined by VARBRUL to be statistically significant in the assignment of antepenultimate stress. The probability with which a word will receive antepenultimate stress is much greater when the antepenultimate syllable of the word is heavy. Thus, the weight of the final and penultimate syllables cannot be seen as directly powerful factors in the determination of antepenultimate stress. However, the roles of final and penultimate syllable weights should not be underestimated. As shown in Table 4, the choice of antepenultimate stress is frequent only when these syllables are light. When this evidence is taken into consideration, it is clear that the choice of antepenultimate stress occurs primarily when only the antepenultimate syllable is heavy. It is disfavored for all other syllable weight combinations.

5. Conclusion

The results of the current study corroborate the claim made in Face (2000) that syllable weights significantly influence the choice of stress placement for novel words and therefore have a very real cognitive effect for speakers. The current study, however, shows that the interaction between these syllable weights is much more complex than that proposed in Face (2000). The differences in the results for the two studies might have been caused by the different methodologies employed. The use of a questionnaire may have lead to the more frequent choice of antepenultimate stress since the subjects were not processing spoken speech and therefore had more time to choose stress. When faced with determining the most logical stress for a nonce word at the very moment of speech, it seems likely that speakers would choose the most frequently occurring stress positions (final or penultimate) while not fully considering the least frequently occurring one (antepenultimate).

This study shows that the weight of the final syllable is not the only statistically significant factor in the assignment of stress to disyllabic nonce words. The weight of the penultimate syllable also significantly influences the choice of stress placement for these words. That is, when the penultimate syllable is light, there is a greater probability that the word will be assigned final stress. If it is heavy, however, it is less probable that the word will be assigned final stress. This interplay of both syllable weights as significant factors in the choice of stress placement for disyllabic nonce words supports the claim that rules do not govern stress assignment. A heavy final syllable alone does not dictate the assignment of final stress.

The weight of the penultimate syllable also influences the choice of stress placement.

The current study shows that a much more complex interaction of syllable weights also determines the placement of stress for trisyllabic words. In the determination of stress placement, the weights of all syllables are significant in one way or another. The weight of the antepenultimate syllable plays a much greater role in the placement of stress than previously thought. For example, when determining final stress placement for trisyllabic words, both the final and antepenultimate syllable weights are significant, not merely the weight of the final syllable (as proposed in Face 2000). The choice of final stress is significantly limited when the antepenultimate syllable is heavy. In the determination of penultimate stress, the weights of all three syllables are significant. Though the weight of the final syllable is consistently the most powerful factor in the placement of stress for nonce words, the importance of the two other syllable weights cannot be overlooked, as these also influence the choice of stress placement. Only the antepenultimate syllable weight directly determines the placement of antepenultimate stress. The choice of antepenultimate stress, however, occurs primarily when the penultimate and final syllables are light. For this reason, the weights of the penultimate and final syllables must also be considered important factors in the determination of antepenultimate stress.

Notes

1. Cutler (1979) defines two senses in which language use may be considered psychologically real. He defines them in the following way:
   In the strong sense, the claim that a particular level of linguistic analysis X, or postulated process Y, is psychologically real implies that the ultimately correct psychological model of human language processing will include stages corresponding to X or mental operations corresponding to Y. The weak sense of the term implies only that language users can draw on knowledge of their language which is accurately captured by the linguistic generalization in question. (79)
2. These variables were chosen for a variety of reasons. The phonemes comprising the nucleus and coda show tendencies with regard to stress placement in Spanish. As described at the outset of the current study, regular stress is assigned to the penultimate syllable for words ending in a vowel whereas it is assigned to the final syllable when the word ends in a consonant other than /s/ or /n/. What is considered regular, however, is based on frequency (which may also be considered the 'unmarked' form) and is general in that this is not a categorical rule. The factors of tense and grammatical person were used in or-

der to better simulate stress assignment when morphological properties are considered. In Spanish, regular preterit verb forms end in stressed vowels for first person (–/é/ and –/í/) and third person (–/ó/).
3. Face (2004) has since made modifications to the nonce words used in this study. In Face (2000), the words were not controlled acoustically for syllable duration, only vowel duration, which could have resulted in added duration of a consonant-final syllable. This factor, however, does not affect the current study since the nonce forms were presented to the subjects in questionnaire form.
4. The factors controlled for in the creation of the 60 nonce words were acceptability among native speakers (which was judged by a native Spanish speaker), dissimilarity among other actually-existing words in Spanish, and non-inclusion of /s/ as a word-final phoneme since words ending in this consonant (also perhaps /n/; see Aske 1990) tend to receive penultimate stress.
5. I would like to thank José Antonio Mompeán González for his help in administering the questionnaires.
6. Some words were not assigned stress by the subjects for reasons unknown.

References

Aske, Jon
  1990   Disembodied rules versus patterns in the lexicon: Testing the psychological reality of Spanish stress rules. In *Proceedings of the Sixteenth Annual Meeting of the Berkeley Linguistics Society*, Kira Hall, Jean-Pierre Koenig, Michael Meacham, Sondra Reinman and Laurel A. Sutton (eds.), 30-45. Berkeley: Berkeley Linguistics Society.
Bárkányi, Zsuzsanna
  2002   A fresh look at quantity sensitivity in Spanish. *Linguistics* 40: 375–394.
Bybee, Joan
  1985   *Morphology: A Study of the Relation between Meaning and Form*. Philadelphia: John Benjamins.
  1988   Morphology as lexical organization. In *Theoretical Approaches to Morphology*, Michael Hammond and Michael Noonan (eds.), 119–141. San Diego: Academic Press.
  2001   *Phonology and Language Use*. Cambridge: Cambridge University Press.
Bybee, Joan and Elly Pardo
  1981   On lexical and morphological conditioning of alternations: A nonce-probe experiment with Spanish verbs. *Linguistics* 19: 937–968.

Cutler, Anne
1979   The psychological reality of word formation and lexical stress rules. In *Proceedings of the Ninth International Congress of Phonetic Sciences*, vol. 2, Eli Fischer-Jorgensen, Jorgen Rischel, and Nina Thorsen (eds.), 79–85. Copenhagen: University of Copenhagen.
Daelemans, Walter, Jakub Zavrel, Ko van der Sloot and Antal van den Bosch
2003   *TiMBL: Tilburg Memory-based Learner, version 5.0, Reference Guide*. Induction of Linguistic Knowledge Technical Report, ILK 03-10. Tilburg, Netherlands: ILK Research Group, Tilburg University. Available at http://ilk.kub.nl/.
Dunlap, Elaine
1991   Issues in the moraic structure of Spanish. Ph.D. diss., University of Massachusetts, Amherst.
Dutoit, T., V. Pagel, N. Pierret, F. Bataille, and O. Van der Vrecken
1996   The MBROLA project: Towards a set of high-quality speech synthesizers free of use for non-commercial purposes. *Proceedings of ICSLP '96*, Philadelphia, vol. 3, 1393–1396.
Eddington, David
1996a   The psychological status of phonological analyses. *Linguistica* 36: 17–37.
1996b   Dipthongization in Spanish derivational morphology: An emperical investigation. *Hispanic Linguistics* 8: 1–35.
2000   Spanish stress assignment within the analogical modeling of language. *Language* 76: 92–109.
2002   Spanish diminutive formation without rules or constraints. *Linguistics* 40: 395–419.
Face, Timothy L.
2000   The role of syllable weight in the perception of Spanish stress. In *Hispanic Linguistics at the Turn of the Millennium*, Héctor Campos, Elena Herburger, Alfonso Morales-Front and Thomas J. Walsh (eds.), 1–13. Somerville, MA: Cascadilla Press.
2004   Perceiving what isn't there: Non-acoustic cues for perceiving Spanish stress. In this volume.
Figueroa, Neysa
2000   An acoustic and perceptual study of vowels preceding deleted post-nuclear /s/ in Puerto Rico Spanish. In *Hispanic Linguistics at the Turn of the Millennium*, Héctor Campos, Elena Herburger, Alfonso Morales-Front and Thomas J. Walsh (eds.), 66–79. Somerville, MA: Cascadilla Press.

Harris, James
  1983   *Syllable Structure and Stress in Spanish: A Non-Linear Analysis.*
          Cambridge, MA: MIT Press.
  1992   *Spanish Stress: The Extrametricality Issue.* Washington, DC:
          Indiana University Linguistics Club.
Hooper, Joan Bybee and Tracy Terrell
  1976   Stress assignment in Spanish: A natural generative analysis.
          Glossa 10: 64–110.
Jackendoff, Ray
  1975   Morphological and semantic regularities in the lexicon. *Language* 51: 639–671.
Pensado, Carmen
  1997   On the Spanish depalatalization of /n/ and /ll/ in rhymes. In *Issues in the Phonology and Morphology of the Major Iberian Languages*, Fernando Martínez-Gil and Alfonso Morales Front (eds.), 595–618. Washington, DC: Georgetown University Press.
Pinker, Steven
  1991   Rules of language. *Science* 253: 530–534.
  1997   Words and rules in the human brain. *Nature* 387: 547–548.
Pinker, Steven and Alan Prince
  1994   Regular and irregular morphology and the psychological status of rules of grammar. In *The Reality of Linguistic Rules*, Susan D. Lima, Roberta L. Corrigan, and Gregory K. Iverson (eds.), 321–351. Amsterdam: John Benjamins.
Pintzuk, Susan
  1988   *VARBRUL Programs.* Philadelphia: University of Pennsylvania Department of Linguistics.
Prasada, Sandeep and Steven Pinker
  1993   Generalization of regular and irregular morphological patterns. *Language and Cognitive Processes* 8: 1–56.
Rand, David and David Sankoff
  1990   *GOLDVARB: A Variable Rule Application for the Macintosh.* Montreal: Université de Montréal.
Schreuder, Robert and Harald Baayen
  1995   Modeling morphological processing. In *Morphological Aspects of Language Processing*, Laurie Beth Feldman (ed.), 131–153. Hillsdale, NJ: Erlbaum.
Sebastián-Gallés, Núria
  1996   Speech perception in Catalan and Spanish. In *Language Processing in Spanish,* Manuel Carreiras, José E. García-Albea, and Núria Sebastián-Gallés (eds.), 1–19. Hillsdale, NJ: Erlbaum.

Skousen, Royal
 1989   *Analogical Modeling of Language.* Dordrecht: Kluwer Academic.
Stemberger, Joseph Paul
 1994   Rule-less morphology at the phonology-lexicon interface. In *The Reality of Linguistic Rules*, Susan D. Lima, Roberta L. Corrigan, and Gregory K. Iverson (eds.), 147–169. Amsterdam: John Benjamins.
Taft, Marcus
 1979   Recognition of affixed words and the word-frequency effect. *Memory and Cognition* 7: 263–272.
 1981   Prefix stripping revised. *Journal of Verbal Learning and Verbal Behavior* 20: 289–297.
 1985   The decoding of words in lexical access: A review of the morphographic approach. In *Reading Research: Advances in Theory and Practice: Vol. 5*, D. Besner, T. Walker, and G. MacKinnon (eds.), 83–124. New York: Academic Press.
 1994   Interactive activation as a framework for understanding morphological processing. *Language and Cognitive Processes* 9: 271–294.
Whitley, Stanley
 1976   Stress in Spanish: Two approaches. *Lingua* 39: 301–332.

Appendix A

Si estas palabras fueran nuevas palabras en español, ¿dónde caería el acento *hablado*?

Considera la palabra tamambi, ¿dónde suena mejor el acento *hablado*?

Si *dirías* "tamambí", pon un acento escrito sobre la /i/, ahora tamambí

Si *dirías* "tamambi", pon un acento escrito sobre la segunda /a/, ahora tamámbi

Si *dirías* "támambi", pon un acento escrito sobre la primera /a/, ahora támambi.

dafantul	torilca	combaltur	dortipor	torencor
tertur	polcada	fafurnal	calseba	tifor
fulanga	salmedad	padorsel	jansoda	tana
landanson	bordanor	silangon	sufapad	pensor
tacamba	tagul	galefa	fandula	bansil
paterba	masapur	linlenton	mentertad	piluca
jurlandil	nijad	fadola	fundamil	terpa
reldon	paba	pirta	mabina	fontal
birsanca	desa	paton	lula	tiroga
nonca	contabal	fandolta	noca	benca
tajonil	cabadon	tortina	soserol	posal
jornenca	pontumba	sobenda	dintalda	fumpa

Así que cada palabra que sigue necesita un acento escrito.

Edad_____

País de nacimiento_____

Lengua nativa_____

Appendix B

Below, the raw numbers and percentages (in parentheses) of choice of stress placement are given for each of the words used in the experiment.

Nonce word	Final stress	Penult. stress	Antepenult. stress
bansil	30 (75)	10 (25)	n/a
fontal	39 (95.1)	2 (4.9)	n/a
pensor	32 (82.1)	7 (17.9)	n/a
reldon	25 (61)	16 (39)	n/a
tertur	10 (24.4)	31 (75.6)	n/a
benca	0 (0)	41 (100)	n/a
fumpa	1 (2.4)	40 (97.6)	n/a
nonca	0 (0)	41 (100)	n/a
pirta	0 (0)	41 (100)	n/a
terpa	0 (0)	41 (100)	n/a
desa	4 (9.8)	37 (90.2)	n/a
lula	0 (0)	41 (100)	n/a
noca	0 (0)	40 (100)	n/a
paba	1 (2.4)	40 (97.6)	n/a
tana	2 (4.9)	39 (95.1)	n/a
nijad	26 (63.4)	15 (36.6)	n/a
paton	31 (75.6)	10 (24.4)	n/a
posal	36 (87.8)	5 (12.2)	n/a
tagul	36 (87.8)	5 (12.2)	n/a
tifor	23 (57.5)	17 (42.5)	n/a
combaltur	28 (68.3)	10 (24.4)	3 (7.3)
landanson	18 (46.2)	4 (10.3)	17 (43.5)
linlenton	29 (70.7)	2 (4.9)	10 (24.4)
mentertad	35 (85.4)	4 (9.7)	2 (4.9)
jurlandil	35 (85.4)	4 (9.7)	2 (4.9)

Nonce word	Final stress	Penult. stress	Antepenult. stress
birsanca	1 (2.4)	39 (95.2)	1 (2.4)
dintalda	1 (2.4)	38 (92.7)	2 (4.9)
fandolta	0 (0)	37 (90.2)	4 (9.8)
pontumba	0 (0)	34 (82.9)	7 (17.1)
jornenca	0 (0)	38 (95)	2 (5)
bordanor	26 (68.4)	7 (18.4)	5 (13.2)
dortipor	23 (56.1)	5 (12.2)	13 (31.7)
fundamil	29 (70.7)	8 (19.5)	4 (9.8)
contabal	22 (53.7)	14 (34.1)	5 (12.2)
salmedad	40 (97.6)	0 (0)	1 (2.4)
fandula	0 (0)	14 (34.1)	27 (65.9)
calseba	0 (0)	32 (78)	9 (22)
polcada	0 (0)	34 (85)	6 (15)
tortina	0 (0)	40 (97.6)	1 (2.4)
jansoda	0 (0)	30 (75)	10 (25)
dafantul	24 (58.5)	7 (17.1)	10 (24.4)
fafurnal	31 (75.6)	7 (17.1)	3 (7.3)
padorsel	32 (78)	5 (12.2)	4 (9.8)
silangon	33 (84.6)	4 (10.3)	2 (5.1)
torencor	25 (61)	12 (29.3)	4 (9.7)
fulanga	0 (0)	38 (92.7)	3 (7.3)
paterba	0 (0)	34 (85)	6 (15)
sobenda	0 (0)	37 (90.2)	4 (9.8)
tacamba	1 (2.4)	39 (95.2)	1 (2.4)
torilca	0 (0)	38 (92.7)	3 (7.3)
cabadon	37 (90.2)	4 (9.8)	0 (0)
masapur	29 (70.7)	9 (22)	3 (7.3)
soserol	38 (92.7)	1 (2.4)	2 (4.9)
sufapad	33 (84.6)	1 (2.6)	5 (12.8)
tajonil	36 (87.8)	3 (7.3)	2 (4.9)
fadola	0 (0)	32 (80)	8 (20)
galefa	0 (0)	39 (97.5)	1 (2.5)
mabina	0 (0)	34 (85)	6 (15)
piluca	0 (0)	39 (95.1)	2 (4.9)
tiroga	0 (0)	39 (95.1)	2 (4.9)

Part III

Segmental constraints

Gestural timing and rhotic variation in Spanish codas

Travis G. Bradley

1. Introduction

In Browman and Goldstein's (1989, 1990, 1991, 1992) theory of Articulatory Phonology, gestures are dynamically, spatio-temporally defined articulatory movements that produce a constriction in the vocal tract. Gestures function not only as units of articulation but also as the primitives of phonological organization. This property sets Articulatory Phonology apart from most theories of phonology which relegate phonetic timing to an implementation component derivationally ordered after the phonology proper. A central claim of the gestural model of Articulatory Phonology is that many phonological processes, such as assimilation, deletion and insertion, can be reduced to two types of modifications occurring in casual speech: reduction in the magnitude of gestures, and temporal realignment of adjacent gestures. Furthermore, the model predicts that overlap between gestures involving different articulators will not affect the trajectory of either gesture, while overlap between gestures involving the same articulator will produce a blending of gestural characteristics, which "shows itself in spatial changes in one or both of the overlapping gestures" (Browman and Goldstein 1990: 362).

This paper explores the role of gestural alignment in the realization of heterosyllabic /rC/ clusters, such as found in *árbol* /arbol/ 'tree' and *carne* /karne/ 'meat', across different Spanish varieties. Many Latin American Spanish dialects are characterized by assibilation, a process whereby an alveolar tap /r/ or trill /r/ is realized phonetically as a strident fricative [ř]. While Colantoni (2001) finds no assibilation of coda /r/ in Argentine dialects, data from Argüello (1978) show that the phenomenon is more widespread in the Spanish of highland Ecuador, where assibilation affects homorganic /rC/ clusters in casual speech.[1] As Colantoni points out, Argüello provides detailed phonetic description of the Ecuadorian rhotic phones but "never demonstrates spectrographically that rhotics are assibilated in syllable coda position" (60). In the present study, spectrographic analysis is presented to show that coda assibilation is empirically attested in this variety. An analysis of rhotic variation in Spanish codas is proposed in which the articulatory preference for overlap between adjacent consonantal gestures conflicts with the competing requirement that underlying clusters be perceptually recoverable. Because it is built directly upon the notion of competition and conflict resolution, Optimality Theory (Prince and Smolensky 1993; McCarthy and Prince 1993a, 1993b, 1995) is an appropriate framework for analyzing cross-dialectal variation in the gestural timing of /rC/ clusters.

This paper is organized as follows. Section 1 reviews previous studies on the realization of /rC/ clusters in Peninsular Spanish and then documents a casual speech alternation between [r] and the assibilated fricative [ř] in highland Ecuadorian Spanish. Section 2 investigates the acoustic properties of assibilation via spectrographic analysis of relevant data collected from highland Ecuadorian Spanish speakers. In Section 3, I provide a phonetically motivated account of coda /r/ assibilation using Browman and Goldstein's gestural model. Section 4 integrates the phonetic explanation into an Optimality-theoretic analysis that captures the attested differences in /rC/ cluster realization across dialects. Section 5 summarizes and concludes.

2. Rhotic variation in Spanish /rC/ clusters

It has long been noted that in Spanish clusters containing /r/, a vowel fragment (a.k.a. *svarabhakti*, Whitney 1889) typically intervenes between the rhotic and the adjacent consonant (Gili Gaya 1921; Lenz 1892; Navarro Tomás 1918). The data in (1) from Malmberg (1965: 34–8) illustrate svarabhakti in /rC/ clusters in Peninsular Spanish:[2]

(1)   *árboles*   [ar³.β]
       'trees'
       verdes   [er³.ð̬]
       'green'
       cargar   [ar³.ɣ]
       'to load'
       fuerza   [er³.s]
       'force'

Although represented here simply as [ᵊ] in narrow phonetic transcription, the svarabhakti fragment has formant structure similar to that of the nuclear vowel appearing on the opposite side of the tap constriction (Quilis 1993: 337–42). Furthermore, the phonetic measurements of Gili Gaya (1921: 277–8) and Malmberg (1965: 10, 35) show that the svarabhakti fragment varies in duration, often approximating that of an unstressed vowel (see Section 2.1 below for more on durational variability).

In addition to the acoustic svarabhakti fragment, /rC/ clusters in Peninsular Spanish also exhibit articulatory characteristics that differ from those of other clusters, such as /lC/. Using the ElectroMagnetic Midsaggital Articulometry technique, Romero (1996) shows that Castilian Spanish [ld] exhibits gestural overlap and blending, while [rð̞] is articulated in sequential fashion.[3] The two-dimensional displays in Figure 1 (a,b) show tongue tip trajectories for the interdental fricative [ð̞], the dental stop [t], the alveolar lateral [l] and tap [r], and the clusters [ld] and [rð̞].

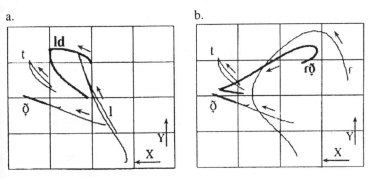

Figure 1. Tongue tip movement paths for intervocalic [l, ð̞, ld, t] in (a) and [r, ð̞, rð̞, t] in (b), both in the context of vowel [o] (taken from Romero 1996: 105–6)

According to Articulatory Phonology, overlap between gestures involving the same articulator will produce a blending of gestural characteristics, which "shows itself in spatial changes in one or both of the overlapping gestures" (Browman and Goldstein 1990: 362). This prediction is confirmed by the tongue tip movement path for the [ld] cluster in Figure 1 (a), whose single constriction is at a location intermediate between those of dental [t] and alveolar [l]. However, the movement path for the rhotic cluster in Figure 1 (b) suggests a sequential articulation of gestures and does not show evidence of overlap or blending. In this cluster, the tongue tip begins at a location close to that of single [ɾ], then subsequently moves forward in a "sliding" motion to form a constriction at a point near that of spirantized [ð].[4] Therefore, /ɾd/ and /ld/ clusters in Castilian Spanish differ in gestural alignment – only the latter exhibits overlap and blending.

Romero hypothesizes that the exceptional articulation of /ɾd/ stems from the inherently short duration of the coronal tap [ɾ]. According to the duration values for Spanish consonants provided by Navarro Tomás (1918), shown in (2), the average duration of [ɾ] is about 25 ms, compared to approximately 65 ms for [l], and 72 ms for [d]:

(2)   [ɾ] 25 ms < [l] 65 ms < [d] 72 ms

The extreme brevity of the tap stems from a ballistic gesture whereby the tongue tip is thrown up against the alveolar ridge (Ladefoged 1993: 168). The tongue tip must be "cocked" back from neutral position to gain momentum for tapping, and it must move away quickly from the point of contact if extra-short constriction is to be achieved. Inouye (1995: 55–6) invokes the metaphor of throwing a baseball, which also involves a ballistic gesture with similar approach and release phases. The throw will be more effective if one's arm is cocked back from rest position in order to gain momentum and if it is also allowed to follow through on its movement trajectory after the baseball is released. As in the case of throwing a ball, the ballistic tapping gesture is most effective when both the approach and release phases are properly executed.

The movement paths in Figure 1 (b) clearly indicate both the approach and release phases of [ɾ] when it occurs intervocalically as well as preconsonantally. I propose that the sequential articulation of Castilian Spanish [ɾəð] stems from the execution of the release phase of the rhotic, which separates the tap constriction from that of the following consonant, thereby ensuring an *open transition* between the two (see Catford 1977: 220). Furthermore, I assume that the svarabhakti fragment observed in (1) is the acoustic result of this transition, which allows some recovery of the underlying nuclear vowel (I return to this issue in Section 3).

Rhotics are known for the considerable phonetic variety they exhibit across languages, dialects, and speech styles. Although the same is true among Spanish varieties, most contemporary generative analyses tend to relegate dialectal phonetic variants to the realm of "low-level" phonetic detail. The following passage from Harris (1983: 62) is representative of the tendency to abstract away from the phonetic reality of rhotics:

There is an astonishing variety of *r*-quality phones in Spanish. A phonetics teacher from whom I took undergraduate courses in Mexico claimed to have identified over 40 types of *r* in the Valley of Mexico alone. Fascinating though this fact is, it leaves open the question of how the phonological system of Spanish works. ... I thus reduce the vocabulary of symbols to just two, [r] and [ř], which will be understood to jointly exhaust the rich phonetic variety ... Of course, these are only the prototypical realizations. I will say little more about phonetic detail...

However, by not investigating rhotic variation, we might fail to recognize other systematic aspects in the cross-linguistic patterning of rhotics, which ultimately deserve some explanation.[5]

One such pattern comes from highland Ecuadorian Spanish (HES), in which rhotics may be realized phonetically as assibilated fricatives in casual speech.[6] Assibilation occurs in many Latin American Spanish dialects but is acoustically more marked in the Andean highlands. Descriptive observations of HES, principally from Argüello (1978), show that the two rhotic phones are in complementary distribution in preconsonantal position in casual speech, with [ř] surfacing before homorganic (coronal) consonants and [ɾ] appearing elsewhere, as shown in (3). Following Argüello's conventions, I employ [ř̥] to denote the devoicing of [ř] before voiceless consonants, as shown in (3b,d). For consistency, I continue to indicate svarabhakti vowels as [ᵊ] in (3a,g).

(3)   a.   *cuerpo*   [eɾᵊ.p]   'body'
      b.   *puerta*   [eř̥.t]   'door'
      c.   *verde*   [eř.ð̞]   'green'
      d.   *persona*   [eř̥.s]   'person'
      e.   *carne*   [ař.n]   'meat'
      f.   *perla*   [eř.l]   'pearl'
      g.   *garganta*   [aɾᵊ.ɣ]   'throat'

The assibilated rhotic appears before a following homorganic consonant, with which it agrees in voicing, as in (3b–f). However, [ř] is unattested in coda position before heterorganic consonants, as in (3a,g).[7]

In contrast to the Peninsular Spanish pattern shown in (1), /ɾC/ clusters exhibit an alternation between [ɾ] and [ř] in casual HES. The assibilated variant has the more limited distribution, appearing before coronal consonants, while [ɾ] appears elsewhere, before labials and velars. Although this distribution is apparent in the transcribed data presented by Argüello

(1978), shown in (3), no laboratory studies have been conducted to verify the claim that preconsonantal rhotics are realized as such in this Spanish variety. The following section presents descriptive evidence of coda assibilation through spectrographic analysis of /rC/ clusters.

3. Acoustic study of highland Ecuadorian Spanish clusters

For the present investigation, data were gathered from recordings of five speakers of HES, the dialect that formed the basis of Argüello's (1978) study. Table 1 lists background information for the subjects:

Table 1.   Background information for five HES speakers

Subject	Gender	Place of origin
EM	Male	Imbabura
GB	Male	Tabacundo
MA	Female	Latacunga
JA	Male	Cuenca
JM	Male	Quito

All of the recorded subjects are native speakers of HES. The first four subjects in Table 1 read a short literary passage (see Appendix) and were recorded on reel-to-reel tape. The recordings were later digitized using audio editing software and stored in MPEG format at 22,050 Hz and 16-bit. The fifth subject was recorded directly to computer reading the same literary passage. All tokens of heterosyllabic /rC/ were extracted from the digitized recordings and were analyzed via waveform and spectrogram with version 1.5 of the SIL Speech Analyzer software.

Overall results indicate that for the five speakers consulted, coda /r/ generally surfaces as such in preconsonantal contexts, except before homorganic consonants, in which case assibilation may or may not apply. Given that assibilation in HES has been associated with casual speech (Argüello 1978), the variability of assibilation observed in the present study is not surprising, since reading tasks tend to promote careful speech styles in laboratory settings. The following sections examine several representative tokens collected in the study, beginning with heterorganic clusters.

3.1. Svarabhakti in heterorganic /rC/

Realizations of coda /ɾ/ before heterorganic consonants in HES are illustrated by the tokens *enorme* 'enormous' (subject GB) in Figure 2 and *cargados* 'loaded' (subject EM) in Figure 3.

In both cases, [ɾ] is phonetically separated from the following consonant by a svarabhakti vowel fragment, whose duration is approximately 24 ms for [ɾᵊ.m] versus 48 ms for [ɾᵊ.ɣ]. Such variability is in agreement with what has previously been shown for Peninsular Spanish /rC/ clusters, in which the duration of svarabhakti typically reaches and frequently surpasses that of the tap constriction: "The duration of the intervening vocalic element is highly variable even in the same word repeated several times by the same individual. This variability probably stems from rate of speech and from the fact that speakers are unaware of the existence of this vowel fragment, even though in most cases it attains a duration greater than that of the *r* [my translation]" (Gili Gaya 1921: 279).

In sum, Figures 2 and 3 suggest that heterorganic /rC/ clusters in HES are realized the same as the Peninsular Spanish /rC/ clusters shown in (1), namely with an intervening open transition and concomitant vowel fragment of variable duration.

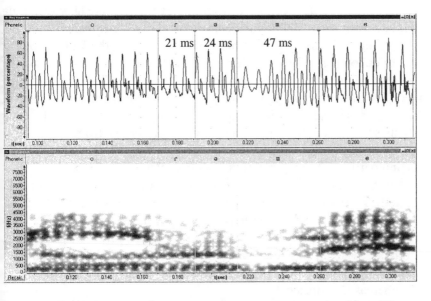

Figure 2. Svarabhakti in [ɾᵊ.m] cluster of *enorme* 'enormous', subject GB

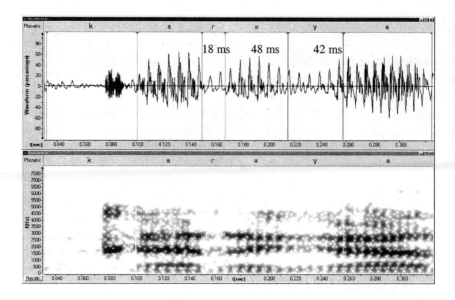

Figure 3. Svarabhakti in [ɾ°.ɣ] cluster of *cargados* 'loaded', subject EM

3.2. Variable assibilation in homorganic /rC/

As noted above, the data collected from the HES speakers show that coda /ɾ/ exhibits variable assibilation before homorganic consonants. The two rhotics [ɾ] and [ř] vary freely in this position, whereas the latter phone is subject to devoicing before voiceless consonants. Figures 4 and 5 show the realizations of /ɾ/ before homorganic /t/ in the tokens *huertas* 'gardens' (subject EM) and *partes* 'parts' (subject MA), respectively. In Figure 4, underlying /rt/ is realized with an intervening svarabhakti vowel of 32 ms in which some trace of formant structure is preserved from the nuclear vowel opposite the tap constriction. In Figure 5, coda /ɾ/ undergoes assibilation and partial devoicing before /t/. Observe that no svarabhakti vowel is present in the assibilated cluster. The assibilated rhotic corresponds to a 47 ms period of strident frication, whose turbulence is indicated by the presence of aperiodic energy in the upper spectra. This variant contrasts with the non-assibilated [ɾ] of Figure 4, which is 17 ms in duration and exhibits no turbulent noise. In sum, the clusters in Figures 4 and 5 differ in that [ɾ°.t] exhibits an open transition and svarabhakti between the adjacent consonants, whereas [ř̥.t] does not.

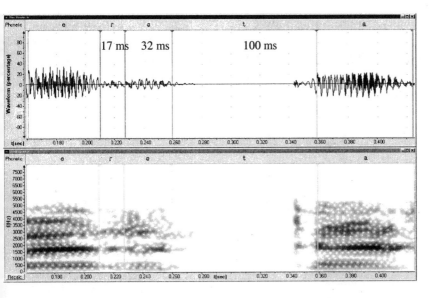

Figure 4.　Svarabhakti in [ɾ˃.t] cluster of *huertas* 'gardens', subject EM

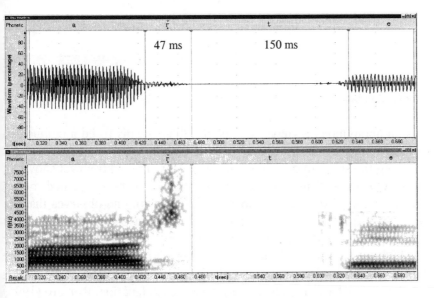

Figure 5.　Assibilation in [ɽ̥.t] cluster of *partes* 'parts', subject MA

Finally, Figure 6 illustrates the assibilation of /ɾ/ before homorganic /n/ in the token *terneros* 'calves' (subject GB). The rhotic in this cluster corresponds to a 52 ms period of turbulent frication, and no svarabhakti vowel is observed between [ř] and the following consonant. Substantial voicing is maintained throughout the assibilated rhotic in [ř.n], in contrast to the partial devoicing of [ř̥] before [t] in Figure 5 above.

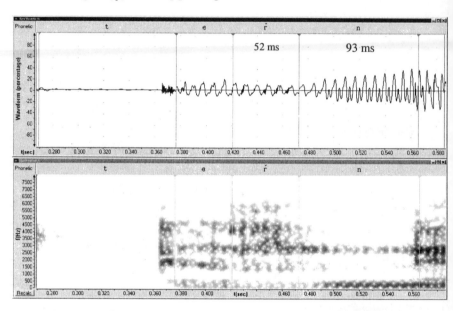

Figure 6.　Assibilation in [ř.n] cluster of *terneros* 'calves', subject GB

As an anonymous reviewer points out, there seems to be a compensatory lengthening effect associated with the assibilation of precoronal /ɾ/. Comparing the sum duration of the tap and the svarabhakti vowel shown in Figure 4 (17 ms + 32 ms = 49 ms total) with that of the assibilated rhotics shown in Figure 5 (47 ms) and in Figure 6 (52 ms), one observes that the absence of svarabhakti entails a longer constriction period for the assibilated phone. I leave it to future research to verify this effect within a more controlled experimental design. However, supposing the same results were obtained in a controlled setting, the relatively longer duration of the assibilated phone may have a plausible aerodynamic explanation. Romero (1995) claims that fricatives must be longer than approximants to allow pressure to be built up at the place of constriction, thus generating turbulent airflow.[8] While the presence of an open transition ensures a brief approximant articulation of the tap, the absence of the transition allows for a durational increase in the assibilated fricative. (See the discussion surrounding Figure 7 below.)

3.3. Summary

The representative spectrograms presented above reveal several properties of /rC/ clusters in HES based on the speech samples collected and analyzed in the present study:

Table 2. Preconsonantal rhotic alternation in HES

Heterorganic /rC/	Homorganic /rC/
– Assibilation unattested	– Variable assibilation
– Extra-short rhotic constriction	– Longer constriction of assibilated
– Intervening svarabhakti vowel of	rhotic
variable duration	– Assibilation and svarabhakti mutually exclusive
	– [ř] subject to partial devoicing

In the remainder of this paper, I illustrate a gestural approach to assibilation in HES clusters within the framework of Articulatory Phonology and then integrate the phonetic explanation into a constraint-based account of rhotic variation in Spanish /rC/ clusters.

4. The role of gestural timing in /rC/ cluster realization

Bradley (1999) proposes a gestural explanation of rhotic assibilation in HES. Specifically, it is argued that the tongue tip gestures for /r/ and an adjacent coronal consonant undergo overlap and blending in casual speech, thereby producing an overall tongue tip trajectory whose duration and constriction degree are sufficient for turbulent airflow. This idea is consistent with Browman and Goldstein's model, in which greater overlap (and blending) yields casual speech forms that differ from their canonical realization in careful speech. In order to see how gestural blending is responsible for assibilation, we must first account for the realization of non-overlapped clusters that exhibit [r] and concomitant svarabhakti. In Articulatory Phonology, consonantal gestures are superimposed on vocalic gestures, which are articulatorily adjacent (Gafos 1999). This explains why the svarabhakti fragment appearing in a [Vɾᵊ.C] sequence is always a continuation of the formant structure present in the nuclear vowel on the opposite side of the tap constriction. Both the full vowel and the vowel fragment stem from the same tongue body gesture, and the superimposed tap constriction produces a brief interruption separating the two.[9] Such an account concords with the definition of Spanish /ɾ/ proposed by Gili Gaya (1921: 279): "It is a vocalic sound interrupted by an alveolar contact that is voiced and more or less intense [my translation]."

Consider the timing relationship depicted in Figure 7 for the hypothetical [Vɾᵊ.tV] sequence. In this gestural representation, the activity of each relevant articulator is depicted on a separate tier. Boxes represent gestures, and the length of a box denotes the period of time during which the articulator is under active control. Gestures that overlap on the same articulatory tier are indicated by broken lines (e.g., the tongue body gestures for V1 and V2). When the tongue tip gesture for /ɾ/ is temporally separated from that of the following /t/, the overlapping tongue body gesture for V_1 is recovered as a svarabhakti vowel fragment. This timing relationship is hypothesized to be responsible for the HES cluster realizations shown in Figures 2 through 4, and more generally for all /ɾC/ clusters in Peninsular Spanish, as shown by the data in (1). The lack of significant gestural overlap between /ɾ/ and the following consonant allows for the successful execution of the tap's release phase, which yields the sliding articulation documented by Romero (1996) in Figure 1 (b).

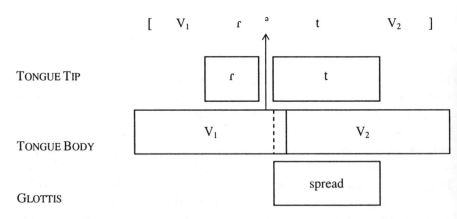

Figure 7. Gestural representation of [Vɾᵊ.tV]

On the other hand, no svarabhakti fragment can be recovered when the tongue tip gestures for /ɾ/ and the following homorganic consonant are overlapped, as in Figure 8. According to Browman and Goldstein (1990), gestural overlap will yield different results depending on whether the two gestures are on the same or different articulatory tiers. The prediction is that same-tier overlap will produce a *blending* of the characteristics of the two gestures, which "shows itself in spatial changes in one or both of the overlapping gestures" (362). Overlap between the gestures associated with /ɾ/ and /t/ in Figure 8 blends the resulting articulatory trajectories, thereby removing the open articulatory transition between the two consonants, along with the svarabhakti vowel it normally produces. Without the open transition to ensure a brief constriction period, the duration of /ɾ/ is increased, yielding a fricative [ř]. In addition, overlap between the tongue tip gesture of /ɾ/ and the glottal spreading gesture of /t/ results in partial devoicing of the former.

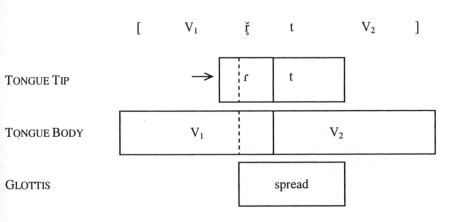

Figure 8. Gestural representation of [Vř̥.tV]

The overlap scenario shown in Figure 8 presumably yields a tongue tip movement trajectory similar to that in Figure 1 (a) for Castilian Spanish [ld]. Further articulatory investigation is required in order to determine whether overlap and blending produces a constriction location intermediate between alveolar [ɾ] and dental [t]. Nonetheless, an overlap account of [ř̥.t] finds some support in the spectrographic results presented in Figure 5, in which svarabhakti is absent and laryngeal coarticulation yields partial devoicing of the rhotic. While the gestural account outlined above provides phonetic motivation for assibilation in homorganic /rC/ clusters, it remains unclear why [ř] is absent from heterorganic ones, as in Figures 2 and 3. Bradley (1999) specifically argues that in HES, /r/ is "*overlapped by adjacent consonantal gestures*, with overlap resulting in gestural blending next to coronals [my emphasis]" (64). Such a general statement of gestural overlap turns out to be descriptively inadequate, since it predicts overlap between /r/ and *any* following consonant. What needs to be explained is why overlap obtains only in homorganic /rC/ clusters but not in heterorganic ones.

5. A phonetically-based Optimality-theoretic analysis

In this section, I develop a constraint-based account of the differences in gestural alignment between homorganic versus heterorganic /rC/ clusters in HES. Section 4.1 introduces the framework of Optimality Theory. Section 4.2 motivates the constraints necessary for the analysis of /rC/ clusters, which is then illustrated in Section 4.3.

5.1. Optimality Theory

Optimality Theory (OT; Prince and Smolensky 1993; McCarthy and Prince 1993a, 1993b) provides a framework for analysis in which ranked and violable constraints apply in parallel to determine the optimal mapping between input and output forms. This approach contrasts with derivational models in which ordered rules apply to yield a series of intermediate representations between input and output. In OT, two functions determine the optimal input-output mapping: GEN, which generates output candidates, and H-EVAL, which selects the output candidate which best satisfies the constraints. The structure of an OT grammar is shown in (4) (Prince and Smolensky 1993: 4):

(4)   a.   GEN (Input$_k$)   → {Output$_1$, Output$_2$...}
       b.   H-EVAL (Output$_i$, $1 \leq i \leq \infty$) → Output$_{real}$

Output candidates are evaluated in terms of their violations of the ranked constraints. Evaluations are shown in the form of a tableau:

Tableau 1. Evaluation of input-output mappings against constraints

Input$_k$	Constraint A	Constraint B	Constraint C
Output$_1$	*!		*
☞ Output$_2$			*
Output$_3$			**!

The input appears in the first cell of the tableau, while output candidates are shown below in the same column. Constraints are given along the top of the remaining columns. A crucial ranking between two constraints is indicated by a solid line separating the two columns. For example, Tableau 1 represents a language in which three hypothetical constraints are ranked as follows: Constraint A » Constraint B, Constraint C. That is, Constraint A outranks both Constraint B and Constraint C, but the latter two constraints are unranked with respect to one another. A constraint violation is indicated by an asterisk. If a violation causes an output candidate to be eliminated from the evaluation, then that violation is said to be fatal, and the symbol '!' appears next to the relevant asterisk. The symbol '☞' marks the winning output candidate (i.e., the candidate that remains after all others are eliminated).

As an illustration, let us consider the evaluation shown in Tableau 1. Output$_1$ violates Constraint A, which is top-ranked, as well as Constraint C. Since there are other candidates that do not violate Constraint A, Output$_1$ is immediately eliminated from consideration, and the lower-ranked constraints are now irrelevant to this candidate. None of the remaining candidates violates Constraint B. With respect to Constraint C, however, Output$_2$ incurs a single violation, while Output$_3$ incurs two violations. A candidate that multiply violates some constraint loses to any candidate that violates the same constraint to a lesser degree. The second violation of Constraint C by Output$_3$ is a fatal one, and Output$_2$ is selected as the winner.

To summarize, OT provides a framework in which phonological systems are expressed in terms of ranked and violable constraints. Grammars consist of "a set of highly general constraints which, through ranking, interact to produce the elaborate particularity of individual languages" (Prince and Smolensky 1993: 198). See Prince and Smolensky (1993) for a more detailed presentation of this formalism.

5.2. Constraints on gestural timing

Cho's (1998a, 1998b) constraint-based account of Korean palatalization offers a means of evaluating gestural overlap in the Correspondence-theoretic version of OT (McCarthy and Prince 1995). In the present analysis, I assume that gestural timing relevant to /rC/ clusters is governed by the constraints in (5).

(5)   a.   IDENT(timing) (cf. Cho 1998a, 1998b)
           The temporal alignment of gestures in the input must be preserved in the output.
      b.   *FAST/SAME (cf. Bradley 2001; Steriade 1995)
           Avoid faster-than usual transitions between adjacent periods of greater stricture involving the same articulator.

Recall that in Articulatory Phonology, gestures function not only as units of articulation but also as the primitives of phonological organization. Gestures have internal duration and are temporally coordinated with each other in the phonological representation. IDENT(timing) in (5a) is a faithfulness constraint that seeks to preserve input timing relationships in the output. More specifically, this constraint enforces the requirement that input gestures be perceptually recoverable. With respect to /rC/ clusters, recoverability entails that the adjacent consonantal gestures be temporally coordinated in such a way as to ensure the presence of an intervening svarabhakti vowel (see Figure 7). The claim that svarabhakti favors the perceptual recovery of underlying /rC/ is reaffirmed in a recent cross-linguistic investigation by Hall (2003). She argues that the presence of the vowel fragment gives the first consonant a stronger release and the second a stronger approach phase, thereby improving the perceptibility of both members of the cluster. Therefore, I assume that IDENT(timing) is satisfied by outputs such as [rᵊ.C], whereas like surface clusters exhibiting substantial gestural overlap violate this constraint. Furthermore, in subsequent tableau, I include the svarabhakti vowel as part of the input in order to indicate that /rᵊC/ clusters are characterized by non-overlap timing, as in Figure 7.[10]

In competition with faithfulness to input timing is the constraint *FAST/SAME in (5b), which encodes the articulatory markedness of an open transition between two homorganic consonants. The claim that open transitions are more marked between homorganic consonants than between heterorganic ones is supported by consonantal transition phenomena in Sierra Popoluca, a Zoquean language spoken in Mexico (Elson 1947, 1956; Foster and Foster 1948). Consonant clusters in this language are realized with an intervening open transition if the consonants are heterorganic, while homorganic clusters lack such a transition, as shown in (6).

(6)   a.   kɛkʰ.paʔ   'it flies'   miɲ³.paʔ   'he comes'
      b.   kɛk.gakʰ.paʔ   'it flies again'   ʔaŋ.kiʔ   'yard'

In (6a), the open transition is realized as aspiration after the voiceless velar stop and as a short schwa-like vowel after the palatal nasal. The homorganic stop sequences [k.g] and [ŋ.k] in (6b) lack an open transition. I argue that *FAST/SAME is responsible for the absence of an open transition in homorganic stop clusters in Sierra Popoluca, as well as in homorganic /rC/ clusters in HES. This constraint is violated by outputs such as [C³.C], in which the adjacent consonants are homorganic (i.e., coronal in the case of /rC/ clusters in HES), whereas like surface clusters without an open transition satisfy this constraint.

It is important to define the notion of adjacency implied by the markedness constraint *FAST/SAME in (5b). Consider the syllabic representations of the hypothetical sequences shown in Figure 9:

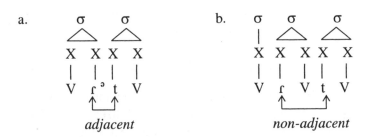

Figure 9. Hypothetical syllabic representations.

In Figure 9 (a), the consonants comprising the heterosyllabic [r³.t] cluster are adjacent on the timing tier, whereas [r] and [t] are non-adjacent in Figure 9 (b) due to the presence of an intervening, lexically sponsored vowel. The syllabic status of the svarabhakti vowel differs from that of a full vowel in that the former does not function as a syllable nucleus. Rather, the fragment in Figure 9 (a) is merely the acoustic result of an open transition between the adjacent consonants, as explained in Figure 7. On this view of adjacency, *FAST/SAME is violated by the presence of open transition between the homorganic consonants in Figure 9 (a), but the constraint is irrelevant in Figure 9 (b) because the homorganic consonants are non-adjacent.

5.3. Analysis of /rC/ cluster realizations

Tableau 2 and 3 illustrate the realizations of heterorganic and homorganic /rC/ under the ranking IDENT(timing) » *FAST/SAME, which character-izes Peninsular Spanish and careful speech in HES. In Tableau 2, [r.m] is a narrow transcription intended to denote gestural overlap, in contrast to [rᵊ.m], which exhibits an open transition and concomitant svarabhakti.[11]

Tableau 2.   Svarabhakti in heterorganic [rᵊ.m] cluster

/rᵊm/	IDENT(timing)	*FAST/SAME
☞ a. rᵊ.m		
b. r.m	*!	

Tableau 3.   Svarabhakti in homorganic [rᵊ.t] cluster

/rᵊt/	IDENT(timing)	*FAST/SAME
☞ a. rᵊ.t		*
b. ř̥.t	*!	

Faithfulness to input timing rules out the (b) candidates, thereby ensuring that both the input clusters /rᵊm/ and /rᵊt/ are realized with an open transi-tion and the associated svarabhakti vowel. The [rᵊ.t] cluster in candidate (a) of Tableau 3 violates *FAST/SAME due to the presence of an open transi-tion between two homorganic consonants, but the violation is tolerated un-der duress of higher ranking IDENT(timing).

Recall the difference between Castilian Spanish [l.d] and [rᵊ.ð̞] shown in Figure 1, as observed by Romero (1996). I assume that the former cluster lacks an open transition because the lateral liquid has a longer duration and, therefore, does not possess the same articulatory release phase to ensure a brief constriction as does the rhotic (see the discussion surrounding (2) in Section 1). As shown in Tableau 4, high-ranking IDENT(timing) favors [l.d] over the hypothetical candidate [lᵊ.ð̞] because the addition of an open transition constitutes an unfaithful realization of the gestural timing relation specified for input /ld/. (Note: I assume that spirantization of /d/ is the result of other constraints not shown in the tableau).

Tableau 4. Overlap in homorganic [l.d] cluster

/ld/	IDENT(timing)	*FAST/SAME
a. lᵊ.ð̞	*!	*
☞ b. l.d		

Since the tap contains an inherent release phase to ensure an extra-short constriction period, IDENT(timing) favors the preservation of the open transition and concomitant svarabhakti vowel in Tableau 5:

Tableau 5. Svarabhakti in homorganic [ɾᵊ.ð̞] cluster

/ɾᵊd/	IDENT(timing)	*FAST/SAME
☞ a. ɾᵊ.ð̞		*
b. ř.ð̞	*!	

Tableau 6 and 7 show the effects of the opposite constraint ranking on the realization of input /ɾᵊC/ in casual HES:

Tableau 6. Svarabhakti in heterorganic [ɾᵊ.m] cluster

/ɾᵊm/	*FAST/SAME	IDENT(timing)
☞ a. ɾᵊ.m		
b. ɾ.m		*!

Tableau 7. Assibilation in homorganic [ř̥.t] cluster

/ɾᵊt/	*FAST/SAME	IDENT(timing)
a. ɾᵊ.t	*!	
☞ b. ř̥.t		*

On the assumption that markedness constraints are promoted in casual speech styles, the violation of *FAST/SAME by candidate (a) in Tableau 7 now becomes fatal. As a result, input /r³t/ maps to output candidate (b) in which gestural overlap and blending yield assibilation and devoicing in the manner shown in Figure 8. Since *FAST/SAME is irrelevant in the case of heterorganic /r³m/, lower-ranked IDENT(timing) decides in favor candidate (a) in Tableau 6, just as it does under the opposite constraint ranking in Tableau 2.

6. Conclusion

While assibilation of rhotics is a common property of many Latin American Spanish dialects, Colantoni's (2001) empirical investigation of Argentine varieties reveals that /r/ fails to surface as [ř] in syllable codas. Moreover, Colantoni questions Argüello's (1978) descriptive observations regarding coda /r/ assibilation in HES. The present study has provided further empirical support for the Ecuadorian pattern via spectrographic analysis of relevant tokens gathered from HES speakers. A gestural account was proposed in which the phonetic realization of /rC/ clusters stems from the ranking of two conflicting constraints, one which requires input clusters to be perceptually recoverable in the output, and another which encodes the articulatory preference for overlap between adjacent consonantal gestures involving the same articulator. By incorporating the notion of gestural alignment within a constraint-based approach, the analysis put forth here captures the phonetic motivation of rhotic assibilation in Spanish codas, as well as the systematic differences in /rC/ cluster realization across dialects and speech styles.

Acknowledgments

This paper is the ongoing extension of research originally undertaken with Erin O'Rourke at the Pennsylvania State University in 1998, with much constructive criticism on the initial stages provided by Holly Nibert. The field recordings utilized in the present study come from a larger corpus of Spanish dialectal data made available by John Dalbor and digitized under the supervision of Eric Bakovic. Results of this ongoing research were presented by the present author at the Laboratory Approaches to Spanish Phonology conference, held September 6-7, 2002, at the University of Minnesota, Minneapolis. I wish to thank the audience members for helpful feedback and discussion, in particular David Eddington, Robert Hammond, José Ignacio Hualde, Anthony Lewis, Geoffrey Stewart Morrison, Pilar Prieto, and Erik Willis. Thanks also to an anonymous reviewer for comments and suggestions on a previous version of this paper. I alone am responsible for any remaining shortcomings.

Notes

1. Assibilation is also frequent in /tr/ clusters in Argentine and highland Ecuadorian varieties. For present purposes, I focus specifically on the realizations of preconsonantal /r/.
2. Spanish /rC/ clusters are overwhelmingly heterosyllabic, except for a few words in which /s/ is parsed along with /r/ in the preceding syllable rhyme, e.g., *pers.pi.caz* 'perspicacious' and *pers.pec.ti.va* 'perspective'. See Harris (1983) for a discussion of Spanish syllabification.
3. Romero does not indicate the svarabhakti fragment in phonetic transcription. Given the discussion surrounding (1), however, [rð̞] is more appropriately transcribed as [ɾᵊð̞].
4. Recasens (2001) observes a similar sliding movement in the same clusters in Catalan: "*rd* does not yield blending but C1-to-C2 sliding in view of the mobility of the tongue tip" (299).
5. Recent investigations have begun to redress the lack of attention given to phonetic detail (e.g., Blecua 2001; Bradley and Schmeiser 2003; Colantoni 2001, Hammond 1999, 2000; and Willis and Pedrosa 1998).
6. Coda liquids in Spanish are subject to a variety of other processes depending on the dialect, such as gliding, assimilation, retroflexion, and neutralization. The present study focuses specifically on the assibilation of preconsonantal /r/ in HES, but see Lipski (1994) for a comprehensive overview of phonological and phonetic variation across dialects.
7. John Lipski (personal communication) points out that in other dialects, fricative rhotics may appear before any consonant regardless of the homorganicity of the cluster (e.g., Mexican Spanish [la βiř.xen] *la Virgen* 'the Virgin'). However, Fanny Argüello (personal communication) maintains the original observation of Argüello (1978) that assibilation in HES affects coda /r/ only before coronals. Furthermore, none of the instances of coda /r/ analyzed in the present study showed assibilation in heterorganic clusters.
8. Recasens (1991) observes via electropalatographic measurements involving Catalan speakers that closure for the tap is seldom complete, as expected from the momentariness of the apical gesture, which suggests that the tap is an ap-

proximant. Similarly, Bakovic (1994) argues that the tap is an approximant in Spanish.

9. A similar gestural explanation is proposed by Steriade (1990) and more recently Bradley (2001, 2002) and Hall (2003).

10. The inclusion of non-contrastive phonetic detail, such as gestural timing, in input representations raises important questions concerning the relationship between phonetics and phonology in the grammar. An adequate treatment of this issue is beyond the scope of the present paper, but see Bradley and Schmeiser (2003) for further discussion.

11. Perhaps a more appropriate interpretation is that overlap in heterorganic /rC/ results in perceptual masking of the rhotic. Browman and Goldstein (1990: 361) cite the apparent deletion of English final /t/ in the casual speech form [mʌsbi] versus the canonical form [mʌst#bi] *must be*. Articulatory measurements via X-ray pellet trajectories indicate that the tongue tip gesture for /t/ is still present in the casual speech form, although its acoustic effects are hidden due to overlap with the following bilabial gesture. See Bradley (2002) for a similar gestural account of rhotic deletion from heterorganic /rC/ clusters in Urban East Norwegian.

References

Argüello, Fanny
    1978   The žeísta dialect of Spanish spoken in Ecuador: A phonetic and phonological study. Ph.D. diss., The Pennsylvania State University.

Bakovic, Eric
    1994   Strong onsets and Spanish fortition. In *MIT Working Papers in Linguistics* 23, C. Giordano and D. Ardron (eds.), 21–39. Cambridge, MA: MIT Press.

Blecua, Beatriz
    2001   Las vibrantes en español: Manifestaciones acústicas y procesos fonéticos. Ph.D. diss., Universitat Autònoma de Barcelona.

Bradley, Travis G.
    1999   Assibilation in Ecuadorian Spanish: A phonology-phonetics account. In *Formal Perspectives on Romance Linguistics,* J.-Marc Authier, Barbara E. Bullock, and Lisa A. Reed (eds.), 57–71. Amsterdam: John Benjamins.
    2001   The phonetics and phonology of rhotic duration contrast and neutralization. Ph.D. diss., The Pennsylvania State University.

2002 Gestural timing and derived environment effects in Norwegian clusters. In *West Coast Conference on Formal Linguistics 21 Proceedings,* L. Mikkelsen and C. Potts (eds.), 101–114. Somerville, MA: Cascadilla Press.

Bradley, Travis G., and Ben Schmeiser
2003 On the phonetic reality of /ɾ/ in Spanish complex onsets. In *Theory, Practice, and Acquisition: Papers from the 6th Hispanic Linguistics Symposium and the 5th Conference on the Acquisition of Spanish and Portuguese,* Paula M. Kempchinsky and Carlos-Eduardo Piñeros (eds.), 1–20. Somerville, MA: Cascadilla Press.

Browman, Catherine, and Louis Goldstein
1989 Articulatory gestures as phonological units. *Phonology* 6: 201–252.
1990 Tiers in Articulatory Phonology, with some implications for casual speech. In *Papers in Laboratory Phonology I: Between the Grammar and Physics of Speech,* John Kingston and Mary E. Beckman (eds.), 341– 376. Cambridge: Cambridge University Press.
1991 Gestural structures: Distinctiveness, phonological processes, and historical change. In *Modularity and the Motor Theory of Speech Perception,* Ignatius G. Mattingly and Michael Studdert-Kennedy (eds.), 313–338. Hillsdale, New Jersey: Lawrence Erlbaum.
1992 Articulatory Phonology: An overview. *Phonetica* 49: 155–180.

Catford, John C.
1977 *Fundamental Problems in Phonetics.* Bloomington: Indiana University Press.

Cho, Taehong
1998a Intergestural timing and overlap in Korean palatalization: An Optimality-Theoretic approach. In *Japanese/Korean Linguistics 8,* David Silva (ed.), 261–276. Stanford: Center for the Study of Language and Information Publications.
1998b The specification of intergestural timing and overlap: EMA and EPG studies. M.A. thesis, University of California, Los Angeles.

Colantoni, Laura
2001 Mergers, chain shifts, and dissimilatory processes: Palatals and rhotics in Argentine Spanish. Ph.D. diss., University of Minnesota.

Elson, Benjamin F.
1947 Sierra Popoluca syllable structure. *International Journal of American Linguistics* 13: 13–17.

1956   Sierra Popoluca morphology. Ph.D. diss., Cornell University.
Foster, M. L., and G. M. Foster
1948   *Sierra Popoluca Speech.* Washington, D.C.: U.S. Government
           Printing Office, Smithsonian Institution, Institute of Social An-
           thropology.
Gafos, Adamantios
1999   *The Articulatory Basis of Locality in Phonology.* New York: Gar-
           land.
Gili Gaya, Samuel
1921   La r simple en la pronunciación española. *Revista de Filología
           Española* 8: 271–280.
Hall, Nancy
2003   Gestures and segments: Vowel intrusion as overlap. Ph.D. diss.,
           University of Massachusetts, Amherst.
Hammond, Robert
1999   On the non-occurrence of the phone [r̃] in the Spanish sound
           system. In *Advances in Hispanic Linguistics,* Javier Gutiérrez-
           Rexach and Fernando Martínez-Gil (eds.), 135–151. Somerville,
           MA: Cascadilla Press.
2000   The phonetic realizations of /rr/ in Spanish: A psychoacoustic
           analysis. In *Hispanic Linguistics at the Turn of the Millennium,*
           Héctor Campos, Elena Herburger, Alfonso Morales-Front, and
           Thomas J. Walsh (eds.), 80–100. Somerville, MA: Cascadilla
           Press.
Harris, James
1983   *Syllable Structure and Stress in Spanish: A Nonlinear Analysis.*
           Cambridge, MA: MIT Press.
Inouye, Susan
1995   Trills, taps and stops in contrast and variation. Ph.D. diss., Uni-
           versity of California, Los Angeles.
Ladefoged, Peter
1993   *A Course in Phonetics.* 3d ed. New York: Harcourt Brace Jo-
           vanovich.
Lenz, Rodolfo
1892   Chilenishe Studien. *Phonetische Studien* 5: 272–293.
Lipski, John
1994   *Latin American Spanish.* London: Longman.
Malmberg, Bertil
1965   *Estudios de fonética hispánica. (Collectanea Phonetica,* I.) Ma-
           drid: Consejo Superior de Investigaciones Científicas.
McCarthy, John, and Alan Prince
1993a   Generalized alignment. *Yearbook of Morphology* 6: 79–153.

1993b   *Prosodic Morphology I: Constraint Interaction and Satisfaction.* Technical Report #3, Rutgers University Center for Cognitive Science.

1995   Faithfulness and reduplicative identity. In *University of Massachusetts Occasional Papers 18: Papers in Optimality Theory,* Jill Beckman, Laura Walsh Dickey, and Suzanne Urbanczyk (eds.), 249–384. Amherst, MA: Graduate Linguistic Student Association.

Navarro Tomás, Tomás
1918   Diferencias de duración entre las consonantes españolas. *Revista de Filología Española* 5: 367–393.

Prince, Alan, and Paul Smolensky
1993   Optimality Theory: Constraint interaction in generative grammar. Manuscript, Rutgers University, New Brunswick, New Jersey, and University of Colorado, Boulder, Colorado.

Quilis, Antonio
1993   *Tratado de fonología y fonética españolas.* Madrid: Editorial Gredos.

Recasens, Daniel
1991   On the production characteristics of apicoalveolar taps and trills. *Journal of Phonetics* 19: 267–280.

2001   Coarticulation, assimilation and blending in Catalan consonant clusters. *Journal of Phonetics* 29: 273–301.

Romero, Joaquín
1995   Gestural organization in Spanish: An experimental study of spirantization and aspiration. Ph.D. diss., University of Connecticut.

1996   Articulatory blending of lingual gestures. *Journal of Phonetics* 24: 99–111.

Steriade, Donca
1990   Gestures and autosegments: Comments on Browman and Goldstein's paper. In *Papers in Laboratory Phonology I: Between the Grammar and Physics of Speech,* John Kingston and Mary E. Beckman (eds.), 382–397. Cambridge: Cambridge University Press.

1995   Licensing retroflexion. Manuscript, University of California, Los Angeles.

Willis, Erik, and M. Begoña Pedrosa
1998   An acoustic analysis of the rhotic system of Spanish: Isolated words, read texts and spontaneous speech. Paper presented at the *Second Hispanic Linguistics Symposium,* The Ohio State University, October 9–11, 1998.

Whitney, William D.
1889   *Sanskrit Grammar*. Cambridge: Harvard University Press.

Appendix

Text employed in data elicitation

Cuando yo era niño, iba todos los años a pasar uno de los meses de vacaciones a casa de mi tío. La hacienda y sus dependencias abarcaban un terreno muy extenso. Estaban rodeadas de un enorme patio. Solía ayudar a mi tío y a sus empleados cuando podía, aunque probablemente no les ayudaba tanto como yo creía. En las cuadras tenía mi tío seis o siete caballos y algunas yeguas. Pero ahora, porque vive todavía, los ha sustituido por tractores y por una camioneta. En los establos tenía magníficos bueyes. Recuerdo como si fuera ayer cuando los vi por primera vez. También había vacas con sus terneros, así como cabras, ovejas y corderos. Menos pintorescos, pero de igual utilidad, eran los cerdos que vivían en sus pocilgas, y los gallos y las gallinas que tenían lo que a mí me parecía entonces un inmenso gallinero. Para un niño que pasaba once meses del año en una gran población, constituyen una novedad los pavos, los patos y los gansos que en otras partes no encontraba sino muertos y preparados para la mesa en la cocina. Uno de los encantos de aquellas visitas era la abundancia de frutas que comía yo en gran cantidad. Generalmente, las fresas y las frambuesas habían pasado ya, pero nos quedaban grosellas y cerezas. Y los manzanos, perales y ciruelos estaban cargados de fruta madura, hermosa y suculenta. ¿Cuáles son las diferentes partes de la hacienda? La casa, el patio, las dependencias y los campos que rodean la casa. ¿De qué constan las dependencias? Constan de las cuadras, los establos, los rediles, las pocilgas y los gallineros. ¿Cuál es, según Ud., el más útil de los animales domésticos? Yo creo que la vaca, no sólo porque da leche, sino porque la leche se transforma en mantequilla y en queso. Y además, la carne de vaca es una parte muy importante en nuestras comidas diarias. ¿No tenía su tío de Ud. abejas? No, Señor. Cuando se instaló en su hacienda hace treinta años, compró una gran cantidad de abejas. Pero la miel le daba tan poco que las vendió. ¿Tenía grandes huertas? No, nada más que una que estaba detrás de la casa. Pero era muy productiva, y daba cada año gran cantidad de frutas y legumbres. Pruebe Ud. una manzana. O, ¿prefiere Ud. ciruelas? Aquí las hay verdes si le gustan más que las maduras. Están muy dulces, gracias. Voy a tomar una de estas manzanas. Las peras y las manzanas son las frutas que más me gustan.

Acquisition of sociolinguistic variables in Spanish: Do children acquire individual lexical forms or variable rules?

Manuel Díaz-Campos

1. Introduction

Previous research in the area of phonological variation has focused on describing internal and external constraints in the speech of adult speakers. These previous investigations have contributed to our understanding of the role played by different groups within the speech community in the process of language change. The study of variation in child language was not taken into consideration for a long period of time in sociolinguistic studies. Pioneer work on the acquisition of variation in child phonology (Labov 1964) proposes that development of stylistic variation probably starts when individuals are 14 years old under the influence of wider contacts with peers beyond the neighborhood or high school. More recently this idea has been challenged by some scholars who have conducted research on the acquisition of variable phonology in English, French, and Spanish (Roberts and Labov 1995; Roberts 1994, 1997a, 1997b; Chevrot, Beaud, and Varga 2000; Díaz-Campos 2001). The assumption in the work of Roberts and Labov 1995; Roberts 1994, 1997a, 1997b, and Díaz-Campos 2001 is that the acquisition of variable phonology entails the encoding of a variable rule. According to Labov (1972), variable rules are based on generative phonological rules with the ingredient of incorporating the probability of application of them when linguistic and social constraints are satisfied. Nonetheless, Chevrot, Beaud, and Varga (2000:295) suggest that children tend to copy adult surface forms instead of acquiring a variable rule. This suggestion that children copy lexical forms is consistent with Bybee's (2001) usage-based model of phonology in which linguistic regularities are not expressed as rules, but rather as schemas. This means that speakers discover generalizations about linguistic units and create a series of connections based on similarities among them.

The purpose of this investigation is to examine whether children acquire sociolinguistically variable phonology as a rule or as a case-by-case copy-

ing of adults' surface forms. The analysis is based on previous work studying the acquisition of intervocalic /d/ in Spanish-speaking children from
Venezuela (Díaz-Campos 2001).

The sections included in this paper will be organized as follows. In the
next section, a discussion of the previous work is presented focusing on the
issues of whether children acquire individual lexical forms or variable rules.
Section 3 describes the corpus and methodology used in the present investigation. Section 4 presents the results. Finally, the summary and conclusions are presented in Section 5.

2. Previous research

Investigations examining acquisition of variable phonology are not very
common in sociolinguistic literature. Nonetheless, one pioneer study
(Labov 1964) and recent studies (Roberts 1994; Roberts and Labov 1995;
Roberts 1997a and 1997b; Chevrot, Beaud, and Varga 2000; Díaz-Campos
2001) have explored the subject in order to describe the role of children
within the speech community.

One of the first investigations examining acquisition of sociolinguistic
variables is that of Labov (1964: 92). This scholar is concerned with the
acquisition of "the full range" of spoken English, including standard varieties as well as regional or vernacular varieties of English. Specifically,
Labov studies the fortition of /θ/ in words such as *thing, think, three*, etc.
and r-deletion word-finally and in preconsonantal position (e.g, *car, board*).
Labov's investigation proposes that children from about 5 to 12 years old
acquire the vernacular variety under the influence of peers in school and in
the neighborhood. Stylistic variation, according to Labov's proposal, would
be acquired around age 14 under the influence of wider contact outside the
immediate community.

This perspective according to which stylistic variation is acquired during teen years has been changed by current research in the field. Sociolinguistic variables appear in the speech of children as young as 3;2 (see Roberts and Labov 1995, Roberts 1994, 1997a, 1997b). Roberts and Labov
(1995) study the acquisition of English short-a, focusing on speech samples
from children born in Philadelphia. The results show that 3- and 4-year-old
children were acquiring the norms of the speech community in regard to
the short-a pattern. Children were acquiring this sociolinguistic variable
even in environments of lexical change in progress (short-a before /l/ and
before inter-vocalic /n/). According to Roberts and Labov, these findings

show that during the preschool period children are able to acquire categorical grammatical rules and variable rules.

Roberts (1997a) also examines the acquisition of variable phonology in children from Philadelphia. She compares her findings with previous results reported by Roberts and Labov (1995). Roberts studies three linguistic variables: 1) The fronting and raising of the nucleus of /aw/, as in *cow*, *crown*, *south*; 2) the raising of the nucleus of checked long /ey/, as in *cake* and *rate*; 3) the backing of long /ay/ before voiceless final obstruents, as in *fight*, *right*, *mice*. Roberts' results show that all children were making progress in learning Philadelphia's vowel system. Children ranged in age from 3 years 2 months old to 4 years 11 months had acquired the fronting of /aw/. Furthermore, even though the conditioning of the raising of the nucleus of /ey/ is more complex, all children acquired this change in progress as well. Based on the findings described above, Roberts claims that 1) children in preschool years are learning their local dialect; 2) the acquisition of sound change in progress seems to be influenced by the dialect background of their parents; and 3) it is the female-dominated sound changes that are advanced in early language acquisition.

Roberts (1994 and 1997b) examines the deletion of final /t/ and /d/ in word-final consonant clusters in children from Philadelphia. Since /t/ and /d/ deletion is a well documented English variable rule, the author considers it an interesting phenomenon to study in children's speech in order to understand the acquisition of variation. As in Roberts' previous work, the results reveal that children acquire patterns of variation at an early age. The author found that children were learning the internal constraints that govern /t/ and /d/ deletion in the Philadelphia dialect. Roberts interprets this outcome as an indication that children simultaneously learn patterns of variation and complex grammatical forms.

In the case of Spanish, Díaz-Campos 2001 has studied the acquisition of sociolinguistic variables in speech samples from 30 Venezuelan preschool children. Two linguistic variables are examined in his work: 1) intervocalic /d/, and 2) syllable-final /ɾ/. Díaz-Campos' results reveal that, from a very early age (i.e. 4 years 5 months old), children begin to use variable phonology with a sociolinguistic value that is similar to that of the adult model. Children acquire first the sociolect of their immediate community, but, with regular exposure to other systems, they begin not only incorporating new repertoires in their speech, but also assigning social value to them.

There are many points in common in the work of Roberts (1994); Roberts and Labov (1995); Roberts (1997a), (1997b), and Díaz-Campos (2001), but the one we need to point out for the present paper is the theoretical assumption that children are acquiring variable rules. Even though current models in generative phonology have abandoned the idea of a rule-based system of phonology, sociolinguistic studies still use this notion for describing social variation. According to Cedergren and Sankoff (1974), variable rules formalize those proposals in sociolinguistic research that examine variability as a core element of linguistic competence. Variable rules incorporate the statistically predicted frequency of its application as an integral part of its structural description. If we take these theoretical considerations into account, we would expect the application of the variable rule any time the structural description proposed is met.

Contrary to the variable rule perspective in the case of acquisition of sociolinguistic variables, Chevrot, Beaud, and Varga (2000) sustain that children copy adult surface lexical forms instead of encoding a variable rule. These scholars study post-consonantal word-final /R/ in French speaking children. Chevrot, Beaud, and Varga (2000) include in their study two age groups children: 6 to 7 year-old and 10 to 12 year-old. According to their findings, they locate variability within the "lexical knowledge internalized for each word" (Chevrot, Beaud, and Varga 2000: 315). The location of variability at the lexical level allows explaining the cognitive nature of speech planning as well as the relationship of variable phonology and social constraints. Chevrot, Beaud, and Varga (2000) point out that cognitive constraints are related to speech production phenomena such as simplification of complex structures. Social factors affecting variability include evaluation of social variants, and the relationship between variants and speech register. In Chevrot, Beaud, and Varga's (2000: 315) words:

> This conception allows us to draw together two opposing tendencies that has divided sociolinguistic approaches to variation: an interactional approach, which supposes that speakers are free to manipulate variants in order to achieve communicative aims, versus a variationist approach, which supposes that speakers' linguistic behavior is constrained by linguistic and sociological factors.

As can be seen in the review of the previous research, the variable rule hypothesis would be triggered any time factors favoring variation increase the probability of application of the rule when the phonetic context is met. If we follow the reasoning behind this proposal, we would expect to find alternation in children's speech in different age groups. In other words, if we think in terms of variable rules, we would expect that children regardless of age will use such rules in the corresponding phonetic context any time internal and external constraints favoring its application are met. In

the specific case analyzed here, we would expect to find alternant production of words such as [kantáðo], [kantáo], *cantado* 'sung'; [laðo], [láo],
lado, 'side'; etc.

Alternatively, if children acquire variation in a case-by-case fashion we
would not find alternation at the beginning stages, but the production of
individual lexical forms and the incorporation of new forms at later stages
where stylistic variation begins to emerge in their speech. Even if we find
alternation, we would need to examine frequency effects as suggested by
Bybee (2001). Following Bybee's proposal, we would expect variability in
frequent tokens as opposed to infrequent ones.

3. Methodology

3.1. Corpus

The corpus of the present investigation consists of recordings in which 30
monolingual Spanish-speaking children were participants. These 30 recordings are part of a larger corpus, *Competencia narrativa en niños de
edad escolar*[1] 'Narrative competence of school-age children' collected by
Dr. Martha Shiro, professor of the Master's Program in Linguistics at the
Universidad Central de Venezuela.

Each interview lasts approximately 45 minutes to 1 hour. The speech
style of the conversation can be described as spontaneous. The recording
session included four different parts. The first one included a conversation
with the children including questions such as: (1) how old are you? (2)
How did you celebrate your birthday? (3) Do you have brothers and sisters? (4) Do you play with your brothers and sisters? (5) Do you get along
with them? (6) What does your father do for a living? (7) What does your
mother do for a living? (8) Does your father or your mother read stories to
you at night? (9) Can you tell that story? (10) Who do you play with at
school? (11) What is your favorite TV program? (12) What is that TV program about? There were several other questions with the same characteristics.

The second part of the interview included a trigger situation in which
the interviewer was trying to obtain a story where the children were emo-
tionally involved. Labov (1972) suggests that topics triggering the
speaker's emotional reaction are more likely to produce casual speech. The
classical Labovian interview includes topics such as the danger of death in
order to initiate the emotional involvement of the speaker during the con-

versation. Labov points out that talking about accidents, sickness, and natural disasters may be appropriate to generate the conditions for emotional speech. The topics suggested by Labov (1972) were adapted to the interviews of the children in this research. The interviewer shared a personal experience with the child as follows: "One day I was in the kitchen serving myself a glass of Coke and I did not hold the glass firmly. The glass fell down and broke, hurting my feet. Have you ever had something like that happen to you?" Another trigger situation included the following: "One day I was very sick and had to go to the doctor. Have you ever visited the doctor? What was that experience like?" The trigger situations worked very well for almost all the children. They were able to narrate a situation and to express their emotional reactions.

The third part of the interview was play activity with toys representing the characters from the movie *Aladdin*. The characters from *The Flintstones* were also used during the interview. The children were able to narrate their own version of the movie or to create new situations playing with the characters. Lower- and upper-class speakers were very familiar with the characters from both *Aladdin* and *The Flintstones*.

Finally, the last part of the interview included a storytelling activity using the tale *La gallinita* 'The little hen'. The child had to retell the story with the pictures of the characters and events in the book. All the situations contained during the interview created a positive environment for obtaining a large amount of discourse suitable for performing a quantitative analysis.

3.2. Analyses

In order to test the variable rule and the case-by-case hypotheses, we have examined the number of times a token was produced and whether there was alternation in its production. If we find alternation we would have to observe whether this variability affects all possible targets where the phonetic as well as internal and external constraints are met regardless of age group if we assume an early acquisition of variability. If this were the case, then we would have enough evidence to support the variable rule hypothesis.

Contrastively, the case-by-case hypothesis would be supported if we do not find alternation at the beginning stages. As explained before, even if we find alternation we will have to analyze whether such variability always applies given the same conditions (e.g., similar internal and external factors affecting the linguistic variables). Following the ideas of Bybee's (2001) usage-based model of phonology, it would be possible to think that frequency may play a role in the spreading of variation in individual lexical forms. Frequency effects were measured in two different ways. First, the cases analyzed were divided according to their frequency in the corpus. Second, the *Frequency dictionary of Spanish words*[2] (Julliand and Chang-Rodríguez 1964) was used to determine the coefficient of general usage for each token.

GoldVarb 2001, a linguistic software program specifically designed for the study of sociolinguistic variation, was used for performing a statistical analysis of the data. Five factor groups were included in the analysis for examining both the variable rule and the case-by-case hypotheses. A description of each factor group is presented below:

1) *Factor group 1* (Alternation vs. no alternation): This Factor group has been taken as the dependent variable. It takes into consideration whether each of the tokens was produced variably or not. As explained above, one way to examine both the variable rule and the case-by-case hypotheses is considering whether there is variably in the production of intervocalic /d/. Two factors are included in this case: 1) alternation, and 2) no alternation.

2) *Factor group 2* (Deletion/retention in non-alternating cases): This Factor group measures what is the predominant production tendency (e.g., /d/ deletion or retention) in the tokens in which alternation was not found. Tokens with no alternation were classified in two categories: 1) cases of /d/ deletion, and 2) cases of /d/ retention.

3) *Factor group 3* (Dictionary frequency[3]): In this case, we examine frequency effects by considering the coefficient of general usage proposed by Julliand and Chang-Rodríguez (1964) in their *Frequency dictionary of Spanish words*. This frequency dictionary consists of 5,024 words coming from 5 different sources including dramatic literature (plays), fictional literature (novels, short stories), essayistic literature (essays, memoirs, correspondence, etc.), technical literature (medicine, engineering, physics, etc.), and journalistic literature (dailies, weeklies, monthlies). Three levels of frequency were taken into account: 1) high frequency (101 or higher coefficient of general usage), 2) mid frequency (50-100 coefficient of general usage), and 3) low frequency (0-49 coefficient of general usage).

4) *Factor group 4* (Corpus frequency): This Factor group takes into consideration the frequency of the tokens within the corpus. The 20 most frequent words containing an intervocalic /d/ were classified as having high frequency. The rest of the tokens were considered as having low frequency. Including this measurement will allow com-

paring whether the tendencies found while examining the Julliand and Chang-Rodríguez (1964) frequency dictionary pattern in the same way.

5) *Factor group 5* (Age): In this case, we distinguish 6 different groups: (1) *42- to 47-month-olds*, (2) *48- to 53-month-olds*, (3) *54- to 59-month-olds*, (4) *60- to 65-month-olds*, and (5) *66- to 71-month-olds*. The motivation for having 6 groups is to track with more detail phonological acquisition at different stages of development. Previous work related to the acquisition of sociolinguistic variables in Spanish has shown that this age division is important for explaining changes in children's speech (see Diaz-Campos 2001).

4. Results and discussion

4.1. Results

This section is divided in two parts. The first one presents the 3 factor groups selected as significant by GoldVarb 2001. The second one discusses the findings in order to answer whether sociolinguistic variables are acquired in a case-by-case fashion or as variable rules.

GoldVarb 2001 allows for clarification of how a group of internal and external constraints are related to the dependent variable. In the particular case of this investigation, factor group 1 (alternation vs. not alternation in the production of intervocalic /d/) is the dependent variable. The application value is factor *alternation* since examining whether or not there is variability across children of different age groups will allow testing the hypotheses proposed at the end of Section 2.2. GoldVarb reveals the probabilistic weight of each one of the constraints not only in relation to a given variant but also the overall effect of significant factors regarding that variant. A weight greater than .500 favors the application value and a lesser probability disfavors it.

The factors found to be statistically significant are presented in Table 1[4] in order of selection. This order of selection is crucially important because it indicates the degree of impact of the factor group selected on the dependent variable from most important to least important. According to this explanation, factor group 3, which measures frequency effects considering the coefficient of general usage proposed by Julliand and Chang-Rodríguez (1964), has the greatest impact on alternant tokens (a discussion of this result is given below). Factor group 4 (frequency within the corpus) is the next in the hierarchy. The next constraint is factor group 5 (age of the consultant). The original analysis also included factor group 2, which considers degree of /d/ deletion or retention in non-alternating tokens. Since this independent constraint contains *knockout factors*, it was discarded in order to be able to perform a probabilistic analysis. A *knockout factor* occurs when there are empty cells and this condition does not allow GoldVarb to run the probabilistic analysis.

Table 1:   Factor groups selected in the acquisition of sociolinguistic variable analysis (input probability = 0.041 (63/344)

Factor group	Factors	No of cases	%	Weight
Dictionary frequency	High	27/58	46	.775
	Mid	3/15	20	.515
	Low	22/174	12	.397
Corpus frequency	High	44/80	55	.991
	Low	19/245	7	.196
Age	42-47 months	19/85	22	.972
	48-53 months	7/41	17	.093
	54-59 months	13/58	22	.288
	60-65 months	13/88	14	.312
	66-71 months	11/72	15	.235

The factor group selected as the most significant is dictionary frequency. The results reveal that high frequency tokens trigger alternation in the production of intervocalic /d/ with a weight of .775. Mid frequency words show a borderline tendency according to which alternation in the production of intervocalic /d/ is neither favored nor disfavored. In the case of lower frequency words, the findings indicate that they disfavor variability in the production of intervocalic /d/. The fact that the factor group dictionary frequency is the one having the greatest impact on the variable pronunciation of intervocalic /d/ is a piece of evidence revealing that acquisition of sociolinguistic variables is more likely to happen in high frequency tokens at the beginning stages. Lower frequency tokens disfavor alternation in the production of intervocalic /d/, so we would expect that stylistic variation would spread to this class of tokens at a more advanced stage. In the following section, we discuss in more detail these findings and explain whether they support the case-by-case or the variable rule hypotheses.

The second factor group selected is corpus frequency. This result is also very important because it is consistent with the factor group dictionary frequency. The weight for high frequency tokens within the corpus is .991, which reveals that this factor highly favors variable production of intervocalic /d/. In the case of lower frequency tokens, alternation in the production of intervocalic /d/ is disfavored. Among the most frequent tokens within the corpus (these tokens also have a high frequency according to Julliand and Chang-Rodríguez 1964) we find *de* 'of/from', *lado* 'side', *donde* 'where', *todavía* 'yet', etc. In all of these tokens, alternation in the production of intervocalic /d/ is the predominant tendency.

Age is the next most important factor group according to the statistical analysis. The factor with the highest weight is 42- to 47- month old children, at .972. This result indicates that the youngest children favor variable pronunciation. In the rest of the age groups, the findings show that alternation in the pronunciation of intervocalic /d/ is disfavored. Is variability in the production of intervocalic /d/ a phenomenon relating to the development of the phonology of the youngest group? How can we explain these tendencies? What is the favored pronunciation in non-alternating cases? In a previous study examining deletion of intervocalic /d/ in this same group of children (see Diaz-Campos 2001), it was determined that the variable pronunciation of intervocalic /d/ is not developmental, but sociolinguistic in nature. Children show in their speech from a very early age the patterns of variation of their immediate community. The fact that older children do not favor variability is reflecting the effect of the variety of language spoken at school where variability is less likely to happen and retention of intervocalic /d/ is the predominant tendency. Retention is favored in the speech of upper class children. Older lower class children begin to retain more intervocalic /d/ in their pronunciation once they are exposed to the school variety of language. This explanation is corroborated by the results of the present analysis according to which in non-alternating cases the predominant pronunciation favors retention of intervocalic /d/ (236 tokens out of 281). In any case, it is important to point out that even though variability is not favored by older children, these age groups did show alternation in their pronunciation of intervocalic /d/ in highly frequent tokens as discussed above.

4.2. Discussion

Since the main concern of this investigation is to determine whether children acquire sociolinguistic variation in a case-by-case fashion or acquire variable rules, we turn our attention to a discussion of the hypotheses presented in Section 2. The statistical results indicate that the two factor groups, dictionary frequency as well as corpus frequency, play a crucial role for predicting variable pronunciation of intervocalic /d/. This piece of evidence will be an important element in the construction of an explanation that we will develop in the next section.

According to the hypothesis presented at the end of section 1, we need to answer whether we find variability in the production of intervocalic /d/ in different age groups. Alternating pronunciation across all age groups could be an indication of acquisition of variable rules, but we will have to explore further pieces of evidence to support this position with solid arguments. Figure 1 shows the patterns of alternation across age groups.

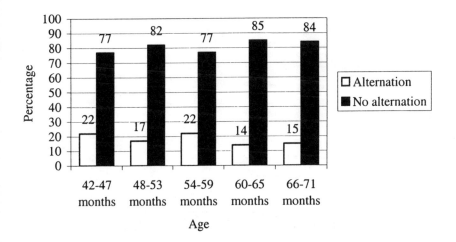

Figure 1. Pattern of alternation in the production of intervocalic /d/ across age groups

Because of the probabilistic analysis presented in section 3.1 we know that 42- to 47- month old children are more likely to produced variable intervocalic /d/. However, figure 1 shows similar percentages across all age groups regarding alternating pronunciation of intervocalic /d/. Recall that alternation is more common in frequent tokens regardless of age group and this fact is reflected in Figure 1. This result could be an indication supporting the variable rule analysis hypothesis because all tokens containing intervocalic /d/ will behave in the same fashion given the internal and external constraints governing sociolinguistic variation of intervocalic /d/ in

Venezuelan children's speech. However, we need to analyze with more detail the role of frequency in the acquisition of sociolinguistic variables.

Can we show that frequency is playing a role in the spreading of variation in a case-by-case fashion? So far we have seen that the probabilistic analysis has provided good indications that alternation is more likely to affect frequent words. Following this finding, we would have to accept that variability is not having the same effect given the same internal and external constraints. In other words, if children were acquiring variable rules we would expect variability any time the conditions are satisfied, but this is not the result that we are observing in the data examined. Figures 2 and 3 show the pattern of alternation according to dictionary and corpus frequencies, respectively.

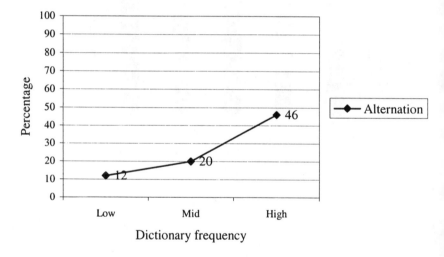

Figure 2. Pattern of alternation according to the factor group dictionary frequency.

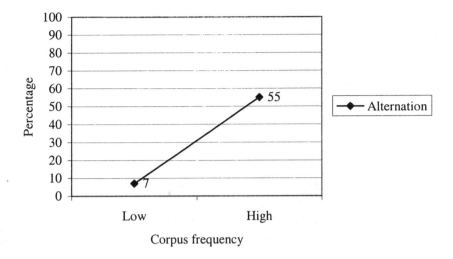

Figure 3. Pattern of alternation according to the factor group corpus frequency.

As can be seen in both Figures 2 and 3, alternating pronunciation of intervocalic /d/ increases in frequent tokens. These findings allow arguing that sociolinguistic variation is first observed in high frequent words and then it spreads to less frequent ones. This would mean that sociolinguistic variables are acquired in a case-by-case fashion contradicting the variable rule hypothesis.

In summary, the statistical results presented here reveal that sociolinguistic variation is first acquired in highly frequent individual lexical forms. Otherwise, we would have had to find alternating pronunciation any time the phonetic context and the internal and external constraints governing variable production of intervocalic /d/ are satisfied.

5. Conclusions

The main goal of this investigation was to answer whether sociolinguistic variables are acquired by individual lexical forms or variable rules. In order to do this we have explored whether the pattern of variation behaves the same across age groups. We also have observed the role of frequency following Bybee's usage-based model of phonology according to which variation would spread first in frequent individual lexical forms. Contrary to our expectations, the first question regarding alternating pronunciation across age groups shows that variability is found in all age groups. It is important to point out that variability is more likely to happen in frequent tokens regardless of age. The probabilistic analysis reveals that the most important predictors of alternating pronunciation of intervocalic /d/ are the factor groups dictionary frequency and corpus frequency. This finding is the most relevant piece of evidence of our analysis for supporting the case-by-case hypothesis according to which variability is first found in highly frequent tokens.

In short, the statistical analysis strongly supports the idea that not all the tokens where the conditions of the variable rule are met behave in the same fashion. Frequency effects explain such contradictory behavior providing a crucial argument to support that children acquire sociolinguistic variables in a case-by-case fashion. These results are consistent with Chevrot, Beaud, and Varga's (2000) interactionist approach for explaining acquisition of variable phonology.

Notes

1. This data collection project was supported by the Consejo de Desarrollo Científico y Humanístico of the Universidad Central de Venezuela (grant #: 07-33.3737.96).
2. We also tried to use the Diccionario de frecuencias de las unidades lingüísticas del castellano prepared by Alameda y Cuetos (1995), but we found that many common words (e.g., donde 'where', todavía 'yet', nada 'anything', todas 'all', etc) are not included in the dictionary creating difficulties for performing a comprehensive analysis.
3. In the results section (see section 4), you will find that this dictionary of frequency based on print sources also reflect very closely frequency in speech. Both dictionary frequency and corpus frequency pattern together in the analysis of acquisition of sociolinguistic variables.
4. The data in Table 1 is organized as follows: the left-hand column shows only the significant factor group in order of selection. The next column indicates the factor values for each factor group selected. The column identified as "No of tokens" has two numbers separated by a slash: the first one refers to the cases the cases of intervocalic /d/ produced variably within the factor considered; the second one indicates the total of tokens of intervocalic /d/ within that same factor or variant. The next column gives the percentage of intervocalic /d/ tokens produced with alternation. The weight column specifies the probabilistic weight for each factor within each group. The range of the weight varies from 0 to 1.

References

Alameda, José Ramón and Fernando Cuetos.
1995   *Diccionario de frecuencias de las unidades lingüísticas del castellano.* Oviedo: Universidad de Oviedo.
Bybee, Joan
2001   *Phonology and Language Use.* Cambridge: Cambridge University Press.
Cedergren, Henrietta
1979   La elisión de la /d/: un ensayo de comparación dialectal. *Boletín de la Academia Puertorriqueña de la Lengua Española* 7: 19-29.
Cedergren, Henrietta and David Sankoff
1974   Variable rules: performance as a statistical reflection of competence. *Language* 50: 333-355.
Chambers, J.
1988   Acquisition of phonological variants. In *Methods in Dialectology,* Alan Thomas and Martin Ball (eds.), 650-665. Clevedon: Multilingual Matters.
Chevrot, Jean-Pierre; Laurence Beaud; and Renata Varga
2000   Developmental data on French sociolinguistic variable: Postconsonantal word-final /R/. *Language Variation and Change* 12: 295-319.
Díaz-Campos, Manuel
2001   Acquisition of phonological structure and sociolinguistic variables: a quantitative analysis of Spanish consonant weakening in Venezuelan children's speech. Ph.D. diss., The Ohio State University.
D' Introno, Francesco y Juan Manuel Sosa
1986   Elisión de la /d/ en el español de Caracas: Aspectos sociolingüísticos e implicaciones teóricas. In *Estudios sobre la Fonología del Español del Caribe,* Rafael Nuñez Cedeño; Iraset Páez Urdaneta; and Jorge M. Guitart (eds.), 135-163. Caracas: Casa de Bello.
Eckert, Penelope
2000   *Linguistic Variation as a Social Practice.* Cambridge, Massachusetts: Blackwell.
Julliand, Alphonse G. and Eugenio Chang-Rodríguez
1964   *Frequency Dictionary of Spanish Words.* The Hague: Mouton.
Kerswill, Paul
1996   Children, adolescents, and language change. *Language Variation and Change* 8: 177-202.

Kovac, Ceil and H. D. Adamson
    1981   Variation theory and first language acquisition. In *Variation Omnibus*, David Sankoff and Henrietta Cedergren (eds.), 403-410. Edmonton, Alberta: Linguistic Research, Inc.

Labov, William
    1964   Stages in the acquisition of standard English. In *Social Dialects and Language Learning*, Roger Shuy, Alva Davis, and Robert Hogan (eds.), 77-104. Champaign: National Council of Teachers of English.
    1972   *Sociolinguistic Patterns*. Philadelphia: University of Pennsylvania Press.
    1989   The child as linguistic historian. *Language, Variation, and Change* 1: 85-97.

Patterson, Janet
    1993   The development of sociolinguistic phonological variation patterns for (ING) in young children. *Dissertation Abstracts International* 53:3, 3196A.

Payne, Arvilla
    1980   Factors controlling the acquisition of the Philadelphia dialect by out-of-state children. In *Locating Language in Time and Space*, William Labov (ed.), 143-178. New York: Academic Press.

Roberts, Julie
    1994   Acquisition of variable rules: (-t,d) deletion and (ing) production in preschool children. Ph.D. diss., University of Pennsylvania.
    1997a   Hitting a moving target: Acquisition of sound change in progress by Philadelphia children. *Language, Variation, and Change* 9: 249-266.
    1997b   Acquisition of variable rules: A study of (-t,d) deletion in preschool children. *Journal of Child Language* 24: 351-372.

Roberts, Julie and William Labov
    1995   Learning to talk Philadelphian: Acquisition of short a by preschool children. *Language, Variation, and Change* 7: 101-112.

Interplay between phonetic and inventory constraints in the degree of spirantization of voiced stops: Comparing intervocalic /b/ and intervocalic /g/ in Spanish and English

Marta Ortega-Llebaria

1. Introduction

Explaining speech variability is a long standing challenge in phonetic sciences that has been addressed from different perspectives. For instance, the great variability encountered in the degree of spirantization of intervocalic voiced stops in Spanish (Quilis 1963; Navarro Tomás 1966; Harris 1969) has often been treated in a categorical manner: Voiced stops have been reduced to two categories, spirantized stops and non-spirantized stops, and their contextual alternations have been interpreted as a case of assimilation. Either the underlying realization was a stop that became spirantized by acquiring the [+continuant] feature from the adjacent vowels (Hualde 1989; Mascaró 1991), or the underlying sound was an approximant that became a stop by assimilating the [- continuant] feature from the preceding consonant (Lozano 1979: 14-29).

However, recent studies have taken into consideration the variation in the degree of lenition and have described spirantization as a gradual phenomenon whose variability is conditioned by phonetic factors or by principles of gestural reorganization. For example, Cole, Hualde and Iskarous (1998) found that the degree of spirantization of Spanish intervocalic /g/ varied according to stress and vowel context. This consonant became most spirantized in unstressed syllables flanked by /o,u/ vowels, like in the word /súgus/ 'candy', and least spirantized in stressed syllables flanked by a /a/ vowels, e.g., /amagár/ 'to show, to indicate'. Moreover, Honorof (2003), after finding de-occlusivization of /n/ in intervocalic contexts, proposes that spirantization of intervocalic voiced stops together with nasal de-occlusivization are patterns that obey the same principle of gestural reorganization in which the gestural magnitude of the consonant is reduced in intervocalic contexts.

In spite of this diversity of perspectives, relating speech variability with inventory constraints has been a long standing proposal (Trubetzkoy 1969) that has proved a productive line of research. Inventory constraints, which are associated to the system of contrasts of the sounds of a language, limit the variation in the production and perception of sounds in order to maintain distinctiveness among contrastive units. Studies, however, have mainly focused on the role of inventory constraints on speech perception (Hume and Johnson 2001; Costa, Cutler and Sebastián-Gallés 1998; Boersma 1998; Best 1995; Khul and Iverson 1994; Otake, Cutler and Mehler 1993). For example, in their (1998) article Costa, Cutler and Sebastián-Gallés demonstrated that the inventory size of a language affected the variability tolerated in the perception of individual sounds. Best (1995) showed that adults perceived sounds of a second language according to the contrast system of their first language. Boersma (1998) quantified articulation and inventory constraints and made them interact in an OT-like fashion in order to account for various perceptual phenomena.

One of the few studies that related inventory constraints with variability in speech production is that of Manuel (1990). She defined inventory constraints as inventory size, and demonstrated that inventory constraints had predictive value with respect to how extensively various phonemes were coarticulated in particular languages. Languages with less crowded vocalic inventories and more acoustic space for individual vowels tolerated more coarticulation than those with more vowels with reduced acoustic space.

This paper extends Manuel's hypothesis to the phenomenon of spirantization. It investigates the interaction of phonetic factors with inventory constraints in determining the variation in the degree of spirantization of intervocalic voiced stops. First, it examines whether the phonetic factors of stress and vowel context, which had an effect in Spanish intervocalic /g/ (Cole, Hualde, and Iskarous 1998), had also an effect in English intervocalic /g/, and Spanish and English intervocalic /b/. Second, this paper studies the interaction of phonetic factors with inventory constraints. Inventory constraints preserve the system of contrasts of a language while phonetic factors provide contexts that favor lenition. Therefore, hypothetically, a consonant will become lenited in a favorable phonetic context only if the resulting sound does not impair a contrast of the language. For example, in English, /b/ contrasts with the voiced fricative /v/ while in Spanish, it does not. However, neither Spanish /g/ nor English /g/ contrasts with a voiced velar fricative sound. Consequently, in contexts favorable to lenition, the difference in the degree of spirantization between Spanish and English /b/ will be greater than that between Spanish and English /g/.

2. Methodology

2.1. Subjects

Ten female subjects participated in the study, 5 native speakers of Caribbean Spanish and five native speakers of American English. Two of the Spanish speakers were from Caracas, Venezuela, one was from Puerto Rico, one from the Dominican Republic, and one from Cuba. Each spoke a dialect of Spanish that tended to strongly spirantize intervocalic voiced stops (Zamora-Munné and Guitart 1982). Each spoke English as her second language, and although four out of the five were highly proficient Spanish-English bilinguals, only one speaker did not have a noticeable Spanish accent when speaking English.

Although the English speakers came from different states, two were from Colorado, one from Wyoming, one from Massachusetts, and one from Wisconsin, their dialectal differences did not affect the pattern under study. Two subjects spoke Spanish fluently, one was proficient in Russian, and the other two were English monolinguals.

The ages of the subjects within each language group ranged from the mid twenties to the early fifties. From birth to adolescence, all participants had received extensive input primarily in their mother tongue to communicate with parents and siblings. They first became literate in their native language, and not until at least age 10, did any of them start learning a second language, nor had they lived in a country where a foreign language was spoken. Presently, all subjects make extensive use of their native language in their daily life. Those who have children choose their mother tongue to communicate with them even if they do not live in their country of origin.

2.2. Materials and task

Subjects participated in a memory game in which they had to recall the names of 12 invented cartoon characters. Their names, which were /bába/, /babá/, /bíbi/, /bibí/, /búbu/, /bubú/, /gága/, /gagá/, /gígi/, /gigí/, /gúgu/, /gugú/, related to the physical appearance of the cartoon characters. The vowels of the character's name were color-coded: red represented vowel /a/, green vowel /i/, and blue vowel /u/. The consonants of the character's name were corresponded to by the shape of the cartoon character's body. A squared body meant /b/ and a rectangular body meant /g/. The stress position in the cartoon character's name was shown by solid color versus a line, i.e. solid color represented stress in the second syllable, line represented stress in the first syllable. For example, the cartoon named /bába/ was red because the vowel /a/, had a squared body due to the consonant /b/, and was drawn with an outline only to represent stress in the first syllable.

Each cartoon character was wearing a piece of clothing. Each subjects' task was to create a sentence in her native language that contained the name of the character and, for example, the piece of clothing it was wearing, i.e. "Mister Bubú is wearing a hat" or "El señor Bubú lleva un sombrero".

The objective of this task was to obtain utterances that contained consonant lenition. Therefore, the task was designed as a game to create a relaxed environment in which participants felt comfortable to speak in an informal register (Lindblom 1990). Moreover, the memory load of the game also aided speakers not to focus on specific sound pronunciation.

2.3. Recordings and measurements

Subjects were recorded in a sound attenuated room. Each subject produced a sentence for each one of the 12 cartoon characters. The same task was repeated four additional times. Recordings were made directly into a computer which digitized sound at a sampling rate of 44 KHz and 16 bytes of resolution.

The intervocalic consonant in each target word was evaluated according to two measures of energy. First, the RMS-amplitude ratio of the intervocalic consonant to the VCV part of the target word was measured. RMS-amplitude indicates acoustic intensity and is calculated by taking the square root of the average of the squared peak amplitudes of each sample in a window. In this case, the windows had the length of the intervocalic consonant and that of the VCV part of the target word (see Figure 1). Thus closer the RMS-amplitude ratio came to 1, the more vowel-like was the intervocalic consonant. A ratio closer to 0 indicated that the intervocalic consonant was produced with a stop closure. For example, the intervocalic /b/ of the word /búbu/ in Figure 1 obtained a ratio of 0.8529 while the intervocalic /b/ in /bubú/ scored 0.6003 indicating that the first /b/ was more similar to a vowel than the second one.

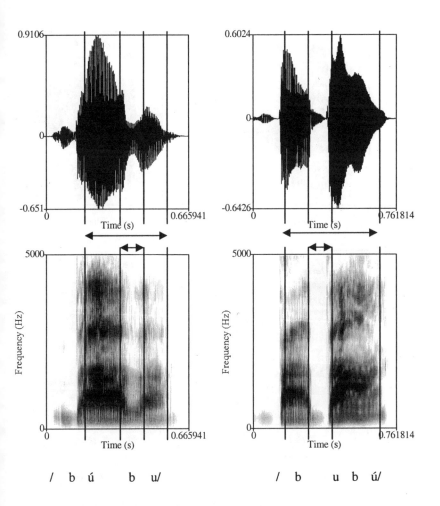

/ b ú   b u/   / b   u b ú/

Figure 1. Waveforms (top) and spectrograms (bottom) of the utterances /búbu/ and /bubú/. RMS ratio of the intervocalic consonant to the VCV part of the target word indicated degree of lenition. The RMS ratio of the intervocalic /b/ in /búbu/ measured 0.8529 and in /bubú/ was 0.6003.

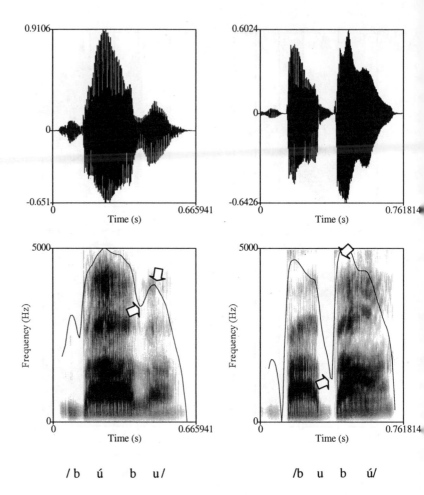

/b ú   b   u/   /b u   b   ú/

Figure 2. Waveforms and spectrograms with intensity contour of the utterances /búbu/ and /bubú/. The arrows indicate the points of maximum and minimum intensity of the intervocalic consonant. Speed of consonant release was measured as difference between the maximum and minimum intensity of the consonant as a function of time. Intervocalic /b/ in /búbu/ measured 79.08 dB/ms., and 199.11 dB/ms. in /bubú/.

Second, the speed at which the intervocalic consonant was released into the following vowel was measured as the difference between the maximum and minimum intensity of the consonant as a function of time. This measurement captures the differences in steepness of intensity changes between glides and voiced stops at their offset, which reflect speed of consonant release: glides going into vowels display more gradual changes in intensity and in consonant release than stops releasing into vowels (Pickett 1999: 105-106). When the formula results in a high number, it indicates that the speed is faster, and therefore the intervocalic consonant will have a faster release and be more stop-like. A lower number signifies a slower release which is more vowel-like. For example, the intensity of intervocalic /b/ in /búbu/ in Figure 2 raised 79.08 dBs per millisecond from its point of lowest intensity in /b/ until reaching the point of maximum intensity in the following vowel. In contrast, this intensity change reached a speed of 199.11 dBs per millisecond in the intervocalic /b/ of /bubú/, indicating that this intervocalic /b/ had a more abrupt release into the next vowel and is realized more like a stops than the intervocalic /b/ in /búbu/.

3. Results

Repeated Measures ANOVA analyses were performed on the RMS ratio measurements and on the speed of consonant release measurements. Each ANOVA contained the within-subject factors of consonant (b, g), vowel (a, i, u), and stress (trochee, iamb), and the between-subject factor of native language (Spanish, English). Post-hoc multiple comparisons used the Bonferroni test.

3.1. Effects of stress

Results indicated that stress influenced the degree of spirantization of intervocalic stops. A significant main effect in RMS measures ($F(1,46)=350.985$, $p<.0001$) and in speed of consonant release measures ($F(1,46)=100.637$, $p<.0001$) showed that speakers of both Spanish and English produced intervocalic consonants in trochee words, i.e. bába, with more lenition than those in iambic words, i.e. babá. As shown in Figure 3, intervocalic consonants in trochees obtained higher RMS scores and slower release motions than did consonants in iambs. Moreover, Spanish consonants were spoken with a higher overall degree of lenition than were their English counterparts, as indicated by the interaction stress*language (RMS measurements: $F(1,46)= 21.735$, $p<.0001$; speed of consonant release measurements: $F(1,46)=8.519$, $p=.005$).

(a)   (b)

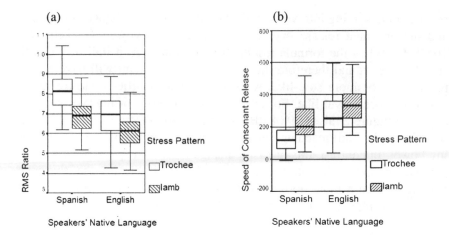

Figure 3. Effect of stress in the degree of lenition of Spanish and English consonants. Spirantization is measured as RMS ratio in (a), and as the speed
of consonant release in (b).

3.2. Interaction of inventory constraints with stress

Consonant type constrained the influence of stress in the degree of spirantization. The interaction consonant*stress*language (RMS measure: $F(2,$
$46)=5.389$, $p=.020$) showed that in trochee words, i.e. bába, Spanish intervocalic /b/ was significantly more lenited than was English intervocalic /b/
(Figure 4a), while intervocalic /g/ in Spanish and in English did not differ
significantly from each other (Figure 4b). No significant cross-language
differences were found for either consonant in iambic words.

Speaker variability contributes to the cross-language differences between the degrees of lenition of /b/ and /g/. Figure (5a) displays the distribution of the lenition scores obtained by the five Spanish speaking subjects
and the five English speaking subjects when producing "búbu" and "bubú"
words. The horizontal line placed at an RMS of .75 dB clearly separates
the Spanish "búbu" utterances, which reached values above .75 dB, from
Spanish "bubú", English "búbu", and English "bubú" utterances, which
generally scored below this value. Thus, in trochees, Spanish subjects consistently produced a more lenited intervocalic /b/ than did English speakers. This cross-language difference, however, is not clear for intervocalic
/g/. As illustrated in Figure (5b), the lenition scores obtained by the 5 Spanish speakers when producing intervocalic /g/ in trochees were above the

horizontal line placed at an RMS of .70. However, the lenition scores for intervocalic /g/ in trochees scored by three of the English subjects, i.e. En1, En3, and En5, also were above the horizontal line, indicating that they produced intervocalic /g/ with as much lenition as did Spanish speakers. The fourth English subject, i.e. En2, produced this /g/ as a stop, while the productions of the 5th English subject, i.e. En4, ranged from strongly spiratized to stop-like. Consequently, the significant differences between Spanish /b/ and English /b/ in trochee words were related to the consistency in which the Spanish and the English subjects produced a strongly lenited /b/ or a stop-like /b/ respectively. The non-significant differences between Spanish /g/ and English /g/ in trochees were associated with the great subject variability among the English speakers.

(a)

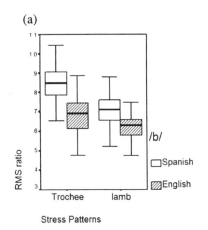

(b)

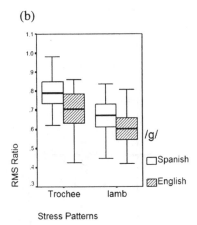

Figure 4. Degree of lenition of /b/ and /g/ in Spanish and English as function of stress.

(a)

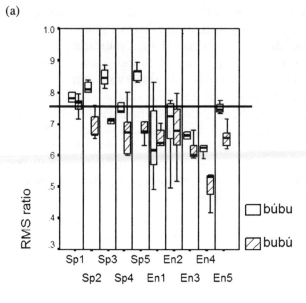

(b)

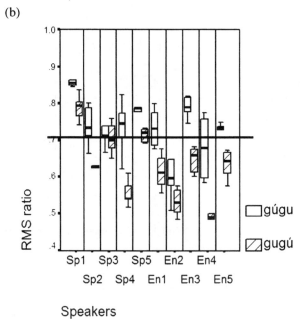

Figure 5. Speaker variability in the degrees of lenition of intervocalic /b/ and /g/.

3.3. Effect of vowel context

Significant results for vowel context were obtained only for the measures of speed of consonant release. A significant main effect ($F(2, 92)=2,607)=20.259$, $p<.0001$) indicated that /a/ scored higher than did /i/ and /u/ in both languages. Moreover, the interaction consonant*vowel ($F(2,92)=9.100$, $p<.0001$) showed that these differences between /a/, and /i/-/u/ took place only in intervocalic /g/. Intervocalic /b/ did not reflect any significant effect of vowel context in either language.

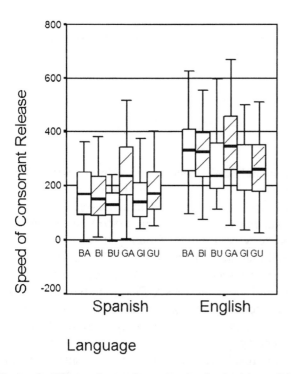

Figure 6. Effect of vowel context in the lenition of /b/ and /g/ in Spanish and English.

In summary, the phonetic factors of stress and vowel context had a significant effect in the degree of spirantization of Spanish and English intervocalic consonants. Both /b/ and /g/ were more lenited in trochaic words. Vowel context had an influence only in /g/, which became more lenited in /i/-/u/ contexts.

In addition to the above similarities, there were notable cross-language differences. First, in trochees, Spanish /b/ was significantly more lenited than was English /b/, while the differences in the degree of spirantization between Spanish /g/ and English /g/ were not significant. This lack of significance was due to the subject variability displayed by English speakers. Secondly, for both phonetic factors, Spanish /b/ and /g/ displayed a higher overall degree of lenition than did their English counterparts. This difference only reached significance for the stress factor.

The phonetic factor of stress differed from that of vowel context in one additional aspect. The influence of stress in consonant lenition was captured by both measures of energy, i.e. RMS ratio and speed of consonant release, whereas the influence of vowel context was captured only by the speed of consonant release measures.

4. Discussion

4.1. Effect of phonetic factors

Both phonetic factors, stress and vowel context had a similar influence on the lenition of intervocalic /b/ and /g/ in Spanish and in English. Consonants are more spirantized when followed by a non-stressed vowel. This result parallels that of Cole, Hualde and Iskarous (1998) for Spanish /g/ and DeJong (1998) in his study on English flapping. It is also consistent with research that has found that articulatory gestures reach a greater magnitude in prosodically strong positions, while it is reduced in weak prosodic positions (Browman and Goldstein 1992; Pierrehumbert and Talkin 1992). This cross-linguistic tendency to reduce segments in unstressed syllables reflects a principle of articulatory economy related to the constraints of the human articulatory system.

As for vowel context, the results indicated that vowel-consonant coarticulation had an effect in /g/, not in /b/; and that /g/ was most lenited in /i/-/u/ words and least in /a/ vowel names. The lack of coarticulatory effects on /b/ was expected given the independence of the articulators used in producing each sound, i.e. lips for /b/ and tongue for the vowel (Farnetani 1997).

Our results for /g/ agreed in part with those obtained by Cole, Hualde and Iskarous (1998). In both studies, /g/ obtained the most stop-like scores when flanked by vowel /a/, and the most lenited scores with /u/. However, for /i/ Cole obtained intermediate scores, while our results indicated a lenition degree equivalent to that of /u/.

These differences can be related to methodological issues between experiments. For example, Cole clustered /i/ with /e/, and /u/ with /o/ in their test materials, while this experiment only included /i / and /u/. Moreover, Cole's results were based on RMS ratio measurements, while in our experiment only speed of consonant release measures, not RMS ratio, yielded significant differences between vowel contexts. One possible explanation is that RMS ratio measures captured energy changes sensitive to an average, while speed of consonant release measures denoted changes of energy over time. Thus RMS measures were less sensitive to dynamic changes such as coarticulation effects than speed of release measures.

In spite of the above differences, Cole's interpretation of the effect of vowel context as a consequence of the Dynamics of Tongue Body Movement theory (DTBM) is also valid for the results obtained in this paper. DTBM theorizes less coarticulation, and therefore a lesser degree of lenition, when the tongue body position is changed in the movement between /g/ and the adjacent vowel. DTMB predicts the most tongue body movement and the least lenition effects for /ga/, while according to Cole, Hualde and Iskarous (1998), Economy of Articulation Theory (Lindblom 1990) and Gesture Overlapping Theory (Browman and Goldstein 1992) conclude that /ga/ would display most lenition. My results for /ga/ confirm both Cole's DTBM theory and results. Similarly, Cole's results and mine for /gu/ coincide in assigning /g/ a high degree of lenition, which DTBM correlates with reduced tongue body movement.

By contrast, my results for /gi/ differ from Cole's. While /gi/ in Cole's experiment obtained intermediate lenition scores between /ga/ and /gu/, in my sample /gi/ scores equaled those of /gu/. If we take into account that /g/ is a sound not resistant to coarticulation since it allows a wide range of points of articulation without loosing its acoustic identity, from velum when adjacent to back vowels to palate when next to front vowels, then the tongue body movement from /g/ to /u/ and from /g/ to /i/ are similarly short. Consequently, DTBM predicts a similar degree of lenition between /g/-/u/ and /g/-/i/.

4.2. Inventory constraints

Even though Spanish and English showed similar patterns of lenition as a function of segmental contexts, i.e. consonants became more lenited in trochee words, the two languages differed in the degree of lenition displayed by consonant /b/ in trochee words as well as in the overall degree of consonant lenition. Inventory constraints explained these observed cross-linguistic differences.

The interaction stress*consonant*language illustrates the first cross-language difference. In trochee words, Spanish /b/ was significantly more lenited than was English /b/ because in English, and not in Spanish, the contrast between /b/ and /v/ had to be preserved. Consequently, in order to maintain the contrast between English /b/ and English /v/, lenition of /b/ in trochee words was inhibited. However, no significant differences were found between Spanish and English /g/ since sound /g/ did not contrast with a velar, voiced, continuant segment in either language. Thus, for both languages, consonant lenition took place in trochee words, the phonetic context that promoted lenition, only if the resulting sound did not impair any segmental contrast of the language.

Secondly, when inventory constraints refer to the contrasts between sound classes rather than to segmental contrasts, inventory constraints motivate the higher overall degree of lenition obtained in Spanish consonants in comparison to their English counterparts. Only in English the class of voiced stops contrasts with the class of voiced fricatives because in the Spanish sound inventory, there are no phonemic voiced fricatives. Consequently, in order to preserve this contrast between sound classes, the sound class of English voiced stops maintained a lower overall degree of spirantization than did their Spanish counterparts.

Speaker variability was also related to inventory constraints. As mentioned earlier, the sound class of English voiced stops maintains a contrast with the class of voiced fricatives preventing the former from reaching high degrees of lenition in favorable contexts. As a consequence, English speakers consistently produced /b/ as a stop in trochees. However, there is no velar voiced fricative to contrast with /g/ in English. As a result of this inventory gap, speakers vary their answers. They either relax the constraint imposed by the contrast between sound classes, producing /g/ with higher degrees of lenition; or they ignore the inventory gap, and pronounce /g/ as a stop, like they did with /b/; or they alternate between the two options.

In comparison to the aforementioned speaker variation, Spanish speakers consistently produced /g/ in trochee words with high degrees of lenition. As in English, Spanish /g/ does not contrast with a velar voiced fricative. This lack of contrast, however, is not due to an inventory gap, but to the lack of the entire sound class of voiced fricatives. The Spanish sound system does not impose restrictions in the degree of lenition of voiced stops. As a consequence, both /g/ and /b/ in Spanish are consistently spirantized among speakers in contexts that promote lenition.

Thus, speaker variability is constrained by the requirements imposed by the sound system of a language. When inventory gaps relax the constraints imposed by contrasting sound classes, speakers produce consonants with varying degrees of lenition. Conversely, speakers produce consonants with a constant degree of lenition when the system of contrasts of a language does not result in conflicting constraints with inventory gaps. In this case, consonant lenition applies in favorable contexts, i.e. unstressed syllables, when the resulting sound does not impair any contrast of the language. Otherwise, consonant lenition will not apply.

5. Conclusion

The phonetic factors of stress and vowel context had similar effects in the lenition of intervocalic /b/ and /g/ in Spanish and English. In both languages, the intervocalic consonants were more lenited in trochee words than did in iambs, and /g/ was most spirantized when flanked by /i/ and /u/ vowels. However, inventory constraints limited the effect of phonetic factors accounting for cross-linguistic and speaker variation. For example, the lack of the contrast between /b/ and /v/ in Spanish explained the higher degree of lenition of Spanish /b/ in comparison with English /b/ in trochee words. Thus, lenition of intervocalic consonants is a gradient phenomenon whose variability is better described by the interaction of phonetic factors with inventory constraints rather than in a categorical fashion.

References

Best, Catherine
    1995   A direct realist view of cross-language speech perception research with adults. In *Speech Perception and Linguistic Experience*, Winifred Strange (ed.), 171–204. Baltimore: York Press.
Browman, Catherine and Louis Goldstein
    1992   Articulatory phonology: An overview. *Phonetica* 49: 155–180.
Boersma, Paul
    1998   Functional phonology. Ph.D. diss., University of Amsterdam.

Cole, Jennifer, José Ignacio Hualde, and Khalil Iskarous
1998   Effects of prosodic context on /g/-lenition in Spanish. In *Proceedings of LP'98,* Osamu Fujimura (ed.), 575–589. Prague: The Karolinum Press.
Costa, Albert, Anne Cutler, and Núria Sebastián-Gallés
1998   Effects of phoneme repertoire on phoneme distinction. *Perception & Psychophysics* 60: 1022–1031.
DeJong, Kenneth
1998   Stress-related variation in the articulation of coda alveolar stops: Flapping revisited. *Journal of Phonetics* 26: 283–310.
Farnetani, Edda
1997   Coarticulation and connected speech processes. In *The Handbook of Phonetic Sciences*, William J. Hardcastle and John Laver (eds.), 371–404. Oxford/Massachussets: Blackwell.
Harris, James W.
1969   *Spanish Phonology*. Cambridge, MA: The MIT Press.
Honorof, Douglas
2003   Articulatory evidence for nasal de-occlusivization in Castillian. In *Proceedings of the 15ᵗʰ International Congress of Phonetic Sciences*, Maria Josep Solé, Daniel Recasens, and Joaquín Romero (eds.), 1759–1762. Barcelona: UAB.
Hualde, José Ignacio
1989   Procesos consonánticos y estructuras geométricas en español. *Lingüística ALFAL* 1: 7–44.
Hume, Elizabeth and Keith Jonhson
2001   *The Role of Speech Perception in Phonology*. San Diego, CA: Academic Press.
Kuhl, Patricia, and Paul Iverson
1994   Linguistic experience and the perceptual magnet effect. In *Speech Perception and Linguistic Experience,* Winifred Strange (ed.), 121–154. Baltimore: York Press.
Lindblom, Björn
1990   Explaining phonetic variation: A sketch of the H&H theory. In *Production and Speech Modeling Speech*, William J. Hardcastle and Marchal (eds.), 403–440. Dordretch: Kluwer Academic Publishers.
Lozano, María del Carmen
1979   Stop and spirant alternations: Fortition and spirantization processes in Spanish phonology. Bloomington: Indiana University Linguistics Club.

Manuel, Sharon
1990   The role of contrast in limiting vowel-to-vowel coarticulation in different languages. *Journal of the Acoustical Society of America* 88: 1286–1298.
Mascaró, Joan
1991   Iberian spirantization and continuant spreading. In *Catalan Working Papers in Linguistics 1991* Albert Bracadell (ed.), 167–179. Barcelona: Universitat. Autònoma de Barcelona.
Navarro Tomás, Tomás
1966   *Estudios de fonología española.* New York: Las Americas Publishing Company.
Otake, T, Anne Cutler, and Jacques Mehler
1993   Mora or syllable? Speech segmentation in Japanese. *Journal of Memory and Language* 32: 258–278.
Pickett, James M.
1999   *The Acoustics of Speech Communication: Fundamentals, Speech Perception Theory, and Technology.* Needham Heigths, MA: Allyn & Bacon.
Pierrehumbert, Janet, and Dennis Takin
1992   Lenition of /h/ and Glottal Stop. In *Papers in Laboratory Phonology II: Gesture, Segment, Prosody*, Gerard Docherty and Robert Ladd (eds.), 90–127. Cambridge, England: Cambridge University Press.
Quilis, Antonio
1963   *Fonética y fonología del español.* Madrid: C.S.I.C.
Trubetskoy, N. S.
1969   *Principles of Phonology.* Berkeley: University of California Press.
Zamora-Munné, Juan, and Jorge Guitart
1982   *Dialectología Hispanoamericana.* Madrid: Ediciones Almar.

Index